Union of Parts

WRITTEN UNDER THE AUSPICES OF THE
CENTER OF INTERNATIONAL STUDIES
PRINCETON UNIVERSITY

A volume in the series

Cornell Studies in Political Economy

EDITED BY PETER J. KATZENSTEIN

A full list of titles in the series appears at the end of the book.

Union of Parts

LABOR POLITICS
IN POSTWAR GERMANY

KATHLEEN A. THELEN

CORNELL UNIVERSITY PRESS

Ithaca and London

TO MY PARENTS,

JOSEPH M. THELEN AND
MILDRED A. ERICKSON THELEN

Contents

Preface

In a sense, this book is an effort to unpack the meaning of an observation made by Peter Katzenstein: "West Germany comes closer than any other large industrial state to the logic by which political life in the small European states is organized" (1985:31). Just how closely, I wondered, did West Germany approximate what had become the dominant account of success at managing economic change peacefully and with the active participation of organized labor? The "democratic corporatism" literature served as my point of departure, but from the start it was clear that the German version of "negotiated adjustment" differs in important ways from that model.

Indeed, Germany has a reputation for being a deviant or only a marginal case of corporatism. Yet cross-national comparisons offer few clues as to what distinguishes Germany and—especially—why it nonetheless "clusters" with the small European democracies in terms of the outcomes typically associated with corporatism. This book, then, is an attempt to understand the institutions and processes that sustained German-style negotiated adjustment through the economic and political changes of the 1970s and 1980s.

As I searched for sources of stability in German labor relations, I became convinced that centralized bargaining is a key element. But centralized bargaining in Germany is quite different from that in the corporatist democracies. Alone it cannot explain the German case. Germany's peculiar and in some ways unique system of plant-level works councils and codetermination contributes greatly to collaborative adjustment. In the corporatist countries, peaceful, negotiated adjustment stems from national tripartite bargaining. In Germany, it is ultimately the interaction of centralized bargaining and works councils (the two levels of Germany's so-called dual system of labor relations) that generates and sustains such outcomes.

Furthermore, the balance between centralized and plant-level bargaining is shifting. This observation led me to further conclusions about the continued stability of German labor relations and the more general issue of union success in the 1980s and 1990s. The mix of centralization and decentralization that is institutionally anchored in the dual system has become, I argue, a crucial asset in the context of the new challenges labor now faces.

I focus primarily on the German Metalworkers' Union, the IG Metall. With over 2.5 million members, the IG Metall is far and away the largest of Germany's multi-industrial unions. In part because of its size, it has served as the informal leader of the German labor movement throughout the postwar period. The union has traditionally assumed a vanguard role in Germany's annual round of collective bargaining, establishing the benchmarks for settlements in other industries. And more generally, it is the IG Metall's policies and strategies (and not those of the relatively weak overarching German Trade Union Confederation, the DGB) that reverberate throughout the economy.

The IG Metall organizes a range of sectors that have long counted as the backbone of German industry and that have been vital to the country's export-led growth. These include the steel, automobile, machine tool, electronics, and shipbuilding industries. Understanding how the IG Metall has responded to long-term decline in steel and shipbuilding, to rapid technological change in autos, and to increased competition from low-wage producers in electronics provides a window on the factors that sustain labor peace in a period of rapid economic change.

This book is organized into three parts. Part I analyzes the particular character of negotiated adjustment in West Germany. As in the corporatist countries, industrial adjustment in Germany has been successful in both economic and political terms. The German model, however, is premised on different institutional arrangements. Germany's negotiated adjustment is on balance more privatized, more decentralized, and more legalistic; it hinges on the interaction of centralized bargaining and plant-level works councils.

Part II examines the political maneuvering that forged the structures of the dual system. My analysis focuses especially on two turning points in the development of the dual system up to 1972: the creation of works councils under conservative auspices in 1952, and the transformation and expansion of their rights under the Social Democrats two decades later, after the shop-floor upheavals of the late 1960s.

Part III explores how labor politics have evolved since the 1970s. I demonstrate how labor representatives in three crisis industries coped with the strains of adjustment at the plant and company levels as relations between union, government, and employers deteriorated at the national level. Moreover, I document the growing importance of works councils to central union strategies since the early 1980s. An examination of bargaining between the IG Metall and employers over working-time reduction and of the IG Metall's strategy toward technological change shows how plant-level bargaining has become an increasingly important locus of conflict (and cooperation) between labor and capital in Germany.

Two final chapters assess the West German model of adjustment in comparative perspective and draw out implications for the future evolution of labor relations. Comparisons of West Germany with Sweden and the United States highlight the distinctive features of the dual system and further illustrate the dynamics of Germany's model of negotiated adjustment. The "hybrid" dual system combines elements of centralization and decentralization that provide the institutional resiliency necessary for continued stability and success.

It is sometimes nerve-wracking to be writing about Germany now, since virtually everything about that country is in flux. The codetermination laws of the Federal Republic were adopted for firms in the East in the summer of 1990, and the incorporation of East German workers into the unions of the West was also formally complete by 3 October 1990, the date of official unification. Thus the key institutional arrangements in my analysis are already in place throughout the "new" Germany. Yet, as this book demonstrates, outcomes are a matter not simply of institutional arrangements but of political dynamics as well. Clearly, the adoption of West German institutions will have an immediate and profound impact on the former DDR (German Democratic Republic). But incorporation is two-way, and it sets in motion new political dynamics whose implications will become clearer only as time goes on.

I owe a great debt to the many institutions and persons who have supported my work over the past few years. The Deutscher Akademischer Austauschdienst (DAAD) provided funding for field research in Frankfurt in 1984–85. Subsequent research in 1988–89, on which the comparisons of the politics of work reorganization in West Germany, Sweden, and the United States are based, was generously funded by the Hans Böckler Foundation in Düsseldorf

My research was greatly facilitated by the active cooperation of its "subjects." I thank the *KollegInnen* at the IG Metall, especially the members of the Department of Automation and Technology, who were always forthcoming with their time and information. I owe double gratitude to Andreas Drinkuth, Bernd Kaßebaum, and Jutta Kneißel, both as teachers and friends. Thanks are also due to the many works councillors, shop stewards, employers, and plant managers with whom I talked. They gave generously of their time and information in a way that far exceeded my expectations. My travels to Frankfurt have been much enriched by my friendship with Gisela Kühne, with whom I shared a hectic but most rewarding year at "Essi 6."

Many colleagues have contributed to this project. Tony Daley, Frank Dobbin, Gerald Feldman, Miriam Golden, Peter Katzenstein, Horst Kern, Tom Knight, Peter Lange, Richard Locke, Andrew Martin, Jonas Pontusson, Jerry Riemer, Stephen Silvia, Sven Steinmo, Lowell Turner, and Kirsten Wever gave me valuable comments and criticisms on various pieces of the manuscript, and some of them on the whole thing. I have also benefited from discussions with Reinhard Bendix, Nancy Bermeo, Marc Blecher, Egon Endres, Robin Gaster, John Gilmour, Jost Halfmann, Peter Hall, Gary Herrigel, Bernd Hofmaier, John Ikenberry, Hirschel Kasper, Christoph Köhler, James McGuire, Evelies Mayer, Frieder Naschold, Åke Sandberg, Christoph Scherrer, Rainer Schultz-Wild, Peter Schulze, Peter Schwartz, Werner Sengenberger, Christian Soe, and Peter Swenson. Jeff Beneke smoothed out my prose in several key chapters; Andrew Lewis's careful copyediting further improved the writing throughout. Roger Haydon provided valuable editorial advice and guidance. I also thank Joshua Dienstag, Kristin Johnson, Marcos Morais, and Ryan Turner for their careful and thorough assistance with research and manuscript preparation.

I extend special thanks to three scholars who have taught many of us much of what we know about contemporary German labor: Christopher Allen, who has been an important source both of intellectual stimulation and of personal support and encouragement over the past several years; Andy Markovits, who in addition to being an excellent scholar generously provided me (and, I know, many others) with valuable leads and contacts for my first round of field research in Germany; and Wolfgang Streeck, whose work on German labor has been an inspiration and set an important agenda for the rest of us. Whoever reads this book will understand the special intellectual debt I owe to these three scholars.

At Berkeley, John Zysman and Harold Wilensky provided crucial ongoing guidance and advice on an earlier version of this manuscript. I profited immensely from my work with John and Steve Cohen at the Berkeley Roundtable on the International Economy, and I thank them for the many opportunities my apprenticeship there afforded me. Harold Wilensky scrutinized this manuscript with his characteristic care and thoroughness. His detailed, extensive, and incisive comments contributed a great deal to making it more coherent.

I have two longstanding debts of a different nature to acknowledge: to Ron Francisco, who guided me toward graduate school in the first place, and to Robert Scheer and Narda Zacchino, who helped get me through it by subsidizing my graduate education with unusual rent policies that provided for "downward flexibility" during lean times.

My greatest debt is to my closest colleague, Ben Schneider.

KATHLEEN THELEN

São Paulo

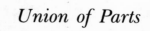

Union of Parts

Introduction: The Argument in Brief

A sense of crisis pervades contemporary labor politics in the advanced capitalist countries. Compared to the 1950s and 1960s, the past two decades have seen great economic turbulence. Beginning with the oil shock of 1973–74, the advanced industrial countries have experienced a variety of pressures to adjust, among them the inflationary effect of rising energy costs, the upheaval in international markets associated with the growing competitiveness of the newly industrializing countries (NICs), and the need to reorganize production in order to keep pace in the increasingly volatile international markets of the 1980s and 1990s. These economic shifts have had important political ramifications as well. They have tested, and in many countries undermined, the "Keynesian consensus" of the 1960s and early 1970s. Unions in many countries have suffered legislative setbacks and political isolation in a neoliberal backlash against organized labor, which is seen to have grown too powerful. Labor organizations in most countries are struggling to hold on to a membership base being whittled away by industrial decline and the shift to the less unionized service sector.

Among the advanced industrial countries, West Germany appears to have weathered the storms of the 1970s and 1980s rather well (Katzenstein 1989b; Wilensky 1981; Zysman 1983; Gourevitch 1986; and Wilensky and Turner 1987). Ask about how well German industry has adapted to these pressures, and you are likely to hear a litany of sectors in which German manufacturing excels in international markets. Ask about labor's role in adjustment, and you will likely hear that German unions are "responsible" social partners in the adjustment process. Ask about the continued viability of Germany's unions, and you will hear that membership levels have held steady or even increased slightly and that labor has scored some significant gains (such as a reduction of working

1

hours) even under the currently difficult political and economic conditions.

This is a study of the sources of stability in German labor relations. Observers who saw labor peace in Germany as a "fair weather" phenomenon that would disappear with the end of the economic miracle of the 1950s and early 1960s were wrong. Harder economic times did not so much expose the hidden weakness of German unions as confirm their strength. Moreover, collaborative labor-capital relations—whether measured in terms of wage moderation, low levels of industrial conflict, or labor cooperation in industrial modernization and restructuring—have survived the transition into the more turbulent economic environment since the 1970s.

The central argument of this book is that the institutional arrangements within which conflicts between labor and capital are resolved have contributed to stable, collaborative adjustment. West Germany's distinctive "dual system" of labor relations has been a key source of institutional resiliency through the economic turmoil and political changes of the past decades. The "dual system" refers to the juxtaposition in Germany of centralized collective bargaining through multi-industrial unions and a statutory system for plant labor representation through autonomous works councils that are formally separate from the unions. This dual system provided a stable avenue for labor participation in adjustment at the subnational level as national-level cooperation between the unions and employers deteriorated in the course of the 1970s. Although they are formally separate from the unions, works councils' legal rights at the plant level have helped shore up central union power as labor's political and market strength waned.

The legal bases of labor's power have been more important in Germany than in other "strong labor" countries. Unions in Sweden and Austria have been able to count on government intervention by sympathetic parties to shield workers from the full impact of recent market changes (e.g., by dampening unemployment and thus bolstering the unions' market power in collective bargaining). German labor lacks similar political clout, and here the legal infrastructure of works councils and codetermination at subnational levels has been more decisive as labor's buttress against political and market vicissitudes.

Works councils were not only important in sustaining peaceful, collaborative adjustment in the 1970s; if anything they became more important to central union strategies in the course of the 1980s. The crisis of Keynesianism and the restructuring of production now underway throughout the advanced industrial world have forced a shift away from the dominance of quantitative (wage) issues toward qualitative issues such as skills and work organization (see, for example, Sabel 1986). This shift has involved a partial decentralization of bargaining, because such qualitative issues are often plant-specific and thus difficult to resolve in the context of uniform centralized negotiations. Hence plant-level bargaining has grown more important in part because of the very nature of the challenges labor now faces. The dual system, combining as it does strong centralized coordination with substantial decentralized labor powers, has given German unions strategic flexibility to meet these new challenges.

Illuminating the sources of stability in German labor relations involves unraveling two puzzles, one theoretical and one empirical. The theoretical puzzle comes out of an extensive literature on democratic corporatism.[1] In this literature West Germany has been considered something of an anomaly. Various cross-national studies of labor politics in the advanced industrial countries find that Germany tends to "cluster" with the corporatist democracies[2] in a variety of outcomes (labor peace, inflation, unemployment, general economic performance, and social policy), but—by virtually any theorist's definition or measures— it lacks the structural features that are considered preconditions for, or attributes of, corporatism (organizational unity of labor, centralization of policymaking, and dominance of a Social Democratic party).[3]

Thus, one of the questions this book addresses is why Germany "behaves" like a corporatist country when it is, as Wilensky (1983) suggests, only marginally corporatist in structure. I argue that the national-level focus of the corporatism literature obscures the special significance in Germany of subnational institutions for labor participation in the adjustment process. The key to the German model of negotiated adjustment lies not in closed sessions of tripartite bargaining in Bonn but rather in the interaction of central unionism and the institutions for labor-management negotiation at various subnational levels.

The empirical puzzle comes out of the history of the dual system itself. West German unions opposed the 1952 law that created works councils in their present form. Among other things, they accused the conservative government that authored the legislation of trying to weaken the unions by creating a second tier of labor representation separate from them. Understanding how the works council system has come to bolster and complement central union strength requires an examination of the political maneuvering that has shaped the dual system over time. I focus on turning points (1950–52, 1969–72, and 1984–89) that have been decisive in shaping its current institutional configuration and functions. I trace how changes in the macroeconomic

1. See, for example, Katzenstein 1984, 1985; Schmitter 1977, 1981; Wilensky 1976, 1981; and Cameron 1984.

2. After two decades of research, "corporatism" is still an ambiguous concept. The definition I use here is based inductively on the characteristics of those cases of corporatism—Austria, Norway, and Sweden—that are considered noncontroversial by scholars working on the topic.

3. See, for example, Korpi and Shalev 1979; Wilensky 1983; Cameron 1984; Hibbs 1977; and Gourevitch 1986.

and political context have periodically produced "openings" that set in motion a reshuffling of relations within the dual system. Political maneuvering among employers, union leaders, and plant labor representatives have provided the dynamic behind institutional adaptation and change.

Unraveling these two puzzles thus involves pursuing two lines of argumentation, one comparative and one historical-institutional. The comparative dimension highlights what is distinctive about the German case and, by contrasting Germany with the corporatist countries, illuminates the general issue of alternative institutional arrangements for reconciling labor strength and successful economic adaptation in rapidly changing international markets. The historical-institutional dimension looks behind and beyond the formal structures at the political conflicts that have shaped them and at the ongoing political maneuvering that helps to sustain them. My thesis is that the stability of German labor relations turns on the resiliency of the dual system, and hence ultimately on subtle changes within it in response to shifts in the political and economic context. Not just static institutional constraints, but ongoing strategic maneuvering and changing political strategies by labor and capital (mediated and constrained, but not determined, by the institutions) account for the continued resiliency of the dual system.

Thus, these two dimensions do not tell different stories, but rather illuminate the German case from two different vantages. The explanation for the comparative stability of the institutions and practices of German labor relations is inseparable from the story of their evolution over time.

In sum, industrial adjustment and economic adaptation to the crises and discontinuities in the international economy in the 1970s and 1980s in West Germany, I argue, have by and large been accomplished *with* and not *against* labor. "Negotiated adjustment" is the shorthand I use to characterize this model based on the participation and cooperation of organized labor.[4]

Negotiated adjustment is not peculiar to Germany, but the institutional arrangements that support and sustain it are. What distinguishes Germany from the corporatist democracies is that negotiations over adjustment are on balance more decentralized, more privatized, and more legalistic. They are more decentralized because labor participation hinges more crucially on labor's plant- and company-level participation than it does (solely) on labor's political clout in national policymaking. They are more privatized because the German government (particularly since 1975) has been less willing than governments in the corporatist democracies to intervene actively in policy trade-offs that sustain centralized,

---

4. The term "negotiated adjustment" follows Zysman's (1983) typology and is close to Katzenstein's (1985) characterization of adjustment in Europe's small states.

cooperative bargaining between labor and capital. Finally, they are more legalistic because of the complex and pervasive statutory framework for labor participation in managerial decision making at various subnational levels. Unlike other varieties, German legalism eschews regulation through detailed rules, instead establishing a broad framework that defines the parameters for competition and conflict in the market. This legal substructure has routinized labor participation in plant decision making and helped sustain cooperative relations between labor and business at the national level.

The economic dislocations of the 1970s and 1980s increased tensions between labor and capital in West Germany, but those tensions were expressed and resolved within stable structures for labor participation at both levels in the dual system. Labor's plant-level rights helped to shore up negotiated adjustment even while relations between the unions, government, and employers deteriorated at the national level.

Political and economic developments since the 1980s, in particular the government's turn toward neoliberalism and employers' growing insistence on greater flexibility in allocating and deploying labor, have exacerbated tensions between labor and capital. Conflicts over these issues have encouraged a shift toward the growing importance of works councils. In contrast, however, to theories that see in these centrifugal pressures an overall weakening of German labor, I argue that centripetal forces are also strong and indeed that labor's strong plant-level rights in the dual system contribute to continued central union strength.

PART I

LABOR AND THE POLITICS OF ADJUSTMENT IN WEST GERMANY

CHAPTER ONE

Continuity through Crisis

Developments since the mid-1970s have tested the political consensus of the period of easy growth in Western Europe and North America that prevailed in the 1950s and 1960s. Economic conflicts, both among countries competing in international markets, and within countries between social groups competing for their share of national wealth, have become more zero-sum. The oil crisis of 1973–74 made international trade more contentious as each country scrambled to increase its exports in order to cover rising energy bills. The growth of the developmental state in Japan and newly industrializing countries (NICs) such as Brazil, South Korea, and Taiwan upset a previously relatively stable international trading order, creating pressures in the advanced capitalist countries for structural change. Upheaval in mass markets has given rise to a new climate of uncertainty and instability (Piore and Sabel 1984). The automation revolution that was only a scare in the 1960s is now in full swing, with the growing application of microelectronics to production and experimentation with competing visions of the "factory of the future."

Having created a world of extreme interdependence and international openness, the advanced capitalist countries are now struggling to cope with its domestic consequences. Finished goods still flow across national boundaries, but in a "market place" made increasingly acrimonious by charges and countercharges of dumping and protectionism.

Stagflation in the early 1970s and growing pressures for industrial adjustment throughout the 1970s and 1980s have reintroduced strains in relations between business and labor in the advanced industrial countries. The decline of bellwether sectors such as steel and shipbuilding cuts into traditional union strongholds. New production technologies

9

and new forms of work organization in other industries throw into question traditional forms of union power and control.[1] The adjustment pressures of the 1980s have changed in a profound way the economic and political landscape faced by organized labor. Where labor had enjoyed decades of full employment and steady growth, it increasingly confronts problems of inflation and structural unemployment. Structural shifts at the macro (international) level, and rapid technological change at the micro (plant) level have broken the link between economic growth and job creation and undermined any direct trade-off between inflation and unemployment.

The political battles of the 1970s began to be dominated by debates over competing interpretations of the crisis and solutions to address it. Although debates over how to restart growth have been cast in technical terms—over the appropriate role of the government in the economy, over the policies and power of unions—the issues themselves are profoundly political. The kinds of technical solutions that various countries have adopted (market liberalism in Britain, state-led adjustment in France, "corporatism" in Sweden) reflect fundamental differences in the political landscape of each of these countries.[2] Political conflict and choice, then, have determined which, if any, technical solution could be implemented. Politics, in short, helps explain why some countries are adjusting and others are not, and also who has benefited and who has lost in the process.

Faced with a similar set of international pressures to adjust, the advanced capitalist countries have varied in (1) the extent to which industry is adapting; (2) how much political and industrial conflict economic change has created; and (3) labor's role in adjustment.

Britain has developed a reputation as the worst case. The "British disease" refers both to the country's now legendary economic decline and to the escalating political and industrial strife that has accompanied it. The crisis has had labor and business locked in a bitter conflict in what is viewed by both sides as an all-or-nothing struggle. The strike of 1984–85 waged by the National Union of Mine Workers over pit closures is perhaps the most spectacular episode. The story of the strike is one of increasing polarization, in which both sides assumed more and more intransigent positions. In the end, miner president Arthur Scargill's eleventh-hour offer to reopen bargaining notwithstanding, a negotiated settlement was not possible.

Less extreme examples of the same syndrome can be found in the

1. In the United States, for example, work rules, job classifications, and in some cases seniority are being renegotiated in many factories (see especially Katz 1985). In Germany, traditional wage systems are being undermined by (and in some cases rewritten to accommodate) new forms of production organization and new technologies.

2. See Zysman, 1983, for an elaboration of these three models in the context of industrial policy and finance.

10

United States: in the politicization of the National Labor Relations Board during the Reagan administration, in the antiunion right-to-work movements, in the migration of industry to the nonunion sunbelt states, and in pockets of industries (like Silicon Valley) where employers fight tenaciously to keep organized labor out. While the form and the rhetoric are different, the common denominator is the same, and it is clear: you don't negotiate with labor organizations, you beat or exclude them; survival depends on a union-free environment.[3]

In other countries, adjustment strategies have been premised less on beating labor than on negotiating with unions. The classic examples of labor inclusion and participation in adjustment are the corporatist democracies, especially Sweden, Austria, and Norway. Studies of these countries' performance in the 1970s and 1980s demonstrate not only that positive adjustment is compatible with strong unions; they show that where labor is strong, adjustment occurs with labor participation or not at all (Lange and Garrett 1985).

Moreover, the adjustment problems faced by industry in the advanced capitalist countries shifted over the course of the 1980s. Employers began to emphasize the need for flexibility in the deployment of labor, and not (primarily) wage restraint, as the key to competitiveness. By "flexibility" employers generally mean one of two things. Labor flexibility may mean the ability to adjust employment levels to fluctuations in demand (through hiring and firing, overtime, or the use of part-time or fixed-contract workers). Or it can mean the ability to reorganize and rationalize production quickly in response to changes in the composition of demand (which includes reassigning workers within a plant).[4]

In some countries, this emphasis on flexibility has found political expression in a push to "free" market forces from the "fetters of the state," in other words, a turn of neoliberalism. Deregulation in the United States, privatization in Britain, and the renegotiation of labor market policies in West Germany in the 1980s are all part of this trend.

These national trends pose new problems for organized labor. Neoliberalism in Britain has been associated with an attack on the unions' organizational position, for example through Margaret Thatcher's drive to "democratize" the unions. In the United States, it has meant an erosion of protection for union organizing and an increase in aggressive employer "whipsawing" strategies that play on competition among

---

3. This is not the only trend in either country, of course. Indeed, individual companies are pursuing very different strategies concerning labor's role in adjustment. Firms like General Motors are currently experimenting with production systems premised on the inclusion and active cooperation of organized labor. An example of this countervailing strategy is the company's "Saturn" project.

4. This distinction corresponds to Cohen and Zysman's (1987) two types of production flexibility.

unions and plants. Elsewhere (in West Germany, for example) neo-liberalism has undermined the "Keynesian compromise" of the early 1970s and in more subtle ways called into question organized labor's role in macroeconomic steering (Sabel 1986).

The drive for greater flexibility is also behind changes at a micro level. Western employers' new fascination with a range of Japanese managerial techniques, such as "just-in-time" production, "quality circles," and teamwork, are examples of this. These shop-floor trends pose a more complicated challenge for labor, combining new opportunities with new dangers (Coriat and Zarifan 1986). The breakdown of rigid Fordist (assembly-line) production techniques opens up possibilities for enhancing the skills of workers and for improving working conditions. Indeed, for these very reasons, German unions have long advocated some of the same kinds of changes in work organization (such as group work) that employers are now eagerly embracing in the interests of economic efficiency and plant flexibility.

Often, however, employers' conceptions of plant flexibility translate into new problems for labor. Quality circles in many of their incarnations are precisely designed to compete with union representation as an avenue for resolving plant conflicts. More flexible work organization can mean greater work autonomy, but it can also disguise old-fashioned speedups and lead to layoffs.

The political and organizational resources the various labor movements brought with them into the 1970s and 1980s have positioned them differently to confront these new challenges. In Sweden, forty-four years of Social Democratic hegemony and a union movement that covers over 80 percent of the work force meant that when the conservative party came to power in 1976, the kinds of radical measures that Margaret Thatcher introduced in Britain in her "conservative revolution" were simply not tenable. Likewise, although West Germany took a marked rightward shift in the 1980s, neoliberalism has had a very different meaning there. Among other things, organized labor's institutional anchoring helped shield unions from the full impact of political isolation and declining market strength (Thelen 1989).

How well unions weather the crisis depends not just on labor's national-level strength, but also on labor's plant-level rights. The extent and character of labor's shop-floor powers influence how well unions are positioned to cope with the breakdown of Fordism. U.S. labor's shop-floor rights are inextricably linked to Fordist production organization, which helps explain why the unions cling to traditional and rigid production practices and work rules despite the potential benefits to workers of other forms of work organization. Where labor's plant rights are not linked to Fordism and are more securely anchored, either politically (as in Sweden) or legally (as in Germany), unions have been both more willing and better positioned to participate in plant restructuring.[5]

Thus, while the symptoms of economic crisis are broadly similar across the advanced capitalist countries, the political challenge to labor takes very different forms. Unions in the United States are fighting for their organizational lives; total membership is down to 17 percent of the labor force (Kochan, Katz, and McKersie 1986:48). Here the question is whether unions have *any* role to play in adjustment. Where labor commands greater political and institutional resources (for example, in Sweden, Austria, and Norway), the question is not whether labor has a role in the adjustment process but what that role will be.

This is also the question in Germany. High unemployment in the 1980s and the Kohl government's neoliberal approach to industrial change intensified conflict between labor and capital in West Germany, but they have not precipitated a general crisis of collaborative labor-business relations. Industrial conflict, while up somewhat in the 1980s, is still very low by international standards. And while the confluence of German labor's political and market weakness in the 1980s put the unions on the defensive, the fact that German labor is institutionally and organizationally entrenched at both the national and subnational levels has given it very different resources to counter neoliberal pressures for greater flexibility in central and shop-floor bargaining.

THE INSTITUTIONAL BASES OF LABOR STABILITY AND PEACE IN GERMANY

The distinguishing characteristic of German industrial relations is the coexistence of two parallel and distinct avenues for labor representation and participation. These are the overarching system of national bargaining by Germany's multi-industrial unions and a set of statutory institutions for labor participation at subnational (company and plant) levels.

Central Bargaining

The main trade union confederation in Germany is the Deutscher Gewerkschaftsbund (DGB), which consists of sixteen multi-industrial unions.[6] The DGB accounts for 83.1 percent of all unionized workers

---

5. This theme is explored fully in Chapter 9.
6. Previously seventeen. In 1989 the artists' and musicians' union (Gewerkschaft Kunst) merged with the printing and paper workers' union (IG Druck und Papier) to form the Media Workers Union (IG Medien).

(Markovits 1986:12).[7] The member unions are centralized and unified both with respect to political tendencies (i.e., individual unions are not affiliated with such competing political programs or parties as Socialist and Communist) and in that all workers—blue and white collar alike— are organized along industrial lines.[8]

Judged in terms of formal organization, organized labor in West Germany is less encompassing than its counterparts in other European countries. The DGB organizes only about 32 percent of all German workers (Löhrlein 1989:69). This puts it well below Sweden's peak trade union confederation, the Landsorganisationen i Sverige (LO) and Austria's Österreichischer Gewerkschaftsbund (ÖGB) (over 80 and 60 percent, respectively), though above the United States and France (where approximately 17 and 15 percent of the labor force is organized by various unions).

Other characteristics of the German system compensate for labor's relatively low organization level. In particular, the high level of organization within the business community, the leadership role played by the powerful German Metalworkers' Union (the IG Metall), and the unions' pervasive presence at the shop-floor level (through the works council system) all give German unions more unity and clout than membership figures alone suggest. Thus, unitary industrial unionism, led informally by the IG Metall, has spared the German labor movement many of the internal programmatic and craft rivalries that characterize labor relations in countries such as France and Britain. Germany's unions may not always speak with one voice, but the fact that they do not compete among themselves for members has contributed to their relative solidarity.

Works Councils and Codetermination

Embedded in this overarching system of national collective bargaining is a relatively strong and stable system of statutory labor participation at the plant and firm levels.[9] The highly touted system of German

7. The remaining 16.9 percent of union members belong to three much smaller trade union confederations: the German Civil Servants Union (Deutscher Beamtenbund, or DBB), which is primarily a lobbying organization prohibited from collective bargaining; the German White-Collar Workers' Union (Deutsche Angestellten Gewerkschaft, or DAG); and the German Christian Trade Union Confederation (Christlicher Gewerkschaftsbund Deutschlands, or CGB).

8. The partial exception to this is that the DAG organizes white-collar workers in a number of industries. In their bargaining with management, however, the DAG and the relevant industrial union informally coordinate settlements in the individual industries.

9. A full text of the laws described here can be found in Kittner 1984; and English translations appear in BAS (Bundesministerium für Arbeit und Sozialordnung) 1980. Streeck, 1983, also contains an excellent discussion of the various codetermination laws.

codetermination is the other crucial element in the German model of negotiated adjustment.[10]

At the plant level, codetermination refers to a comprehensive system of labor participation through works councils. Workers in any plant or enterprise employing more than five workers are entitled by law to elect a works council (*Betriebsrat*) to represent them. The rights and privileges enjoyed by plant works councils are specified in the 1952 Works Constitution Act and the 1972 revised Works Constitution Act (*Betriebsverfassungsgesetz*). The law stipulates that management consult with the works council on a range of plant issues (consultative rights), and in some areas requires management to reach an agreement with the works council before implementing a plant policy (codetermination rights). Works councils' rights are strongest in the general area of personnel policy (hiring, firing, overtime, and plant payment systems). Works councils possess weaker consultative rights on a range of other issues, including the introduction of new technologies and changes in the organization and flow of the production process.

At the company level, there are two forms of codetermination within German industry. The stronger and more far-reaching exists only in the coal and steel industries.[11] Here, labor representatives sit on company supervisory boards (*Aufsichtsräte*) in equal numbers with management (parity codetermination), and participate in long-term company planning (e.g., investment and rationalization decisions). In the event of ties, a neutral chairperson (elected by the entire board) casts the deciding vote. The chairperson cannot be appointed to the board against the opposition of labor. Labor representatives also sit on the executive boards (*Vorstände*) of companies in the coal and steel industries (which are responsible for the day-to-day operation of the firm). The labor director on the executive board is an representative of labor itself, generally chosen by the union in collaboration with the works councils of the company's various plants.

Labor-management relations at the company level outside the coal and steel industries are governed by a weaker form of codetermination. The 1976 Codetermination Law (*Mitbestimmungsgesetz*) provides for labor representation on the supervisory boards of all firms employing over two thousand workers.[12] Although labor representatives are allot-

10. "Codetermination" is sometimes used to refer only to labor participation in company supervisory boards. Throughout this book, I will use the term in its broader sense, to refer as well to the works council system at the plant level. Technically speaking, it is the formal separation of the works councils from the unions (and not codetermination per se) that makes the system a "dual" one.

11. This form of codetermination is known as *Montanmitbestimmung*.

12. Firms employing between five hundred and two thousand workers are covered by the previous codetermination legislation contained in the 1952 Works Constitution Act, which gave labor representatives one-third of the seats on the supervisory board.

15

ted 50 percent of the seats on the supervisory boards of such firms, one seat must go to a senior manager (*leitender Angestellte*), who generally votes with the stockholders. Moreover, the chairperson—always a representative of capital—casts the deciding vote in the event of a tie. In addition, and again unlike the *Montan* (coal and steel) industries, the labor director on the executive board of firms covered by the 1976 Codetermination Law is not generally labor's candidate.

THE INTERACTION OF INDUSTRIAL UNIONISM AND CODETERMINATION

The two levels in the dual system are mutually reinforcing. This structure has both sustained negotiated adjustment in West Germany and helped counterbalance the unions' waning political and market power since the 1970s.

This argument seems paradoxical in light of the history of works councils in the dual system. Although codetermination has long been the centerpiece of German labor's agenda for social and economic reform, the way codetermination at the plant level was institutionalized in 1952 was very different from the unions' conception. At that time, the goal of Konrad Adenauer's conservative government was to circumscribe the powers of Germany's national labor unions by constructing a system of labor representation at the plant level that emphasized the formal separation of works councils from the unions (see especially Markovits 1986:80–82). The conflict over the Works Constitution Act of 1952 pitched employers and the conservative government against the unions and the Social Democratic party in a battle over the unions' position in the plant and their role as sole intermediary between management and the rank and file.

The unions lost in 1952. Although not interfering with the unions' collective bargaining monopoly, the Works Constitution Act established a system of plant representation parallel to the unions and underscored works councils' independence from them. As Andrei Markovits puts it, the law "banned the unions as the official shop-floor representatives of West German workers" (1986:81). Furthermore, the law bound works councils to negotiate with management not only in good faith, but "in the interest of the workers *and the plant*."[13] It prohibited them from undertaking actions that could endanger the welfare of the company.[14] In stressing works councils' responsibilities to the firm while weakening their formal links to the unions, the law's framers intended for it to

---

13. Emphasis added. For a text of the law in its entirety, see Kittner 1984. Here and elsewhere translations are my own unless I have noted otherwise.

14. For example, works councils were prohibited from striking and from divulging company secrets to the union or other "outsiders."

foster cooperative plant labor relations by encouraging labor's cooptation at the plant level.

When the Bundestag (parliament) passed the law on 19 July 1952, the DGB condemned the act, calling it a "dark moment for democratic development in the Federal Republic."[15] A contemporary observer of German unionism has characterized the conflict over the Works Constitution Act as "the single most disappointing struggle in the post–World War II history of German labor" (Markovits 1986:80).

Although the 1952 law constituted a major setback for the unions, the issue of union influence in the plant was by no means settled. Since that time, the relationship between Germany's national unions and plant-level works councils has gone through many phases. In the course of the 1950s and 1960s the unions succeeded in "capturing" a large majority of works councils. Currently over 80 percent of all works councillors belong to the unions in the DGB. Union dominance in the works councils and the subsequent evolution of the relationship between them and the unions have turned the "logic" of the dual system on its head.

The peculiar and paradoxical history of German works councils distinguishes them from similar institutions in other European countries, where works council systems were generally designed and implemented by labor-sympathetic governments, or as a concession to labor in the wake of rank-and-file militancy in the late 1960s (Stephens and Stephens 1982:221, 223–24). German labor as well was able to capitalize on the Social Democratic victory in 1969 to extend works councils' rights, so that by the 1970s Germany's works council system was the second strongest in Western Europe.[16]

This history helps explain what is something of an anomaly in Evelyne H. and John D. Stephens's analysis. They demonstrate a strong correlation between the strength of organized labor (measured in terms of socialist incumbency and the degree of labor organization) and the comprehensiveness of worker participation schemes (1982:238–39). West Germany's works council system is stronger than one would expect, given the national labor movement's somewhat lower organizational strength (1982:240). Of the six countries with the strongest worker participation schemes, only Germany has an organization level under 50 percent.

West Germany's more circuitous path to strong works councils is also important for its contemporary political consequences. The works coun-

15. Quoted in Markovits 1986:81.
16. Stephens and Stephens (1982:238–39) rank the strength of worker participation systems according to the formal provisions of the laws in each country. In their ranking, Sweden is first and Germany is second, followed by Austria, Denmark, Norway, Belgium, the Netherlands, and distantly by Britain, Finland, France, Switzerland, Ireland, and Italy.

cil system is stable and pervasive because of its legal anchoring, but what is crucial politically is that works councils in even little-organized plants are overwhelmingly comprised of representatives of DGB unions. The result of its peculiar development is that German's strong works council system only partly reflects the political power of the unions; in many ways—and more so here than in the other countries with similar systems—it actually amplifies the presence of unions in the economy.

The Rigidities and Flexibilities of the Dual System

Negotiated adjustment in Germany hinges on the interaction of the two levels of the dual system. Labor's relative strength at both levels has given German labor relations adaptability, and thus also stability and strength, in the face of the macroeconomic and political changes since the 1970s. These two different avenues for labor representation are parallel in that they operate on different economic planes. Central collective bargaining is conducted on an industry level and often (de facto, though informally) on a national level; and codetermination, on the plant and company levels. They are also distinct in that they operate on different logics. Unionism is voluntary, though relatively pervasive. Codetermination is statutory, and nearly universal (at least at the plant level). Central bargaining by the unions establishes general standards for labor; plant bargaining responds to the particular issues confronted by workers in a given plant.

The many legal constraints on works councils' behavior have long made the dual system the object of criticism (see Erd 1978; Crouch 1978: especially 202; and Hoffmann 1978: especially xxv–xxvii). However, Wolfgang Streeck (1979, 1981) has persuasively argued that the dual system in Germany has performed the important function of stabilizing central unionism in years of prosperity. In particular, he argues that because works councils are prohibited from calling strikes and are legally bound to uphold centrally negotiated agreements at the plant level, they insulate central unions from "syndicalist" pressures by shielding top business and labor negotiators from militant appeals from the shop floor. In addition, works councils in economically strong plants and sectors often bargain *informally* with employers over supplemental wage increases; the resulting "wage drift" has served as a safety valve that has helped sustain central union wage restraint (Teschner 1977).

But where Streeck's "stabilization" argument rests on an analysis of what works councils cannot do in a period of prosperity, mine stresses instead what they *can do* in a period of economic downturn and crisis. The same "rigidities" and "flexibilities" that worked during good times continue to stabilize negotiated adjustment in the crisis years since the mid-1970s. The works councils' (legal) inability to undercut (as opposed to informally supplement) centrally bargained wage agreements has meant that wages cannot be pushed downward for particular plants or firms. Hence, the kind of concession bargaining that has plagued unions in the United States is structurally ruled out in the German context.[17]

Moreover, the flexibilities inherent in the dual system have helped shore up the position of the central unions when the national political and economic balance of power shifted against labor. Works councils have provided a channel for negotiating the terms of adjustment in plants and sectors differently affected by the economic upheavals since the 1970s. Particularly since Germany's Keynesian compromise began to come apart in the mid-1970s, the works council system has given unions a "second avenue" for diffusing conflicts over the "flexibility" of central bargaining and for continuing to pursue labor demands even as labor's political and market power waned.

Labor's plant-level rights on a range of personnel and production issues became, if anything, more important in the course of the 1980s. The significance of the legal structures that sustain labor participation and power at the plant level was largely obscured in the heyday of centralized bargaining (over wages, primarily) in the 1970s. In the current period, however, a shift in emphasis away from wages and toward qualitative issues—employment, technology, skills—has reinforced the importance of labor's subnational strength as a complement to national union power. Central coordination remains essential to labor's role in Germany's negotiated adjustment, but contemporary trends point to a shifting balance in the dual system, and the subnational plant and company levels are increasingly becoming the locus of negotiation and conflict.

My argument runs counter to that of many other students of German labor, who emphasize *instabilities* in the dual system in a period of economic crisis and high unemployment. Many theorists have argued that the dual system encourages the growth of "plant egoism," which complicates unions' problems of central control.[18] In years of prosperity, the dual system successfully held in check *militant* syndicalist tendencies; however, Streeck and others have argued that under conditions of high unemployment the dual system and strong works councils foster syndicalism of a *cooperative* variety that dovetails with employer efforts to decentralize bargaining and "relax . . . corporatist controls over the workplace" (Streeck 1984c: 297; see also Hohn 1988). In effect, the "plant egoism" argument asserts that the dual system operates (in a

17. More precisely, in order to escape the provisions of the central bargain, firms must withdraw from the employers organization itself. They are generally reluctant to do this since it means they must bargain separately and alone against the union.

18. See, for example, Streeck 1984c: especially 303–14; Hohn 1988; Kotthoff 1979; and Windolf and Hohn 1984.

period of economic crisis, in any event) in precisely the way that the conservative framers of the Works Constitution Act intended, namely to drive a wedge between the central union and the shop floor and to encourage the cooptation of labor at the plant level. Streeck's own works avoids mechanistic and zero-sum characterizations (see especially Streeck 1989). However, in many other versions of this theory, the growth of plant egoism and the decentralization of bargaining on the one hand and the weakening of central unionism on the other hand are two sides of the same coin (see especially Hohn 1988:168–76).

My own analysis confirms some of the same tendencies toward "plant egoism" stressed by these authors. However, it challenges theories that mechanically deduce outcomes (and especially the "breakdown" of centralized bargaining in Germany) from formal institutional arrangements. Applying a sort of "stress analysis" to assess the capacity of institutions to withstand new external pressures, these theories often overemphasize the formal autonomy of works councils. The legal separation of plant-level labor representation from the central unions is what appears to make the German system particularly vulnerable to breakdown through decentralization.

What remains quite mysterious in light of such theories, however, is the actual resiliency of centralized bargaining in West Germany throughout the crisis, and the continued strength of central unions despite plant egoism. Unions throughout the advanced capitalist world are on the defensive, but German unions have scored some comparatively impressive collective bargaining victories recently, including reducing the regular workweek to thirty-five hours. Centrifugal forces may be at work in Germany, but apparently centripetal forces within the labor movement are also still strong. Accounting for this requires an explanation that is less mechanical and more political.

A further problem with the "plant egoism" thesis (and, I would argue, most of the literature on the breakdown of corporatism generally) is that it builds on an essentially dichotomous conception of union strength and weakness. The implication in this literature is that any decentralization of bargaining necessarily comes at the expense of central union strength. This zero-sum treatment of the centralization/decentralization question, however, obscures two points. First, it ignores the many areas in which the interests of labor representatives at the plant level are identical with those of the central union. In Germany, even egoistic works councils perform vital functions in the plant that shore up central union strength. To cite but one example, local non-wage gains bolster union loyalty. Second, it fails to realize that decentralization as such need not imply the fragmentation of labor interests and the growth of "company unions," which would of course undermine central union strength. In fact, the character of the problems that confront organized labor has shifted, and the growing importance of productive restructuring at the plant and firm levels makes a strict centralization/decentralization dichotomy somewhat misleading. Because some of the challenges unions now face present themselves at the plant level, strong shop-floor rights are part of the *solution* to maintaining union strength, rather than part of the problem.

In short, where others stress what works councils can do to weaken the central union, I emphasize how labor's plant-level strength in West Germany has been an asset for central unions in the current crisis. If we accept the dichotomous characterization in which decentralized strength poses problems for continued central union strength, then we must characterize the Swedish unions' drive for legislation to bolster plant-level powers in the 1970s as an act of organizational masochism. Only by viewing the question of centralization and decentralization in other than zero-sum terms can we understand why German unions would rather live with strong works councils (even egoistic ones) than do without them.

The dual system has given German labor considerable room for maneuver at a time when its bargaining position has weakened, thereby putting unions in a position to meet the new challenges of the 1980s and 1990s. Labor benefits from some of the virtues of centralized bargaining while at the same time gaining crucial flexibility for action at the plant and company levels. Central bargains impose a floor on plant-level negotiations, thus allowing German labor to avoid the worst of concession bargaining. Parallel subnational avenues for labor influence that are based in law and hence less sensitive to labor's changing fate in the market have contributed to stability in labor relations in a period of rapid political and industrial change.

The fundamental continuity in West German labor relations does not mean that nothing has changed. It does mean that labor relations are characterized less by an all-out attack on labor's position in the economy than by a complex jockeying for position within established and stable structures at both the national and plant levels. Contemporary conflicts between labor and capital in Germany are largely conflicts over the *balance* between the two levels of organization in the dual system.[19]

THEORETICAL APPROACH

The analytic approach adopted here is broadly informed by a "new institutionalist" perspective.[20] Like other scholars in this tradition, I am

19. This argument resonates with the major message of Katzenstein 1989. See especially Katzenstein's concluding chapter.

20. See also March and Olson 1984; Zysman 1983; Hall 1986; Skocpol 1985; and Ikenberry 1988.

concerned with illuminating how institutional arrangements shape political outcomes by structuring the relationships among contending societal groups.[21] I argue that the institutions of labor relations in West Germany have channeled conflict between labor and capital in ways that have simultaneously sustained labor's strength and contributed to successful adjustment. The comparative dimension of my research thus points to the usefulness of an institutional perspective for identifying broad inter-sectoral and cross-national differences.

However, my analysis differs from many varieties of new institutionalism by emphasizing the political dynamics within the formal structure of labor relations that have shaped it over time and that continue to contribute to its resiliency. Not just structural constraints, but also strategic choice and political conflict within and over these institutions are part of the story. My focus on politics within the dual system is a necessary antidote to the otherwise excessively formal and static institutional analyses that characterize much of the literature on German labor relations, especially the literature on codetermination. But my approach also runs counter to a general tendency in the institutionalist literature to allow the analysis of institutional constraints to lapse into institutional determinism or functionalism.[22]

The underdevelopment of explicit theorizing about the interaction of politics and institutions within the "new institutionalism" becomes evident when we consider the dominant model of change associated with this approach. Most institutionalists subscribe either explicitly or implicitly to a theory that Stephen D. Krasner, invoking the work of evolutionary biologists, calls "punctuated equilibrium" (1984:240–44).[23] Briefly, this model focuses on the fit between institutional structures and their external "task environments." Institutional arrangements help explain policy outcomes during periods of institutional stability, since they structure political conflicts in distinctive ways. Long periods of institutional stability are periodically interrupted by crises, often emanating from the external environment, that strain the institutions beyond their capacity to absorb change. Such crises throw the institutions themselves into question and precipitate intense political conflict as the rules and procedures that normally constrain and govern politi-

---

21. Indeed, it would be difficult to ignore institutions in a study of labor politics in Germany since the formal framework of codetermination is prominent and pervasive and affects relations between labor and capital in obvious and important ways.

22. Cross-national studies, especially, often lean toward somewhat static institutional comparisons that are powerful for explaining variation across systems but cannot easily account for change within particular systems over time (see, for example, Zysman 1983; Olson 1982; and Steinmo 1989, among others). See also Steinmo and Thelen, forthcoming, for a discussion of the strengths but also the limitations of these more static institutional arguments, as well as a related discussion of institutional change.

23. Skocpol's (1979) theory of institutional change, for example, seems to fit this model.

cal behavior are open for renegotiation. When a new equilibrium is reached, a new period of institutional stasis begins.

The punctuated equilibrium model offers a very elegant theory of institutional breakdown, but it is ultimately premised on a simplistic characterization of the relationship between politics and institutions. That relationship is unidimensional and noninteractive: during periods of stability institutions shape politics; when institutions break down, the relationship is reversed and politics shape institutions. The focus in the punctuated equilibrium model on external strains and the adaptive capacities of the institutions themselves largely "blackboxes" the politics *within* the institutions. It treats the political actors who inhabit these structures as passive spectators whose positions in the internal political balance of power are either enhanced or undermined by shifting external conditions.

The model elaborated here, in contrast, hinges on the notion of "dynamic constraints." I emphasize political strategies within institutions and demonstrate how ongoing political conflict and compromise can influence the institutional parameters themselves. I argue that in contrast to a strict punctuated equilibrium model, institutional breakdown is not the only source of institutional dynamism, and that it is not just in moments of institutional crisis that political strategies matter.

Two types of change figure prominently in my analysis of the dual system, and have provided a source of institutional dynamism within that system. First, the meaning and functions of an institution can be transformed as a result of changes in the external context, with implications for shifting strategies within stable institutions. For example, the IG Metall came to accept the dual system as the economic context shifted and dualism became an asset rather than a liability in light of the new opportunities and challenges the union faced in the 1960s. Second, political conflict does not just occur *within*, but also often *over* institutions, and the outcome of such conflict can influence the institutional parameters within which subsequent battles take place. Organizational struggles within the IG Metall in the late 1960s over the relationship between shop-floor labor representation and central union leadership drove forward the development of the dual system, although in ways unanticipated by the instigators of these conflicts. More recently, conflicts between the IG Metall and employers over flexibility in central contracts have been resolved through a partial decentralization of bargaining and a renegotiation of relations between the central union and works councils within the dual system.

While these two sources of change are analytically distinct, they are often empirically intertwined. The typical pattern is one in which changes in the larger political and economic context confront political actors with new challenges or present them with new strategic "openings," which they try to exploit in order to enhance their positions and achieve their ends. Such strategic maneuvering in turn sets in motion political conflicts, the outcomes of which can reshape in subtle ways the institutional parameters themselves.

In short, the external forces that are central to the punctuated equilibrium model constitute an important source of institutional dynamism, but they interact with internal political struggles in more complex ways. By focusing on strategic and goal-oriented maneuvering within institutional parameters and on the interaction of political strategies and institutional constraints, I show how ongoing political conflict and compromise between labor and capital in West Germany have stabilized the institutions of the dual system while subtly transforming them over time.

CHAPTER TWO

Negotiated Adjustment in West Germany

Labor conflict affects both political stability and economic perform-ance. As a large body of literature demonstrates, supposedly economic problems like inflation often have their sources in political-distributional conflicts.[1] Indeed, political economy as a field of study takes as its point of departure the interface between political conflict and economic phenomena in an attempt, in Goldthorpe's words, "to understand [economic] problems as being generated—quite intelligibly if not usual-ly intentionally—[by] divisions and conflicts between groups and classes (and their organizations, movements, and parties)" (1984a:3). In the current period, industrial adjustment is the subject of intense political conflict not just because social groups vie to protect their short-term interests, but also because the decisions taken now will affect the balance of power among competing political and economic interests in the longer run as well.

The entanglement of markets and politics means that in democratic political economies, industrial adjustment is both an economic task and a political challenge. Successful adjustment policy means more than just implementing technical solutions to market shifts; it implies also achiev-ing a political settlement among the major actors—business, labor, and the state—over the pace and terms of economic change (Zysman 1983: especially chapters 1 and 2). The literature on democratic corporatism tells us that strong unions are not only compatible with successful economic adjustment; in countries where labor is politically and eco-nomically well organized, labor's cooperation is essential to that adjust-ment (Katzenstein 1985; Lange and Garrett 1985). The more general point for all advanced industrial democracies is that how conflicts over economic dislocations are "mediated and channeled" is important for understanding those arrangements "that do not seriously impede eco-nomic efficiency and may even perhaps enhance it" (Goldthorpe 1984a:4).

1. See, for example, Hirsch and Goldthorpe 1978; and Lindberg and Maier 1985.

Although organized labor's strength is hard to measure precisely, few would quibble with the assertion that German labor is strong compared to its counterparts in most other advanced capitalist countries. In terms of labor's legal rights, works councils in Germany enjoy rights at a plant level that would make American managers shudder.[2] Moreover, German labor's legal rights at the plant and company levels place it second only to Swedish labor in the strength of worker participation schemes.[3] By dint of labor's relative strength in collective bargaining, most West German workers now enjoy among the longest paid vacations (five to six weeks per year) and the shortest regular working hours (in the metalworking and printing industries, thirty-seven hours per week) in Western Europe (*New York Times*, 8 March 1989:D1; Kurz-Scherf 1989:96, 123–24).[4]

Organized labor's influence in German society is also pervasive: the nonunion options available to American managers (e.g., the migration of industry to the "right-to-work" states in the sunbelt) are blocked in Germany both by the encompassing nature of central collective bargaining and by the nearly universal presence of plant works councils. Under these circumstances, employers have no choice but to come to terms with labor. Against almost any other backdrop, "negotiated" adjustment is unlikely. But given labor's presence in the German economy, any other kind of adjustment is unthinkable.

A PORTRAIT OF ADJUSTMENT IN WEST GERMANY

West Germany has adjusted relatively successfully to the economic dislocations of the last two decades. My definition of "successful" adjustment follows Katzenstein's, which measures "the extent to which social coalitions, political institutions, and public policies facilitate or impede shifts in the factors of production that increase economic efficiency with due regard to the requirements of political legitimacy" (1985:29). My claim for Germany is that adjustment has been successful in both economic and political terms. Indicators of successful economic adjustment include measures of international competitiveness, inflation, growth, and unemployment. Successful adjustment can be measured politically in the relative peace of labor relations (using strike rates as an indicator) and—more qualitatively—in terms of the comparatively mild rhetoric of class conflict that has accompanied adjustment in West Germany.

2. One observer has even made the claim that West German codetermination has weakened capitalism (Pejovich 1983:101).

3. For a ranking of thirteen European countries, see Stephens and Stephens 1982:238–39.

4. And regular weekly working hours will drop to thirty-five in the metalworking industries beginning in 1995. See Chapter 7 below.

Economic Measures of Adjustment

Competitiveness. Economic growth in West Germany since 1945 has depended on a strong export base in manufacturing (Kreile 1978). Even before World War II, foreign trade was important to German business, but the division of the country after the war deprived the industrial west of a major internal market for its manufactured goods, making it even more dependent on foreign markets. Manufacturing exports fueled West Germany's "economic miracle" in the 1950s and 1960s, and their importance to the economic well-being of the German economy has not diminished since then. West Germany sells a third of its production abroad, twice the proportion as in Japan (*New York Times,* 6 October 1988:D1; *Economist,* 6 December 1986:20).

Compared to that of other countries in the Organization for Economic Cooperation and Development (OECD), the performance of the German export sector has been spectacular. West Germany is the only OECD country able to boast of trade surpluses every year since 1952. Even in 1974, when Germany's raw materials imports soared, the country booked a net trade surplus of nearly DM 51 billion (Kohl and Basevi 1980:8–9). Table 1 shows why West Germany has earned the reputation of being "an unstoppable export machine" (*New York Times* 6 October 1988:D1).

Table 1. German trade balance, 1972–88

Year	Trade balance (billion DM)
1972	20.3
1973	33.0
1974	50.8
1975	37.3
1976	34.5
1977	38.4
1978	41.2
1979	22.4
1980	8.9
1981	27.7
1982	51.3
1983	42.1
1984	54.0
1985	73.4
1986	112.6
1987	117.7
1988	128.0
1989	134.7

Source: Statistisches Jahrbuch für die Bundesrepublik Deutschland (Stuttgart: Metzler-Poeschel Verlag, 1990:256; 1989:241; and 1988: 251).

Germany's consistent trade surpluses contrast with the relatively weaker performance of other countries in international markets. Table 2 compares the German trade balance for 1981–89 with that of the other major OECD countries. It shows that German trade has remained strong relative to other countries through the 1980s.

Table 2. Trade balance for various countries (billion dollars, monthly averages)

Country	1981	1982	1983	1984	1985	1986	1987	1988	1989
W. Germany	1.0	1.8	1.4	1.6	2.1	4.3	5.5	6.1	6.0
Japan	0.8	0.6	1.8	2.8	3.8	6.8	6.7	6.4	5.4
U.S.	−2.3	−3.6	−5.8	−10.3	−11.6	−12.9	−12.7	−9.9	−9.1
France	−1.6	−1.2	−0.5	−0.2	−0.3	0.0	−0.4	−0.5	−0.6
U.K.	—	−0.2	−0.7	−0.9	−0.7	−1.6	−2.0	−3.7	−3.7
Italy	−1.3	−1.0	−0.6	−0.9	−1.0	−0.2	−0.7	−0.8	−1.0
Austria	−0.4	−0.3	−0.3	−0.3	−0.3	−0.4	−0.5	−0.5	−0.5
Norway	0.2	0.2	0.4	0.4	0.4	−0.2	−0.1	−0.1	0.3
Sweden	0.0	−0.1	0.0	0.2	0.2	0.4	0.3	0.3	0.2

Source: OECD, *Main Economic Indicators* (Paris: OECD).

If we look at comparative trade balances as a percent of gross domestic product (GDP), we find that West Germany outtraded all other major OECD countries for each of the periods 1960–67, 1968–73, 1974–79, and 1980–88 (see Table 3).[5]

Table 3. Trade balance as percentage of GDP

Country	1960–67	1968–73	1974–79	1980–88
W. Germany	1.8	2.5	2.4	2.8
Japan	0.2	1.5	0.4	2.1
U.S.	0.7	0.1	−0.4	2.1
France	0.8	0.5	0.3	−0.2
U.K.	−0.7	−0.1	−0.9	0.5
Italy	0.1	0.4	−0.2	−0.4
Austria	−0.1	0.6	−0.7	−0.2
Norway	−1.8	0.0	−4.7	3.9
Sweden	−0.1	0.7	−0.7	1.1

Source: OECD, *Economic Outlook: Historical Statistics: 1960–87* (Paris: OECD, 1989), 68.
Note: Last column recalculated (simple averages) through 1988 using data from OECD, *Economic Outlook* (Paris: OECD).

As for the Japanese, manufacturing exports are a vital lifeline for the German economy and the centerpiece of that country's economic repertoire. Indeed, manufacturing exports are even more important to

---

5. The one exception to this is the 1980–88 period, where Norway ranks first, largely because of North Sea oil.

the Germans, since their domestic market is about one-half the size of the Japanese.

While all of the advanced capitalist countries are shifting away from manufacturing toward services, the rate of change varies. Some observers have noted with horror the pace at which Britain and the United States, for example, seem to be abandoning traditional manufacturing (Cohen and Zysman 1987; Blackaby 1978).

Adjustment in Germany, more than in most other countries, has been adjustment within rather than out of manufacturing. "Deindustrialization" is far less advanced in Germany than elsewhere. Stephen Cohen and John Zysman's (1987) dictum that "manufacturing matters" would be greeted in West Germany with enthusiastic—if somewhat bemused—approval. No German needs to be convinced that the strength of the economy lies in manufacturing. Proportionally more people are employed in manufacturing in Germany than in any other major OECD country (see Table 4).

Table 4. Employment in manufacturing as a percentage of total civilian employment in various countries (averages)

Country	1960–67	1968–73	1974–79	1980–87
W. Germany	35.3	36.6	35.1	32.7
U.S.	26.8	25.8	23.0	20.2
Japan	23.7	26.9	25.4	24.7
France	27.6	27.6	27.2	23.9
U.K.	37.4	36.1	32.6	26.3
Italy	26.0	27.9	27.5	24.5
Austria	31.7	32.1	31.2	28.7
Norway	26.1	—	22.6	18.3
Sweden	31.4	28.3	26.4	22.8

Source: OECD, *Economic Outlook: Historical Statistics: 1960–87* (Paris: OECD, 1989), 37.
Note: Comparable data beyond 1987 not yet available.

Manufacturing in Germany is an enormously important component of the country's gross domestic product as well. Comparing Germany to other major OECD countries reveals that value added in manufacturing as a percentage of GDP is again well above the OECD average (see Table 5).

Manufacturing exports, then, continue to form the cornerstone of German economic strength, and comparing German export performance to the other OECD countries reveals that German industry has remained highly competitive in international markets through the 1980s.

Inflation. A second measure of Germany's performance is price

Table 5. Value added in manufacturing as a percent of GDP for various OECD countries

Country	1960–67	1968–73	1974–79	1980–87
W. Germany	39.9	37.3	34.6	31.8
U.S.	28.0	25.5	23.3	20.6
Japan	34.5	35.2	30.5	29.3
France	29.0	28.4	26.7	22.6
U.K.	30.0	28.2	26.3	21.7[a]
Italy	27.9	27.1	28.5	25.0
Austria	33.6	32.8	28.7	27.0
Norway	21.2	21.4	19.7	14.6
Sweden	27.4	24.8	24.0	20.8

Source: OECD, Economic Outlook: Historical Statistics: 1960–87 (Paris: OECD, 1989), 59.
[a] 1980–86 only (from OECD Historical Statistics: 1988).
Note: Comparable data beyond 1987 not yet available.

stability in the face of inflationary pressures since the 1970s. Table 6 shows that inflation in West Germany was the lowest of the major OECD countries in 1968–73 and again in 1973–79. In 1979–88, German inflation was lower than in all other countries save Japan.

Table 6. Average percent annual change in consumer price index

Country	1960–68	1968–73	1973–79	1979–88
W. Germany	2.7	4.6	4.7	2.9
U.S.	2.0	5.0	8.5	5.6
Japan	5.7	7.0	10.0	2.5
France	3.6	6.1	10.7	7.8
U.K.	3.6	7.5	15.6	7.4
Italy	4.0	5.8	16.1	11.8
Austria	3.6	5.2	6.3	4.0
Norway	3.9	6.9	8.7	8.8
Sweden	3.8	6.0	9.8	8.1

Sources: OECD, Economic Outlook: Historical Statistics: 1960–1987 (Paris: OECD, 1989), and Main Economic Indicators (Paris: OECD, April 1989).

Economic growth. In terms of economic growth, Germany looks somewhat less formidable. Germany recorded moderate growth rates through the 1970s, but then slowed considerably relative to the other OECD countries. Very slow growth in the early 1980s can be traced directly to the deflationary fiscal and monetary policies the government began pursuing in 1979. Fearing inflation, the powerful and autonomous German Central Bank (Bundesbank) deliberately put the brakes on growth after the second oil crisis of that year (Scharpf, 1984:281–82, 284–85). Thus, growth figures for Germany in the early 1980s must be interpreted against the backdrop of a conscious political decision to head off inflation by, among other things, raising interest rates. Between 1979 and at least 1982, Germany actively chose not to grow. This helps explain the pattern depicted in Table 7.

Table 7. Economic growth: Average percent annual change in real GDP

Country	1960–68	1968–73	1973–79	1979–88
W. Germany	4.1	4.9	2.3	1.7
U.S.	4.5	3.2	2.4	2.9
Japan	10.2	8.7	3.6	4.0
France	5.4	5.5	2.8	1.9
U.K.	3.1	3.3	1.5	2.0
Italy	5.7	4.5	3.7	2.4
Austria	4.2	5.9	2.9	1.9
Norway	4.4	4.1	4.9	3.0
Sweden	4.4	3.7	1.8	1.8

Sources: OECD, *Economic Outlook: Historical Statistics: 1960–1987* (Paris: OECD, 1989), and *Main Economic Indicators* (Paris: OECD, April 1990).

Unemployment. Until 1973, German unemployment was the lowest of the major OECD countries. However, it rose somewhat over the late 1970s, and quite sharply in the early 1980s. While average unemployment in Germany for 1980–88 was still below that of other comparably sized economies in the OECD (except Japan's), it has grown well beyond that of Europe's smaller economies (Sweden, Norway, and Austria), as Table 8 shows.

Table 8. Unemployment as percent of total labor force

Country	1960–67	1968–73	1974–79	1980–88
W. Germany	0.8	0.8	3.5	6.8
U.S.	5.0	4.6	6.7	7.4
Japan	1.3	1.2	1.9	2.5
France	1.5	—	4.5	9.0
U.K.	1.5	2.4	4.2	9.9
Italy	4.9	5.7	6.6	9.7
Austria	2.0	1.4	1.6	3.6
Norway	1.0	—	1.8	2.5
Sweden	1.6	2.2	1.9	2.6

Sources: OECD, *Economic Outlook: Historical Statistics: 1960–1987* (Paris: OECD, 1989), and *Main Economic Indicators* (Paris: OECD, January 1990).

Interpreting German unemployment figures requires some background on the political decisions that lie behind them. Chapter 5 treats in more detail the policy shifts in the late 1970s and 1980s that have exacerbated rather than alleviated unemployment in Germany. Here it is sufficient to note that some of the employment promotion programs the Social Democrats instituted in the late 1960s were subsequently cut back as part of Helmut Schmidt's austerity package of 1975, and further dismantled after 1982 under the conservative Kohl government.

With these caveats, and taking all four measures of economic adjustment together, it is nonetheless clear that the German economy has weathered recent economic crises relatively more gracefully than most comparably sized economies. On all four counts—competitiveness, inflation, growth, and unemployment—Germany does no worse than the OECD average (growth), or slightly better than average (unemployment), or much better than the OECD average (competitiveness and inflation).

These indicators of German economic performance suggest that Germany has adjusted quite successfully in economic terms compared to the other advanced capitalist countries. Has German adjustment been politically successful as well? Has adjustment been accomplished, in Katzenstein's words, "with due regard for the requirements of political legitimacy"? Again the evidence suggests that it has.

Political Measures of Adjustment

As the postwar German boom began to wane in the early 1970s, many observers predicted the breakdown of the German model of collaborative, peaceful industrial relations. Scholars on the left argued that economic downturn would reveal the contradictions that had been inherent in the cooperative policies of German unions all along (see, for example, Bergmann, Jacobi, and Müller-Jentsch 1979: especially 42–44). Other observers foresaw a more straightforward deterioration of collaborative relations between labor and capital as the economic context became more zero sum (see for example Thimm 1980: especially 60). Despite their differences, both saw the German model as a "fair weather system." The buoyant economy of the 1950s and 1960s had papered over the contradictions by allowing both German business and labor to benefit, but more difficult economic times would render German labor relations more contentious and/or reveal the real weakness of German labor.

The end of the German economic miracle and the upheaval in international markets starting in the 1970s did fundamentally change the context of labor politics. Yet, despite the end of "easy growth" in Germany, the character of labor-capital relations has turned out to be far less fragile than these observers had predicted. The main ingredient of the German model—relatively peaceful labor relations premised on labor strength—survived the transition from the prosperous 1960s to the more turbulent economic and political context of the late 1970s and 1980s.

Strikes. Strike statistics show that West German industrial relations are still very peaceful compared to those of other countries. The single worst strike year in Germany in the postwar period (1984, when 226 working days per 1,000 workers were lost to industrial conflict) was well below an average year in Britain or Italy. The German average over the years 1976–87 was thirty-eight working days lost per 1,000 workers; only Japan and Austria experienced less industrial strife in this period. Table 9 shows that the German pattern is closest to Europe's small states, which are often held up as models of peaceful labor relations.

Table 9. Average working days lost per 1,000 workers 1976–87

West Germany	38
United States	158
Japan	17
Austria	2
France	85
Italy	915
Norway	78
Sweden	121
United Kingdom	435

Source: Calculated on the basis of figures in ILO, *Yearbook of Labour Statistics* (Geneva: International Labour Office, 1988).
Note: Comparable data beyond 1987 not yet available.

Qualitative indicators. Strike statistics, however, tell only a part of the story. More qualitative indicators, gleaned from statements by leading politicians, unionists, and employers, corroborate the conclusion that German labor relations are still informed less by polarization and class conflict than by what we might call "cooperative antagonism." There is no truce between labor and capital in Germany, and conflict between the two intensified somewhat in the 1980s. However, on all sides—government, employers, and unions—the rhetoric is less vitriolic and the policies less radical than in many other countries.

Katzenstein notes that despite Chancellor Helmut Kohl's promise to effect a "big change" (*Die Wende*) in Germany when he took office in 1982, his government's policies in fact turned out to be much more moderate than those of his conservative counterparts in other countries (1987:349).[6] Both Ronald Reagan and Margaret Thatcher "went to the mat" with organized labor in the course of implementing their conservative programs.[7] Deep political cleavages of course separate Kohl and the German unions (particularly the IG Metall). While his policies have run counter to labor's interests on many issues, his government has certainly not undertaken an all-out attack on organized labor's institutional

6. *The Economist* makes the same point in its 6 December 1986 survey of West German politics and economics.

7. For example, Reagan's firing of PATCO workers in 1981 and Thatcher's war with the British miners in 1984–85.

position. Kohl has even made overtures to the unions to reopen regular discussions between labor, business, and the government along the lines of the "concerted action" (*Konzertierte Aktion*) discussions of the late 1960s and early 1970s (*Stuttgarter Zeitung*, 15 December 1986).

Ironically perhaps, the Social Democrats' former coalition partner, the Free Democratic party (F.D.P.), has turned out to be the unions' greatest foe in the current conservative coalition. For example, the F.D.P. was the instigator behind legislation to enhance the chances of "minority" (read "non-DGB") candidates in works council elections, which the DGB unions viewed as an attack on their position in the plant.[8]

Relations between German unions and employers became somewhat more strained in the early 1980s. But while German employers in many ways benefited from the unions' political and market weakness, they have shown no signs of wanting to seize this opportunity to defeat labor decisively. The business community in fact opposed the F.D.P. proposal to change works council election rules (*Frankfurter Allgemeine Zeitung*, 2 February 1985; *Westdeutsche Allgemeine Zeitung*, 11 June 1987). A representative of the Association of West German Employers in the Metalworking Industries (Gesamtmetall) explained the business community's position in this way:

> We would rather have the whole works council composed of DGB members. As soon as you get splinter groups in the plant, you get unrest in the plant as well. We would rather deal with one union, with a unified works council. A single, unified opponent is more reliable and trustworthy [*verläßlich*]; more than one faction fosters competition among them as each tries to outdo the other. We would rather have a single strong and self-confident union to work with. [Interview, 1987]

These sentiments, while perhaps not universal, are nonetheless very widely held in the German business community.

Even after the difficult conflict in 1984 in the metalworking industry over weekly working-time reduction, conciliatory tones could be heard from the employers' camp. In recent years the head of Gesamtmetall, Werner Stumpfe, has at least twice suggested that the IG Metall and Gesamtmetall initiate a regular and ongoing dialogue in order to reduce tensions between the two (*Handelsblatt*, 5 September 1986).[9]

---

8. For a text of the bill, see "Entwurf eines Gesetzes zur Verstärkung der Minderheitenrechte in den Betrieben und Verwaltungen," Bonn: Deutscher Bundestag, 10. Wahlperiode, Drucksache 10. The debate over this legislation is covered in *Stuttgarter Zeitung*, 13 December 1984; *Der Spiegel*, Nr. 50, 1984; *Wirtschaftswoche* 51 (14 December 1984); and *Handelsblatt*, 25 January 1985 and 24 May 1985. For the unions' position see IG Metall, 1985a, and the DGB's "Umfassender Angriff auf Arbeitnehmerrechte und Einheitsgewerkschaft" (DGB Nachrichtendienst, 22 May 1985).

9. The head of the IG Metall, Hans Mayr, rejected the idea as a publicity ploy on the part of Gesamtmetall.

Also, in a particularly telling exchange on the question of including apprentices in the 1987 agreement reducing working time in the metalworking industries,[10] Stumpfe said that although employers had serious reservations about including trainees in the deal, they conceded the point because this is the group among whom the union recruits many of its new members. According to Stumpfe, "We saw that if we want to preserve the IG Metall's strength, we cannot weaken the union on this point" (*Kölner Stadt Anzeiger,* 12 June 1987). In sum, Hans-Peter Stihl (head of the Employers' Federation for the Metalworking Industries in Baden-Württemberg) speaks for much of the business community when he says that German employers still want "strong unions... who are capable of enforcing the rules they agree to" (quoted in Bahnmüller 1985:24).

The rhetoric on the union side is generally sharper and less conciliatory, but the underlying tone still reflects "cooperative antagonism." Union leaders in Germany are often praised for being "sensible" and "responsible."[11] While this characterization is frequently overstated, the evidence does suggest that the huge bureaucratic apparatus of German trade unionism does encourage moderation by its leaders. In 1986, for example, Franz Steinkühler, long considered the IG Metall's enfant terrible by employers, was elected president of the all-important Metalworkers' Union.[12] With Steinkühler's election, the union's leadership passed from an older generation of unionists who had participated in the rebuilding of Germany after the war (such as Steinkühler's predecessors Eugen Loderer and Hans Mayr), to a younger one, whose politically formative years and experiences were those of the student movement in the late 1960s. Many observers worried that this generational change posed a threat to Germany's "social peace."

Since his election, however, it has become amply clear that Steinkühler is not the "loose cannon" many feared. Particularly in the 1987 collective bargaining round, Steinkühler established a reputation within the business community as a "determined opponent, but a reliable and responsible one, with whom one can reach sensible compromises" (interview with representative of Gesamtmetall, 1987; see also *Manager Magazin,* October 1986:30-36, and Chapter 7). Although Steinkühler's rhetoric is often rather inflammatory, those employers who have dealt most with him praise his fundamental pragmatism. Stihl, who for years was Steinkühler's opponent in regional collective bargaining, calls the

---

10. Apprentices had been excluded from working-time reduction under the previous (1984) agreement.

11. See the discussion in Flanagan, Soskice and Ulman 1983:260–75.

12. For various views on Steinkühler's election, see *Neue Ruhr Zeitung,* 23 October 1986; *Handelsblatt,* 9 and 10 July 1986; *Frankfurter Allgemeine Zeitung,* 9 July and 24 October 1986; *Stuttgarter Zeitung,* 9 July 1986. For an interview with Franz Steinkühler see *Die Zeit,* 24 October 1986.

new president "a very pragmatic man ... who does not seek conflict for its own sake" ("Der Arbeitskämpfer," *Wirtschaftswoche*, 17 October 1986). The head of Gesamtmetall, Werner Stumpfe, concurs, calling Steinkühler "a responsible and reliable bargaining partner" ("Unter Ehrenmännern," *Der Spiegel*, 27 April 1987).

This brief survey of qualitative indicators of the character of relations among the German government, employers, and unions points to the same conclusion as the strike statistics presented above. Conflicts between labor and capital are hard fought in Germany, but the atmosphere of labor relations favors compromise over all-or-nothing battles. The kind of "social partnership" that characterized labor relations in the "easy growth" period of the 1950s and 1960s came under strain in the more turbulent 1970s and 1980s, but compared to other countries the tone and character of labor conflict in Germany are relatively mild.

Quantitative and qualitative measures of labor conflict since 1970 indicate that adjustment in Germany has been relatively successful in political as well as economic terms. It is this combination of positive adjustment in both technical/economic terms and in political terms that qualifies Germany as a case of negotiated adjustment.

THE "DEMOCRATIC CORPORATISM" MODEL

A number of authors have argued that corporatist countries are the most successful in adjusting peacefully to economic change[13] (see, for example, Schmitter and Lehmbruch 1979; Lehmbruch and Schmitter 1982; Lange and Garrett 1985; Cameron 1984; Katzenstein 1984, 1985; Wilensky, 1976, 1981; Wilensky and Turner 1987; Korpi and Shalev 1979; and Goldthorpe 1984a). Despite great diversity in their definitions of corporatism, one of the striking features of this literature is the widespread agreement that exists at the empirical extremes. Virtually all corporatism theorists, regardless of the particulars of their model or definition, agree on Sweden, Norway, and Austria as instances of corporatism and consistently rank Britain and the United States as clearly noncorporatist. Disagreement still exists, however, on a range of other cases, including West Germany.[14]

13. When referring to democratic political economies, authors variously qualify the term "corporatism" as "neo-, liberal, societal, or democratic." For ease of exposition, I will refer simply to "corporatism," with the understanding that in all cases I am referring to the variant that characterizes some democratic political economies.

14. Schmitter's (1981) measure of corporatism puts Germany squarely in the middle. Using combined rankings of organizational centralization and associational monopoly, Germany scores an *8* on a scale that runs from *1* (Austria) to *14* (Britain). Miriam Golden (1986) categorizes the Federal Republic of Germany (along with the United States, Australia, Canada, and the United Kingdom) as a case of "pluralist" policymaking networks in her sixfold typology. For Wilensky (1976, 1983), Germany is "marginally corporatist."

Rather than enter this conceptual quagmire with yet another definition and categorization scheme, I find it more useful to highlight the logic of corporatism by constructing an ideal-typical model of it. Such an ideal type can then serve as the basis for identifying what is distinctive about the German case and for generating hypotheses about what sustains negotiated adjustment there. The characterization of corporatism offered here is inductively derived, and based on those empirical cases that are broadly seen as noncontroversial.

Two factors occupy a privileged position in corporatism literature and form the basis for constructing such an ideal-typical model. These are the *structure of interests* that characterize corporatist countries and the *bargaining process* through which consensus between labor and capital is achieved.

Structure of Interests

Most cross-national analyses of corporatism are based either explicitly or implicitly on Philippe C. Schmitter's definition of corporatism:

> Corporatism can be defined as a system of interest intermediation in which the constituent units are organized into a limited number of singular, compulsory, noncompetitive, hierarchically ordered, and functionally differentiated categories, recognized or licensed (if not created) by the state and granted a deliberate representational monopoly within their respective categories in exchange for observing certain controls on their selection of leaders and articulation of demands and supports. [Schmitter 1977:9]

This definition emphasizes the structure of economic interests. Many authors have operationalized this concept of corporatism in terms of the organizational characteristics of the labor movement, generally assuming that business interests are similarly organized (Wilensky 1976, 1983). The unity and centralization of labor appear to be necessary preconditions for corporatism. However, while the requisite structures may be necessary for corporatism, in themselves they are not sufficient to explain how consensus between labor and capital is achieved in corporatist countries. The way these centralized socioeconomic interest groups interact is a second component of the corporatist model.

Bargaining Processes

In many cross-national and nearly all quantitative studies of corporatism, the structural and organizational attributes of economic interest groups are used as a proxy for a set of attitudes and processes that theorists argue are central to the corporatist model of negotiated adjustment.

Some authors are more explicit than others on the processes that occur within these structures. Katzenstein's qualitative study of corporatism in Europe's small states (1985), for example, emphasizes an ideology of "social partnership" between labor and business as a defining feature of the corporatist model. In small countries like Sweden and Austria, the shared perception of vulnerability and exposure to the vicissitudes of international markets helps sustain the "voluntary and informal coordination of conflicting objectives through continuous bargaining between interest groups, state bureaucracies and political parties" (Katzenstein 1985:32). Wilensky's definition of corporatism captures the same process: "By democratic corporatism I mean the capacity of strongly organized, centralized economic interest groups interacting under government auspices within a quasi-public framework to produce peak bargains involving social policy, fiscal and monetary policy, and incomes policies—the major interrelated issues of modern political economy" (1981:345).

This process is often overlooked by authors who rely heavily on quantitative measures of the structural attributes of economic interests groups, but it is crucial to understanding the logic of the corporatist model. This logic is best summarized by Wilensky: "Labor, interested in wages, working conditions, social security, and, to a lesser extent, participatory democracy, is forced to take account of inflation, productivity, and the need for investment; employers, interested in profit, productivity, and investment are forced to take account of social policy" (1983:53). This notion of trade-offs that centralized labor and business organizations negotiate—formally or informally—under state auspices is an essential aspect of the logic of corporatism. The structures may be necessary preconditions for the trade-offs, but the trade-offs and not the structures are what sustain corporatist bargaining over time and what ultimately explain how peaceful change in these countries is achieved. In short, particular structures *and* processes are necessary (and sufficient) to explain corporatist outcomes.

GERMAN CORPORATISM?

As I mentioned above, the Federal Republic of Germany is a much-disputed and somewhat anomalous case in the corporatism literature. Corporatism theorists tend to have trouble with the German case no matter what they are trying to explain. Germany regularly scores high on the "dependent variable" side of corporatist studies, whether the outcome is general economic performance (Cameron 1984),[15] social

15. Although Cameron does not use the term "corporatism" except in the title of his article.

and economic policies (Wilensky 1976, 1983; Wilensky and Turner 1987), or industrial conflict (Korpi and Shalev 1979). However, Germany generally ranks anywhere from medium to low on most measures of corporatism (the independent variable in these studies). Harold Wilensky (1976) considers Germany "marginally corporatist," citing several functional equivalents for the structures and processes he sees as critical components of corporatism. David Cameron (1984) increases Germany's corporatism "rating" by including works councils and codetermination. Walter Korpi and Michael Shalev throw up their hands and conclude that Germany is the "most baffling" of the eighteen cases they examined (1979:183).

Most corporatism theorists disqualify Germany from the ranks of the "clearly" corporatist countries on the grounds that it lacks the structural prerequisites. Usually they mean that organized labor appears not to be sufficiently centralized or unified to fit the model. The German union movement is—formally at least—neither as centralized nor as encompassing as the countries most regularly associated with corporatism. Not only do the DGB unions organize a smaller proportion of the total German work force than their counterparts in Austria and Sweden; the central confederation does not perform the same leadership role, for example, in collective bargaining rounds. Instead, the individual industrial unions in West Germany formulate their policies and strategies largely independently of the DGB.[16]

The problem in West Germany, however, is not so much that it lacks the requisite structures, or functional equivalents, but rather that the processes that characterize "classic" (national level) corporatism are absent or weak. Most cross-national studies of corporatism are insufficiently detailed to uncover the other structural characteristics of the political economy of labor in Germany that compensate for the relative weakness of the DGB. Two important factors are the informal coordinating role played by the IG Metall within the union movement and the organization and centralization of German business interests. At the same time, however, most cross-national studies of corporatism miss what remains truly distinctive about the German model of negotiated adjustment, even if functional equivalents for its structural prerequisites can be found. What really distinguishes the German case from the corporatist countries is the role of the state and the channels and processes through which industrial adjustment is negotiated.

---

16. DGB policies follow rather than lead those of Germany's industrial unions. The sometimes odious task of finding the common denominator among them and defining German labor's position on particular issues often falls to the DGB. This has not always been easy. For instance, the individual unions have taken quite different positions on the question of working-time reduction and organized labor's relationship to the Green party.

GERMAN CORPORATISM: THE ORGANIZATION OF ECONOMIC INTERESTS

Unions

The formal decentralization of labor in Germany is compensated for to a certain extent by the informal leadership role played by the IG Metall. With over 2.6 million members, the IG Metall is far and away Germany's largest union (Löhrlein 1989:66). It has twice as many members as the second largest union, the public sector workers (Öffentliche Dienst, Transport, und Verkehr, or ÖTV), and four times as many as the third largest union, the chemical workers' union (IG Chemie-Papier-Keramik, or IG Chemie). Alone, the IG Metall accounts for 33.7 percent of total DGB membership (Löhrlein 1989:66, 68).

The IG Metall occupies a pivotal role within the German labor movement. Wage negotiations are conducted separately by each of the sixteen unions, but in most cases, the other unions wait for a settlement by the IG Metall, which then serves as a benchmark for subsequent negotiations in the other industries.[17] The IG Metall has led the German union movement through many important struggles. In the 1950s and early 1960s the IG Metall succeeded (after the DGB had failed) in negotiating a reduction in the regular workweek from forty-eight to forty hours in a series of bargains that were subsequently extended (through collective bargaining in the other industries) to the entire economy.[18] The IG Metall was also behind other important union breakthroughs such as six-week paid holidays. The union first achieved this in a strike in the steel industry in 1978, and currently 66 percent of all German workers have six or more weeks of annual paid vacation, and another 28 percent have between five and six weeks (Bundesministerium für Arbeit und Sozialordnung 1988:4.8).

In addition, since the IG Metall commands a huge bloc of votes (though not a majority) within the DGB, this union has the single most important voice in DGB policy. While important differences among the individual unions exist on certain issues, such as the unions' relationship to the Green party, the IG Metall remains nonetheless the leading voice of German unionism.[19] Thus, while the IG Metall technically

17. There have been exceptions to this. In the 1971 wage round, for example, the public sector workers' union (ÖTV) served the "pilot" function. And, some of the DGB unions (led by the Chemical Workers' Union, the IG Chemie) have taken a different approach to working time reduction in the 1980s.

18. The importance of the unions' industrial victories in Germany can hardly be overstated. The forty-hour workweek was never codified in law. Nor, for that matter, does Germany have a minimum wage.

19. In the late 1970s and early 1980s some significant differences emerged between "left" and "right" factions within the DGB. The IG Metall leads the left, or what Markovits calls the "activist" unions; the Chemical Workers' Union (IG Chemie) is considered the leader of the right, what Markovits calls the "accommodationist" or "social

organizes only 10.9 percent of the total dependent German labor force,[20] its policies reverberate throughout the economy. The size and position of the IG Metall within the union movement and in the economy compensate on the labor side for Germany's weaker scores on structural measures of corporatism.

Employers

A second important structural attribute of the German case is the extraordinarily high degree of organization among business interests. The corporatist literature tends to use the organizational unity and centralization of labor as a measure of the degree of centralization of socioeconomic interests generally, more or less assuming that business interests are organized in a parallel fashion. In Germany, business interests are arguably much more centralized and organized than labor interests.

West German business is organized into two main associations. The Bundesverband der Deutschen Industrie (BDI) coordinates the business community's lobbying and other political activities. Eighty to ninety percent of all firms belong to the BDI (Katzenstein 1987:25). The business community's economic activities are coordinated by the Bundesvereinigung der Deutschen Arbeitgeberverbände (BDA). The BDA coordinates the collective bargaining strategies of its industrial and regional member organizations (*Verbände*), which do the actual negotiating with the unions. The BDA also provides its member firms with legal support and financial assistance in the event of strikes. At least eighty percent of all employers belong to the BDA (Katzenstein 1987:25).

Membership in the BDA does not imply casual obligation. The BDA has established guidelines for its member organizations in their dealings with the unions, including an enumeration of certain areas in which employers' negotiations with the unions are to be coordinated at the national level.[21] The centralization of German business interests and strong coordination by these two associations compensates for labor's relatively lower level of organization and centralization.

In Germany, whether the employer belongs to the business federation is in many ways more important than whether the employees

partner" unions (Markovits 1986: especially chaps. 4 and 5). However, contrary to analyses predicting that these cleavages would grow and eventually paralyze the labor movement, coordination rather than competition among the unions continues to be the dominant pattern in West Germany.

20. Calculated on the basis of 1987 figures in Löhrlein (1989:66, 69).

21. The BDA calls this list "The catalogue of wage and collective bargaining issues to be centrally coordinated" (*Katalog der zu koordinierenden lohn- und tarifpolitischen Fragen*). The unions call it the "Tabu Katalog." For a text of this document, see Degen et al. 1979. Chapter 5 below contains a discussion of the Tabu Katalog.

belong to the union. Firms that do not belong to the employers' association are not officially bound by contracts the association concludes with the union.[22] On the other hand, though nonunion workers in a given plant are not in a formal sense parties to collective contracts negotiated by the unions, such contracts are in fact applied to all workers in the plant, union members or not.[23]

Within industries, however, membership in the employers' organizations is pervasive. In the metalworking industries, for example, the IG Metall's bargaining partner, the Gesamtverband der metallindustriellen Arbeitgeberverbände (Gesamtmetall) bargains directly for its member firms. With its 8,200 member firms (employing 2.9 million workers), Gesamtmetall speaks for virtually the entire metalworking industry. Gesamtmetall has organized 42 percent of all firms in the metalworking industries, and these account for 72 percent of all employees in these industries (Gesamtmetall 1989:1–2).

Thus, we can find functional equivalents for the structural attributes of corporatism, factors that compensate for German labor's weaker organizational unity and lower degree of centralization. But what of corporatist *processes* in Germany? Where and how are the trade-offs negotiated?

GERMAN CORPORATISM: THE ROLE OF THE STATE

Most authors assign an important role to the state in facilitating the kind of stable, centrally negotiated deals that are the hallmark of corporatism. This is as true for theorists who argue that social democratic (or labor-sympathetic) governments play a necessary convening role in corporatist bargaining (Luebbert 1987; Korpi and Shalev 1979; and Hibbs 1978) as for those who see corporatism as compatible with other political constellations (Wilensky 1981). As discussed above, the logic of corporatism hinges on the trade-offs produced by bargaining among peak associations, and this is where the role of the state is crucial in sustaining the negotiated adjustment that characterizes corporatist countries.

Again drawing on Wilensky (1983), the key to corporatist, negotiated adjustment involves trade-offs among policies in which all parties have an interest: fiscal, incomes, monetary, social, and, often, active labor

22. However, the government can, and regularly does, extend the terms of collective bargaining agreements to many of these firms as well (*Allgemeinverbindlichkeitserklärung*, Declaration of General Applicability).

23. There is no closed or union shop in Germany. Also, the extension of contract provisions to nonunionized workers was formalized in the specific area of wage contract law when the Federal Labor Court (Bundesarbeitsgericht) ruled that "wage contracts that differentiate between union-organised and nonorganised employees are invalid" (Müller-Jentsch and Sperling 1978:276).

market policies. Corporatism works in those countries where labor unions temper their demands on those issues in which they have an interest (e.g., wages, through their participation in formal or informal incomes policies) and ensure industrial peace in exchange for concessions in other policy areas. In Sweden, for example, active labor market policies have greased the wheels of corporatist negotiations since the 1960s. In Austria, the government's policy of sustaining employment in the late 1970s through the expansion of the public sector was an important concession to labor and a part of the trade-offs that have helped to sustain the collaborative business-labor relations that characterize that country.[24] According to the classic democratic corporatist model, Keynesian demand management, countercyclical state spending, and active labor market policies are all contributions that governments in the corporatist countries make in order to sustain growth and ease labor market rigidities, which in turn help to sustain centralized bargaining and promote labor-business cooperation.

The politics among business, labor, and the state in Germany most closely approximated the processes with which corporatism is associated between 1967 and 1974. After the Social Democrats first came to power (in the Grand Coalition of 1966 with the Christliche Demokratische Union (CDU); three years later as senior partner in a coalition with the F.D.P.), the German government aggressively pursued Keynesian fiscal policies and also increased government spending for active labor market policies. It was in this period, too, that the government initiated "Concerted Action" discussions (Konzertierte Aktion) among business, labor, and the state, which included an informal incomes policy.

However, peak-level bargaining in West Germany was always a pale imitation of tripartite negotiations in the corporatist countries. As Robert Flanagan, David Soskice, and Lloyd Ulman point out, the "Concerted Action" discussions provided a forum for debate, but they did not "function as policy-making sessions," nor did they hammer out trade-offs, for example, by "integrat[ing] monetary and fiscal policies with wage and price setting" (1983:285). The informal incomes policy that was worked out in 1967 broke down in a wave of spontaneous strikes in 1969, never to be revived in its former version. "Concerted Action" meetings became increasingly meaningless; and when they petered out in 1977, hardly anyone noticed.

The fact that peak-level bargaining in Germany had a very limited

---

24. By now it is clear that union cooperation in national incomes policies is not necessarily simply a matter of government coercion, as some authors once suggested (cf. Panitch 1976, 1977). Unions cooperate over the long run in state-sponsored incomes policies because there is a payoff for their cooperation. The benefits for labor are generally material (Cameron 1984; and Schwerin 1984). But as Peter Lange (1984) points out, the "rational basis" for union cooperation in wage restraint can be symbolic, but based on expectations that state policy will benefit them in the longer run.

43

and largely symbolic function is reflected in industrial trends in Germany in this period. In the early years of labor's incorporation into national-level bargaining, the unions delivered neither industrial peace nor wage restraint. Although strike levels remained low in Germany compared to other countries, they rose rather than fell in the early years of German "corporatism."[25] And real hourly wages in manufacturing increased at a rate of 5.2 percent for the 1968–73 period, up from 4.3 percent for 1960–68 (OECD 1986a:91).[26] Indeed, between 1969 and 1972 wages outpaced productivity gains for the first time since 1963 (Flanagan, Soskice, and Ulman 1983:224).

The early years of the social-liberal coalition saw the passage of a substantial amount of prolabor legislation. But after the initial flurry of activity, and especially after the oil crisis of 1973–74, the German state behaved quite differently from its more corporatist neighbors. Beginning with the Budget Structure Law of 1975 (Haushaltsstrukturgesetz), the Social Democratic government began successively cutting back spending in precisely those areas in which labor has the keenest interest. Though unemployment was rising in the late 1970s, Chancellor Helmut Schmidt cut spending on active labor market policies as part of a more general fiscal austerity package. Meanwhile, the Bundesbank moved aggressively toward a restrictive monetary policy that ultimately exacerbated the German recession in 1981–82. The government in a sense pulled out of its countercyclical steering role and increasingly let the market identify the winners and losers.[27] The Swedish and Austrian governments, in contrast, both continued to pursue full-employment policies (though the instruments were different), while the German government abandoned demand management, cut active labor market policies, and focused on price stability at the expense of rising unemployment (Scharpf 1984).

This line of analysis leads us to the same conclusions as some studies of corporatism, but via a different route. Germany is a marginal case of corporatism not so much because it lacks the structural prerequisites, but because, as a more micro perspective reveals, the German case does not conform to the "logic" of the corporatism model. If by corporatism we mean peak bargaining among business, labor, and the state over trade-offs among fiscal, monetary, social, active labor market, and incomes policies, then Germany is not corporatist. The reasons, however, do not lie with labor or with the organization of economic interests in the German political economy, as corporatism theorists relying on

25. Average annual strike activity rose from 102 working days lost per 1,000 workers for 1964–68 to 1,084 for 1969–74. These figures were calculated on the basis of ILO statistics (ILO 1986).

26. Hourly rates for manufacturing (not adjusted for inflation) rose from an annual average of 7.1 percent for 1960–68 to 10.3 percent for 1968–73 (OECD 1986a:91).

27. On this period, see especially Riemer, 1983: chap. 3, and Allen 1989d.

aggregate data stress. As I argued above, labor and business interests in Germany are more centralized than most measures of corporatism give them credit for.

The problem is not the interest organizations; it is the German state.[28] Two characteristics of the German political economy in particular complicate national bargaining processes and trade-offs that tend to characterize the corporatist countries. These (state-level) impediments to corporatism in Germany are both institutional and political.

Institutional Impediments

The Nazi legacy and the Allied occupation had important ramifications for the reconstruction of the West German state after World War II. The idea was to diffuse central state power; federalism and a strong and autonomous central bank were important elements in the institutional reconfiguration of the German state (see also Shonfield 1969:268–69). Both limit in important ways the national government's ability to intervene directly and selectively in the economy.

Federalism is stronger in Germany than in most other West European countries. Among the occupying forces after World War II, the United States in particular favored strong state-level powers. However, it is important to realize that federalism also has deep roots in German history. Federalist structures are firmly anchored in longstanding indigenous tradition (Allen 1989a:154).[29] State authorities in Germany today are somewhat less powerful than their American counterparts, but they nonetheless have substantial powers, and this limits central government authority. The *Länder* (states), for example, control a substantial share of tax revenues, which enhances their independence from the central government.

A further institutional check on central state authority is the German Central Bank (Bundesbank). In its autonomy from the government, the Bundesbank resembles the U.S. Federal Reserve Bank, and this distinguishes it sharply from the central banks of most comparably sized European countries (Shonfield 1969:269). As with federalism, the occupying forces favored an independent central bank, but the idea also commanded the support of crucial actors within Germany such as the Freiburg school economists, who shared the aversion to a strong, state-centered economy (Allen 1989d:264).

The autonomy of the Bundesbank complicates enormously the kind

28. Katzenstein's (1987) description of German politics as being characterized by a "centralized society" and a "decentralized state" dovetails with my analysis.

29. In addition, as Allen notes, West German federalism is no simple copy of the American model. There is more coordination among the states (*Länder*) and relations between them and the central government are characterized more by a "sharing" than a "division" of powers (Allen 1989a:154; see also Scharpf, Reissert, and Schnabel 1976).

of national-level trade-offs that are negotiated as a matter of course among business, labor, and government in the corporatist countries. The bank coordinates its policies with the German government, but operates with few restrictions. Its wide scope for independent action allows its leaders to insulate monetary policy from political pressures. To the extent that the Bundesbank's policies are therefore less "negotiable" in Germany than elsewhere, it is difficult to incorporate monetary policy into a package of nationally bargained policy trade-offs. Experience shows that the Bundesbank's traditionally intense commitment to price stability can outweigh other policy goals such as low unemployment. Scharpf (1984), for example, points out that the Bundesbank's restrictive monetary policy was directly at odds with the Social Democratic government's fiscal policy in the mid-1970s. The result of deflationary monetary policy in Germany in that period—in contrast to Austria and Sweden—was a sharp rise in unemployment in Germany.

Government policymakers negotiating with business and labor cannot trade off what they do not control. Strong federalism and a highly autonomous central bank in Germany make national-level bargaining of the sort that is routine in Sweden and Austria unlikely and difficult to sustain. The institutional fragmentation of economic policymaking in Germany, then, is one factor that inhibits German corporatism.

Political Impediments

If federalism and the Bundesbank are the most important institutional factors mediating against (national-level) corporatism in Germany, then the Free Democratic party counts as perhaps the most significant *political* force operating in the same direction. Despite its small size,[30] the Free Democratic party is pivotal in German politics. With very few exceptions, neither the Social Democratic Party (SPD) nor the Christian Democratic Union/Christian Social Union (CDU/CSU) has been able to form a national government without the F.D.P.[31] A coalition shift by the Free Democrats brought the Social Democrats to power in 1969, and another threw them out again in 1982.

Of all the German political parties, the Free Democrats have the strongest commitment to a free market economy, government at arm's length, and market-driven adjustment. The F.D.P. has close links to German industry and is particularly oriented toward small business and the more antiunion professional classes. If the immediate cause of the turn away from Keynesianism since the mid-1970s can be located in the

30. The Free Democratic party generally wins between 5 and 10 percent of the votes in federal elections, compared to about 30 to 45 percent by the SPD and CDU/CSU (*The Economist*, 6 December 1986).

31. One notable exception is of course the "Grand Coalition" between the SPD and the CDU in 1966–69, which excluded the F.D.P.

policies of the Bundesbank, the F.D.P. played a strong supporting role.

Political struggles within the F.D.P. itself help explain what precipitated the policy shift away from support for strong prolabor policies over the course of the 1970s. As Katzenstein points out, there are two factions within the F.D.P., a "social-liberal" wing and a "national-liberal" wing (1987:14). Agreement between the F.D.P. and the SPD on foreign policy issues originally facilitated the formation of a coalition between them in 1969. In the F.D.P. Willy Brandt found a ready ally for his *Ostpolitik* (Markovits 1986:130). At that time, the "social-liberal" faction was in ascendance within the party. This faction was amenable to economic reform and relatively strong macroeconomic intervention. This constellation of interests provided the political basis for the reforms of the early 1970s: Keynesianism, active labor market policies, and labor legislation such as the revised Works Constitution Act of 1972.

By the mid-1970s, however, the "national-liberal" wing, which favors market forces over government intervention, was gaining strength within the F.D.P. (Katzenstein 1987:14). The conflicts that plagued the SPD–F.D.P. coalition in the late 1970s and ultimately led to its collapse were in large measure the consequence of this shift in the balance of power within the F.D.P. and its adoption of a more rigid market orientation. At several critical junctures, the Free Democrats were able to rein in the Social Democrats on policy issues of central concern to the unions. The Free Democrats, for example, were behind the watering down of the Codetermination Act of 1976.[32] Wielding strength beyond its numbers, the Free Democratic party thus became an important political drag on the trade-offs—especially between fiscal and incomes policy—that the Social Democrats had pursued in the early 1970s.

In "classic" corporatist democracies, state policy complements and helps sustain national bargains between labor and employers by compensating the unions for their cooperation in dampening inflation and promoting adjustment. As the Swedish case shows, state intervention in the economy need not override the market, but government policy nonetheless plays an important role in sustaining growth and easing labor market rigidities. As Katzenstein puts it, corporatist countries pursue the goals of economic efficiency, but in all cases "compensatory political gestures are essential for maintaining consensus on how to adjust" (Katzenstein 1985:29).

32. Economic policy was also a contentious issue within the SPD in the late 1970s, with Chancellor Helmut Schmidt assuming a position on the "Right" of the party. Indeed, many authors have suggested that Schmidt used the Free Democrats as a smokescreen, for example justifying his austerity program of the late 1970s to labor as having been the F.D.P.'s doing (*Koalitionszwang*) (Markovits 1986:130; Allen and Riemer 1985:8). No doubt there is much truth to the assertion that Schmidt himself pushed these policies very hard within his own party. The shift in the F.D.P. probably served to strengthen the chancellor's position. See also chapter 5.

As we have seen, Germany does not fit the corporatist model. Yet numerous studies demonstrate that Germany achieves many of the same outcomes in terms of economic performance and labor peace that are commonly attributed to corporatism. Or, in Katzenstein's words: "West Germany comes closer than any other large industrial state to the logic by which political life in the small European states is organized" (Katzenstein 1985:31). That "logic" is what I have been referring to as "negotiated adjustment." But if adjustment in Germany is not negotiated in tripartite national agreements, where is it negotiated, and what sustains peaceful, negotiated adjustment in Germany over time? Codetermination is central to the answer to this question.

THE LEGALISM OF INDUSTRIAL RELATIONS IN GERMANY

Numerous labor scholars have noted the high degree of legalism that governs labor relations in West Germany.[33] An intricate web of rules regulates many aspects of labor relations, including national collective bargaining.[34] However, it is the pervasive framework of codetermination that especially justifies the characterization of German labor relations as "legalistic." As of 1979, 18.6 million German employees (or 84.5 percent of the total labor force) were covered by one or more of four different codetermination laws that give labor participatory rights at various levels and specify both labor's and management's obligations under the law (German Press and Information Office 1979:235; see also Thimm 1981).[35]

The legalism of German industrial relations has its critics,[36] but for a number of other authors it forms the basis for an alternative explanation of negotiated adjustment. A long line of labor scholars have credited codetermination with providing an important channel for the peaceful resolution of labor-management conflict (Shuchman 1957;

33. See, for example, Aaron and Wedderburn 1972; Erd 1978; Wedderburn, Lewis, and Clark 1983; Crouch 1978:201–2; and Müller-Jentsch and Sperling 1978:276–77.

34. For example, the conditions under which unions can strike and employers can lock out.

35. These laws are the Montanmitbestimmung law (for the coal and steel industries); the 1976 Codetermination Law for companies outside the coal and steel industries employing over two thousand workers; the Works Constitution Act (Betriebsverfassungsgesetz) for plants employing over five workers; and the version of the Works Constitution Act that applies to the public sector (Bundespersonalvertretungsgesetz).

36. Colin Crouch (1978) and Rainer Erd (1978) have been perhaps the most outspoken critics of the legalism of industrial relations, which in their view hinders the effective representation of workers' interests (Erd 1978: passim), and which Crouch even sees as "coercive" (1978:206). Walther Müller-Jentsch and Hans-Joachim Sperling (1978:276–77) also stress the limits that various legal regulations place on union activities. As will become apparent, my evaluation of the net effect of legalism in German industrial relations is very different.

Spiro 1958; Tegtmeier 1973; Diamant 1977; Jenkins 1973: especially 121, 130; Macbeath 1973; and Kissler 1989). Codetermination laws establish permanent dialogue and ongoing bargaining between labor and capital at the plant and company levels and encourage, if not require, constant negotiation and renegotiation of their competing interests (see also Helm 1986).

In his empirical study of the effects of German codetermination, Werner Tegtmeier concludes that this system has contributed decisively to social stability (1973:247). His characterization of labor-capital relations under codetermination is reminiscent of the give and take between labor and capital that is the hallmark of national-level corporatism (1973:246–47). Tegtmeier notes that labor relations under codetermination are not always tension-free, but he demonstrates that they are generally characterized by constructive cooperation (1973:246). Alfred Diamant arrives at similar conclusions in his 1977 study, which also argues that the "corporative features" of the German political economy "tend to be strengthened by codetermination" (1977:39).

An important report on the effects of codetermination on German business concluded that worker participation in company-level decision making does not significantly interfere with the economic efficiency of German firms, but it does give labor a forum for negotiating over the social consequences of economic decisions (Biedenkopf Commission 1970: especially 41–48).[37] According to this report, the main impact of codetermination is not so much to reverse management initiatives as it is to consider their social impact and revise them accordingly (*soziale Korrektur*) (1970:43). On the basis of statements by members of executive and supervisory boards of German companies that report concludes:

> Worker participation...has led to a greater emphasis on the social aspects...of company activities, but has not called into question the validity of the profit motive as the guiding principle of company initiative and planning. Thus, for example, rationalization measures aimed at reducing [production] costs never encountered labor resistance so long as adequate provisions were taken to maintain the social [standard] of the workers in the firm. [1970:42]

The same goes, according to the report, for worker participation in plant works councils (1970:42). Indeed, the commission "had the impression that a consideration of the social consequences of plant and company decisions has become a standard feature in company behavior" (1970:46).

The influence of codetermination laws also runs in the other direction, as labor moderates its own demands to conform to the requirements of economic efficiency. Unions gather information on the eco-

37. The Biedenkopf Report, named after its primary author, was commissioned by the government prior to its reconsidering legislation to enhance labor's rights in codetermination.

nomic situation of particular firms through their participation in supervisory boards. But the Biedenkopf Commission found that this flow of information "does not lead to greater demands by the union, but rather that in difficult economic situations, labor is more willing to consider the firm's actual economic situation" (1970:47–48).

More recent empirical studies point to similar conclusions. Jutta Helm (1986), for example, argues that codetermination brings economic benefits for workers and enhances employee influence in corporate decision making. While the system does not provide an absolute guarantee of job security, bargaining between labor and capital under codetermination can reduce or delay layoffs and cushion the impact on the affected workers. Most important, perhaps, she finds that both the economic benefits workers derive from codetermination and the enhanced influence over company decision making it provides them are effects that result independently of the company's economic situation. That is, her evidence suggests that workers derive these benefits even "in lean years when losses rather than profits are accrued" (Helm 1986:42).

One can scarcely afford to ignore codetermination in explaining the particular features of Germany's negotiated adjustment. But analyses that focus exclusively on these subnational institutions for labor participation are incomplete, for they miss the overarching context of national unionism in which these institutions are embedded. The weakness of the codetermination literature is thus the mirror image of that of the corporatism literature, which stresses national level organization and virtually ignores the shop floor.

A comprehensive explanation of Germany's negotiated adjustment demands attention to the interaction of both levels of the dual system. In the absence of national labor unity and strong central coordination (if not formal centralization) the institutions of codetermination would operate very differently. Without the countervailing centripetal pull of centralized unions, the incorporation of labor at the plant and company levels might amount to enterprise unionism. Germany would resemble Japan rather than Sweden.

Thus, both codetermination and centralized collective bargaining figure into the explanation of West Germany's negotiated adjustment. German labor's influence over the pace and terms of industrial adjustment is accomplished less in the context of national trade-offs among macroeconomic and political policies than it is in the sum of myriad decentralized deals between labor and business in the context of plant and company-level codetermination. The overarching system of industrial unionism plays a crucial unifying and coordinating role, representing labor interests at the national level both politically and in centralized bargaining with employer associations. Nonetheless, negotiated adjustment in Germany—by virtue of codetermination—is on balance more decentralized, more privatized, and more legalistic than in the classic corporatist democracies.

Labor participation at lower levels of economic decision-making helps explain how Germany's negotiated settlement process has survived the rather dramatic shifts in government policy in the last two decades, particularly in the late 1970s and early 1980s. It also helps explain why the breakdown in 1977 of state-sponsored, tripartite "concerted action" discussions did not put an end to negotiated adjustment in Germany. Collaborative labor-business relations at the subnational level have persisted even in the face of increasingly tense relations between the unions and the national government.

THE STATE IN GERMANY'S NEGOTIATED ADJUSTMENT

The fact that negotiated adjustment in Germany rests not only on centralized bargaining between labor and capital and labor's national political presence, but also on the sum of the many deals struck decentrally between business and labor (only sometimes involving the state) does not mean that the government has played no role in Germany's negotiated adjustment.[38] What distinguishes Germany from the corporatist countries is the manner in which the government intervenes in labor relations. The German government has been less involved in actively mediating between labor and capital in national-level policy trade-offs, but it has obviously been important in creating and shaping the subnational institutions within which labor and capital meet in the market. After all, the legalism of industrial relations is the work of state policy. Outcomes are still decided in the market, but the German state has influenced mightily the legal parameters within which labor and business negotiate these outcomes.

This point can be made clear by distinguishing different models of state interaction with labor and the market. Picture a continuum that runs from the "minimalist" state, in which the government pursues a hands-off approach to industrial relations, to a highly activist state, in which the government preempts the market and intervenes actively in regulating labor relations.

All advanced capitalist countries fall somewhere in between these two ideal types, of course, but important differences exist cross-nationally in the dominant tendencies within individual countries and the extent to which they approach one or the other extreme. The United States

38. Organized labor's national-level strength, of course, makes it a strong political lobby, and government policies reflect this. My discussion here focuses on the role of the state in actively mediating conflicts between labor and capital, rather than on those policies that simply reflect the fact that labor is a political force to be reckoned with in Germany.

generally takes a more hands-off approach to labor relations, but even the United States has established some ground rules to govern labor and capital's interactions in the market. Occupational safety and health requirements and the rules governing the right of unions to organize workers are examples of this. At the other extreme, some governments pursue policies that involve the state directly in labor relations. Nationalization of industries in Britain in the 1970s and France in the 1980s, for example, had this effect.

Between these extremes are countries like Sweden where state intervention has been more indicative than direct. While the Swedish Social Democrats have undertaken some nationalizations, state intervention has consisted mainly in changing the market incentives economic actors face and in this way influencing their behavior. Sweden's corporate tax laws offer incentives for firms to invest when the market would otherwise tell them not to—during recessions. Sweden's well-developed active labor market policy operates in the same way, though the target group is not business but labor. Active labor market policies reduce the barriers to worker mobility and hence ease labor market rigidities.

The German government's policies resemble those of the corporatist countries on social and welfare issues, but have been less consistent in manipulating market signals in a conscious effort to mediate conflicting interests between labor and capital. The German state, especially since the mid-1970s, has been more reluctant to intervene in this way, either directly through nationalization or indirectly through monetary and fiscal steering. In this sense, the German government seems to approach the laissez-faire model. However, as Andrew Shonfield (1969) and, more recently, Christopher S. Allen (1989b, 1989d, 1990) have argued so persuasively, important differences exist between an American-style "laissez faire" capitalism and Germany's "organized capitalism." In the realm of labor relations, this difference turns on a very different meaning of "legalism."

Rahmenbedingungen versus Rules

In the American context, the term "legalism" tends to conjure up images of the kind of detailed, uncoordinated regulation common in many facets of American public policy.[39] The legalism of industrial relations in the United States fits this image. Derek C. Bok has characterized U.S. labor law as a "tangled web of statute and prece-

39. Christopher Allen's comments helped clarify and sharpen the argument presented in this section. My characterization of the legalism of West German industrial relations parallels and draws on Allen's analysis of banking and finance in the United States and West Germany, in which he develops the contrast between America's antistatist laissez-faire tradition and Germany's very different tradition of "organized capitalism" (Allen 1989b, 1990).

dent" (1971:1394), in which "an early articulation of simple standards is typically followed by a constant embellishment of exceptions, qualifications, complex reformulations, and ad hoc decisionmaking" (1971:1462). The result is a "web of regulation that is highly complex and extremely litigious" (1971:1460).

As the discussion of codetermination makes clear, however, the legalism of German labor relations is premised on a very different kind of state intervention. Unlike the American model in which interventions are ad hoc and uncoordinated, the German state's involvement in labor relations (like many other aspects of public policy) establishes a general framework (*Rahmenbedingungen*) that structures relations between actors in the market without dictating outcomes directly. This pattern of setting Rahmenbedingungen rather than strict rules is related to Germany's tradition of "organized private enterprise" (Shonfield 1969: chaps. 11 and 12). On the one hand, this model features strong private sector organizations that have their roots in the country's late industrialization—what Katzenstein (1987) calls Germany's "centralized society." On the other hand, it also bears the imprint of efforts in the postwar period to curtail the powers of the once formidable central state, which now coordinates outcomes more than it controls them (Katzenstein's "decentralized state"; Shonfield's "divided authority").

Recent work by Allen (1989b, 1989d, 1990) draws out the implications of the difference between Rahmenbedingungen and rules for banking and finance in West Germany and the United States, but this distinction is equally illuminating when applied to state involvement in labor relations. Codetermination sets the framework that structures labor conflict without, however, removing it from the market. In this sense, Wilhelm Röpke's description of the "framework" philosophy that characterizes many aspects of German public policy fits as well the kind of legalism that codetermination embodies:

> [The program] consists of measures and institutions which impart to competition the framework, rules, and machinery of impartial supervision which a competitive system needs as much as any game or match if it is not to degenerate into a vulgar brawl. A genuine, equitable, and smoothly functioning competitive system can not in fact survive without a judicious moral and legal framework and without regular supervision of the conditions under which competition can take place pursuant to real efficiency principles. This presupposes mature economic discernment on the part of all responsible bodies and individuals and a strong and impartial state. [quoted in Allen 1990:7]

In sum, the German state, like the American, eschews direct intervention in labor relations where it can. Instead, both systems are characterized by a more "arm's-length" pattern premised on a high degree of legalism. But, as Allen points out for the field of financial regulation, there is a big difference between a system that has a multitude of rules and no overarching framework (the United States) and one that has a broad but clearly articulated framework which contains a coordinated set of general rules (Germany). As in the United States, the context of German labor conflict is the market, but the ground rules that govern interactions between unions and employers are very different.

Institutionalized Conflict and "Liberal Pluralism"

By emphasizing the institutions that channel labor conflict, my argument bears a superficial resemblance to the "liberal-pluralist" school of industrial relations of the 1950s and 1960s.[40] However, my argument differs from liberal pluralism in important ways.

Theorists in the liberal-pluralist school posited that the institutionalization of labor relations would promote labor peace and cooperation. They argued that political democracy and the development of specialized institutions (e.g., collective bargaining) for regulating and channeling industrial conflict would eliminate the basis for labor's opposition to capitalism and encourage the separation of political from industrial conflict. Consensus about the "rules of the game" would ensure the relatively peaceful resolution of industrial disputes. Ultimately, this separation of political and industrial conflict and the "rationalization" of industrial disputes would lead to a "withering away of the strike" (Ross and Hartmann 1960: chap. 5).

The "institutionalization of conflict" thesis works in the German context to the extent that labor conflict is indeed usually played out within a stable institutional framework to which all parties generally agree. As the Biedenkopf Commission's report showed, employers have come to terms with codetermination in large measure because it does not impede their ability to run capitalist companies successfully. Labor's main criticism of codetermination is that it does not go far enough.

Beyond this, however, the liberal-pluralist version of the "institutionalization of conflict" thesis is inaccurate on two counts. First, the thesis overstates the separation of political and industrial conflict. Even in Germany's highly legalistic system, conflict resolution is not a straightforward matter of dispute adjudication. As the case studies in Chapter 6 demonstrate, the institutions of codetermination channel conflicts between labor and employers, but the outcomes reflect the interplay of the institutional and political resources available to both labor and capital.

Second, the liberal-pluralist argument rests on a convergence theory that comparative research flatly belies (Ingham 1974). Cross-national

40. See, for example, Dunlop 1958; Kerr et al. 1960; Ross and Hartmann 1960; and Clegg 1960.

analyses clearly demonstrate that the stability of labor relations over time hinges not just on *whether* conflicts between labor and capital are institutionalized,[41] but also on *how* they are institutionalized. Not all institutions have proved equally resilient through the economic and political changes since the 1970s. Chapter 9 shows how important elements of the very structure of labor relations in the United States (e.g., work rules) have themselves become the object of contention between labor and capital. In contrast, the way labor's plant rights have been institutionalized in Germany has proved more stable and resilient in the face of changing macroeconomic and political circumstances. The institutions of German labor relations have allowed both labor and capital greater strategic flexibility to adapt to new challenges and opportunities (Katz and Sabel 1985). In short, the emphasis of the liberal pluralists on the process of institutionalization fails to discriminate adequately among different kinds of institutions and their effects on stability over time.

THE INTERACTION OF CENTRALIZED BARGAINING AND CODETERMINATION

Both the corporatism and codetermination literatures feature important elements of the German model of negotiated adjustment, but neither alone captures fully the dynamics of the system. Both centralized collective bargaining and decentralized negotiation within Germany's legal substructure of codetermination are important to the continued stability and relative success of Germany's negotiated adjustment, but a simple juxtaposition of the two will not suffice. Understanding the resiliency of the dual system requires a dynamic model of how centralized bargaining and codetermination interact.

In order to clarify this interaction, I will first sketch out the basic contours of the relationship between centralized bargaining and codetermination using the analytical categories (structure and process) from the corporatist model. Subsequent chapters set this static model in motion, looking at how the dual system has evolved and at the political maneuvering within this system that has maintained it, even as it has transformed it, over time.

Structures

A high degree of centralization and organizational unity in the labor movement is important in the corporatist model because the character

41. They are, of course, institutionalized to one extent or another in all the advanced industrial democracies.

of national bargaining requires it. Centralization means that labor commands the political and industrial clout to make *negotiated* adjustment attractive, if not imperative, to employers and the state. In addition, a high degree of centralization means that union leaders can bargain for large numbers of workers and (usually) make national agreements binding at lower levels.

A highly inclusive and encompassing labor movement is also important for giving labor leaders a national perspective in their interactions with employers and the state. As Mancur Olson has convincingly argued, organized labor's centralization and breadth shape how unions view their interests (1982:47–53). Thus, strong and encompassing labor movements in corporatist countries like Sweden and Austria regularly do not play their full market strength in wage rounds, but formulate their wage demands with an eye toward the general state of the economy taking into account issues of inflation, productivity, investment, and growth.

Labor's national perspective also allows it to take a longer view of adjustment. Decades ago Sumner Slichter (1941) observed that the structure of unionism (craft, industrial, or multi-industrial unionism, for example) strongly influences how union leaders view adjustment and technological change. Unions that organize a single plant, firm, or sector would be committing organizational suicide if they failed to try to save jobs (through protectionism or militant opposition to layoffs and plant closings, for example) should the industry run into competitive difficulties. Likewise, it is perfectly rational for craft unions to try to obstruct the introduction of technological innovations that directly threaten the interests of their members. Unions encompassing a range of industries do not have the same interest in intervening to save particular plants or even industries, or in blocking particular technological developments. Indeed, the survival and success of broadly based unions hinges less on the fate of particular groups of workers than it does on successful national adjustment, which may shift workers across industries or occupations, but not out of the union (or union federation). For these reasons, a labor organization with a national perspective is an important prerequisite for negotiated adjustment.

Processes

The other element in the corporatist model is the process through which adjustment is negotiated. The structural attributes of a union movement may make top labor leaders more or less predisposed to take a positive view of adjustment, but labor's continued cooperation and participation in that process depends, as I argued above, on concrete trade-offs. This is true because workers and leaders at lower levels in the union will not (and historically have not, as the British experience with incomes policy shows) cooperate with adjustment strategies if workers do not benefit in some way from such arrangements.[42] Thus, the stability of corporatist arrangements hinges crucially on what labor gets in return, be that generous social welfare policies or other policies that protect workers from the whims of the market, or policies that ease the transition for those workers who are "shifted" (through retraining or relocation plans, for example) by adjustment.

I have argued that Germany's negotiated adjustment deviates from the corporatist model in important ways. Yet the outcomes in Germany closely resemble those achieved in the corporatist countries. The key to resolving this apparent discrepancy is understanding how these two components of the corporatist model—labor's national orientation and labor participation in adjustment—are achieved in the German context.

Centralized Bargaining

The IG Metall's pivotal position in the labor movement compensates to a great extent for the weakness of Germany's central trade union confederation. The IG Metall assumes the national perspective that is important to negotiated adjustment. The range and character of the industries this union organizes force it to take a broad and nonparochial view. Many of these sectors have been or still are Germany's most dynamic export industries (steel and shipbuilding for example were; automobiles and machine tools still are). The dependence of these industries on foreign markets rules protectionism out of the union's repertoire. While some of these industries have encountered competitive pressures in international markets, the livelihood of others still depends on foreign trade. Under these circumstances, the union has traditionally favored industrial change over protectionism. Similarly at a more micro level, rank-and-file appeals for central union support for factory occupations in the face of plant closures have consistently fallen on deaf ears.

On wages as well, the IG Metall has in general been a "responsible" leader. An OECD study credits German unions (led by the IG Metall) with having consistently pursued a "flexible" wage policy, in which union wage demands respond more to unemployment than to inflation (*The Economist*, 1 November 1986:72).[43] This study chastises British unions, on the other hand, for a "rigid" wage policy that exacerbates inflation and perhaps even unemployment (see also Flanagan, Soskice, and Ulman 1983:222–75).

42. Sabel (1981), for example, describes the internal conflicts that can lead to the formation and success of rival union factions.

43. The OECD economists who wrote the report define real wage flexibility as "the elasticity of money wages with respect to prices . . . divided by the elasticity of wages with respect to unemployment."

Codetermination

The other component of the corporatist model emphasizes labor participation in the adjustment process and negotiations over the consequences of adjustment for workers. It is at this point that the micro level in Germany becomes particularly important, for to a significant extent it is at the plant and company levels that such labor participation is accomplished. Organized labor in Germany constitutes a strong political lobby, of course, and this has affected national policy in a broad sense, even if German unions have never achieved the kind of stable presence in national-level policymaking that their Swedish and Austrian counterparts have. But plant- and company-level codetermination provide a crucial second avenue for labor participation in industrial adjustment in Germany. While current codetermination legislation still falls short of the goals German labor has set historically, the subnational channels for labor participation that do exist are an important feature of Germany's negotiated adjustment process.

Works councils enjoy rights in a number of areas that are particularly important in a period of adjustment. Their strongest rights (codetermination rights) are in the area of personnel policy—for example, negotiations over hirings and firings, wage rates, and wage guarantees in the event of transfers. Works councils have weaker (consultative) rights on other issues, such as changes in the organization of production and the introduction of new technologies.

As discussed above, codetermination encourages a consideration of both economic and social factors in adjustment strategies at the company level. Within the context of labor's national political and industrial power, the trade-offs that characterize negotiated adjustment are also made at the subnational (plant and company) levels. In other words, in Germany labor influence over the terms of adjustment is accomplished in part through the exercise of codetermination.

The argument presented here resembles in some ways recent scholarship on what is now being called "meso-corporatism" (see especially Cawson 1985b).[44] Studies in meso-corporatism focus on "corporatist" interest intermediation at subnational levels—in specific sectors and policy areas, for example. Some meso-corporatist studies even point to "islands" of corporatism, or corporatist "strategies" in countries where the traditional corporatism literature would lead us least to expect them, namely in such "noncorporatist" countries as Canada and Britain (Burgi 1985; Atkinson and Coleman 1985; and Cawson 1985a).

44. I question the wisdom of burdening corporatism with yet another prefix. It adds additional baggage to an already heavily laden and often confusing concept. In addition, since "meso-corporatism" can apparently be found in the classic "noncorporatist" countries (e.g., Britain, Canada, and the United States), the difference between corporatism and meso-corporatism seems to be greater than just their manifestations at the national versus the subnational levels.

What the present analysis shares with studies of meso-corporatism is a focus on decentralized channels for negotiated adjustment. The similarities end there, however, for two reasons. First, in contrast to the emphasis on subnational levels common in meso-corporatist analyses, centralized bargaining is a crucial complementary feature in Germany's negotiated adjustment. Negotiated adjustment in Germany is not just the sum of so many instances of meso-corporatism; it is the interaction of centralized bargaining and codetermination. Second, in contrast to the emphasis on "islands" of corporatism in meso-corporatist analyses, decentralized channels for labor participation in adjustment are far more pervasive in Germany than elsewhere. The kind of plant- and firm- (or even industry-) level deals that German codetermination facilitates are not peculiar to Germany. What is distinctive about the German case is the breadth and scope of such negotiations and arrangements. Workers in all plants in Germany employing over five workers are entitled to elect a works council to represent them in negotiations with management. Isolated and sector-specific instances of meso-corporatism are one thing; continuous labor participation in industrial adjustment on the basis of structures for codetermination that exist economy-wide is quite another.

The stability of the dual system is related to the rigidities and flexibilities it institutionalizes. The critical rigidity in the dual system, as Streeck (1979) points out, is that the two levels do not compete with each other. Plant works councils are prohibited from calling strikes and negotiating wages, and they must uphold collective bargaining agreements in the plant. This division of labor is an important stabilizing force in German labor relations. As Streeck has argued, these limits on works council powers "contribute substantially to the solution of one of the most crucial organizational problems of industrial unions, the preservation of the 'strike monopoly' and the 'bargaining monopoly' of the extra- and supra-plant organizational bodies" (1979: abstract). Thus, Streeck's analysis suggests that codetermination has shored up industrial unionism by protecting central union leadership from having to confront the unmediated demands of the rank and file.

The flexible side of the dual system, which Streeck does not emphasize, relates to the way decentralized bargaining complements central bargaining. Recall that although works councils are formally autonomous from the unions, over 80 percent of all works councillors in Germany are members of the DGB unions. Union dominance in works councils provides a crucial link between these statutory bodies and the larger system of voluntary unionism in which they are embedded. What this means is that the unions participate in adjustment in virtually all sectors of the economy. Even where union membership in a given plant is very low—say, 10 to 20 percent—the works council is generally composed overwhelmingly (if not entirely) of union members. Hence, despite (or perhaps because of) its formal autonomy from the unions, the works council system more than compensates for the unions' rather low overall membership levels.

A brief comparison of this situation with that in other countries will clarify the point from another perspective. Certain industries in the United States (the automobile and steel industries, for example) are well organized by very strong unions. But the unionized sector of the economy as a whole is small and shrinking. Union strength is highly concentrated and does not cover huge sectors of the economy. In addition, regional differences in union organization and in labor laws allow employers to escape union influence altogether, for example, by moving to less unionized regions or by attempting to expel or exclude unions from their plants.

Contrast this situation with that faced by Swedish employers. In that country, the central trade union confederation, the LO, organizes a full 80 percent of the national work force, and over 90 percent of blue-collar workers. A nonunion option simply does not exist. Unable to escape union influence, Swedish employers have to come to terms with organized labor.

West Germany lies somewhere in between these two extremes. German unions organize a substantially lower percentage of the national work force than do the Swedish. But German employers, like their Swedish counterparts, face fewer nonunion options than American employers. German unions are not strong because they organize *everyone* (as in Sweden); they are strong because through central collective bargaining and through the works council system they organize *everywhere*.

The institutions and processes sketched out above constitute the basic components of Germany's negotiated adjustment. The static model of relations within the dual system presented so far, however, cannot account for the dynamic interaction of centralized bargaining by unions and decentralized bargaining within codetermination. My analysis of the dynamics of the dual system focuses on the case of the IG Metall, and how relations between the central union and the shop floor have evolved in response to changing market and political trends.

Part II

CODETERMINATION AND THE DEVELOPMENT OF THE DUAL SYSTEM

CHAPTER THREE

The Origins of the Dual System

The dual system was created and consolidated not according to some master plan, but in fits and starts, and it emerged in its present form as the unintended consequence of a series of battles among labor, capital, and the state over the position of the unions in the plant, and within the unions over relations between the central leadership and the rank and file. This chapter and the next examine how works councils have fit into the evolving struggle over labor's role in the German political economy.[1]

The story of the creation and development of the dual system demonstrates the dynamic interaction of institutional constraints and political strategies. The evolution of this dualism has been driven forward both by changing macroeconomic and political conditions and by political conflict within the system itself. Changes in the political and economic context have affected the meaning and operation of the dual system over time, and thus help account for changing union strategies within and toward the "dual" structure. The outcomes of the political

1. There are several excellent and more detailed analyses that focus on various parts of the story laid out in this chapter and the next, and my own account draws on these. Koopmann (1979, especially vol. 1) discusses the reaction of the unions to the Works Constitution Act of 1952 and the IG Metall's subsequent policies toward shop stewards; and Schmidt (1975), Krusche and Pfeiffer (1975), and Zoll (1981) examine the shop-floor unrest of the late 1960s. Most existing studies emphasize continuity over time, especially in the formal structure of dualism, which in turn often becomes an important independent variable to explain other outcomes such as the "underdevelopment" or "weakness" of plant-level labor representation, on which Germany's cooperative unionism is allegedly premised. My own account, in contrast, highlights changes in the meaning and operation of the dual system over time, both in response to changes in the macroeconomic and political context and as the result of conscious strategic maneuvering among the major actors—central union leadership, shop-floor labor representatives, employers, and the state.

struggles within the institutions of the dual system have also shaped its development, though often in ways unanticipated by those who initiated such conflicts.

My analysis highlights the interaction of these three variables—context, institutions, and politics—during two critical turning points in the development of the dual system in the post–World War II period: the passage of the Works Constitution Act of 1952, and shop-floor militancy in the late 1960s, which was the first major crisis of relations within it. These turning points shaped relations within the dual system and thus form a crucial backdrop to developments in the 1970s and 1980s.

The basic structure of the dual system dates back to the Weimar period, though its legalistic foundations, and even its "dualism," had very different meanings then than they would assume later. Weimar's dominant "free" trade unions benefited from the legalism of the system because it bolstered their position on the shop floor and helped neutralize the revolutionary council movement that was challenging the reformist leadership by organizing the rank and file. Furthermore, the "dualism" of the 1920 Works Council Law stressed the subordination of the works councils to the unions, rather than their autonomy.

The works council system was recreated after World War II in a political and economic context very different from the one that had produced the 1920 law. Authored by a conservative government acting without the participation of the unions, the 1952 law put a new spin on the system's legalism and dualism. It emphasized the legal constraints on the activities of works councils, defined their responsibilities for the welfare of the company, and underscored their independence from the unions. The law passed against the unions' bitter opposition.

The IG Metall coped with the dual system by promoting the development of union shop steward committees and by campaigning aggressively for seats in works council elections. Despite its successes in both endeavors, the union remained suspicious of plant autonomy and strove for greater centralization of authority. Auspicious economic conditions in the 1950s and early 1960s facilitated the union's emphasis on centralized collective bargaining to consolidate its power over the shop floor. These events paved the way for labor's incorporation into an informal incomes policy when the Social Democratic party entered the government in 1966.[2]

Union centralization and incorporation into state incomes policy set the stage for the second turning point in relations between works councils and the central union, a rank-and-file challenge to central union authority in the late 1960s. The leadership responded to calls for a decentralization of power within the union in a way that made use of and indeed reinforced the dualism of the dual system while vigorously

---

2. The IG Metall also emerged as the leading union in the DGB in this period.

defending central union power. Plant militancy forced the IG Metall to back off from its policy of highly centralized wage negotiations and delegate somewhat more authority to its ten regional bargaining districts. But union leaders sidestepped full-scale decentralization and thwarted the bid from the shop floor for greater influence within the union. Bargaining in the crucial area of wages may have been delegated to the union's regional districts, but it still never got anywhere near the plant.

Instead, the central union channeled calls for greater shop-floor power into a debate over legislation to extend the rights of works councils in the plant. That is, the union redirected demands for increased influence for plant representatives *within the union* into a battle to enhance their powers *in the plant*. The revised Works Constitution Act of 1972, passed with the support of the Social Democratic government, strengthened the rights of works councils vis-à-vis management, even as it explicitly reinforced their subordination to the central union.

Auspicious market and political conditions made it possible for the central union to maneuver successfully between defending central authority and addressing the demands of plant militants. Rapid economic growth in the early 1970s allowed the union to obtain significant wage concessions through aggressive centralized bargaining, which helped shore up central authority. At the same time, the Social Democratic victory in 1969 created the political space necessary to reopen the debate on codetermination and renegotiate the powers of works councils on organized labor's terms. Thus, the union roundly defeated all challenges to central union control in part by recasting the demands of the rank and file for more power within the union into political reforms that enhanced their rights vis-à-vis management.

In sum, the maturing of the relationship between central unions and works councils since World War II was accomplished in two phases. The first, a political defeat for labor in 1952, emphasized the independence of works councils from the unions. The second, a political victory two decades later, reemphasized their subordination to the unions, while also bolstering their powers in the plant.

These outcomes are important in their ambivalence: two separate channels for labor representation, central union dominance but significant plant rights. This ambivalence is the institutional expression of the political battles that have shaped relations within the dual system. These outcomes are also important because, moving into the 1970s and 1980s, the character of the dual system defined the options open to both labor and capital and influenced the strategies each has adopted to meet the new challenges of the last two decades.

Understanding labor relations in the dual system today requires that we consider how codetermination came to be the centerpiece of labor's political agenda in Germany and how conflicts over codetermination as an ideology were translated through politics into the concrete institutions we now associate with codetermination as a system of labor relations. This background is crucial to an understanding of German labor's continuing commitment to codetermination as a goal, and also to a grasp of how the institutions that emerged in their efforts to achieve it have affected labor's and capital's struggles over and within them.

WORKS COUNCILS IN THE WEIMAR REPUBLIC

C. W. Guillebaud put it most elegantly when he wrote that the first Works Council Law of 1920 was "the child of two parent ideas—the one constitutional, the other essentially revolutionary" (1928:1).[3] The Weimar works council system was forged out of the political struggles of 1918–1920, as Germany's reformist trade unions negotiated a troubled and sometimes contradictory course between the revolutionary appeals of the labor movement's radical wing and their own commitment to parliamentary democracy and the reform of capitalism from within.

The general idea of worker participation in plant decision making has a longer and more varied pedigree.[4] In the nineteenth century conservative and Catholic reformers promoted the idea of the "constitutional factory," but with antiliberal and largely antidemocratic goals in mind (Shuchman 1957:14). The council system they envisioned was one dominated by paternalistic employers, in which Germany's unions had no role.[5] Meanwhile, on the left, reformist Socialist leaders such as Friedrich Albert Lange developed and promoted an alternative, union-oriented notion of works councils, where labor would "serve its apprenticeship in Socialism" (Shuchman 1957:46).

Worker participation in factory councils was first institutionalized on a broad basis and with the support of organized labor in the course of World War I. The German government conceded labor participation at the plant level through *Arbeiterausschüsse*, or workers' committees, in order to enlist the cooperation of the unions in the war effort (Reich 1938:41; Braunthal 1978:29; and Berthelot 1924:5–6).

The transition from these temporary wartime councils to the institutionalization of a works council system in 1920 was rocky. Although the

3. The focus in this section is on plant-level works councils. The Weimar Constitution in fact sketched out a more elaborate and multitiered system for labor representation at the district, regional, and national levels, but in the end only works councils became law.

4. Hans Jürgen Teuteberg (1961) has written a comprehensive history of the development of codetermination as an ideology and pre–World War I institutions for worker representation in industry.

5. Indeed, in 1891 the SPD defeated a proposal in the Reichstag to institutionalize worker committees along these lines (see Winschuh 1922:20–21; and Reich 1938:160). Some employers, nonetheless, implemented this kind of system on a voluntary basis.

unions ultimately participated in the process, they certainly did not control it. Rather, the force that drove the process forward came from labor's radical left wing, which competed with and opposed the reformist unions in defining labor's strategy for the transition to socialism.

In the period immediately following the collapse of the Imperial German government, revolutionary "workers' and soldiers' councils" sprang up in a number of large industrial and commercial concerns.[6] These rival councils opposed the integration of labor that the wartime *Arbeiterausschüsse* had represented. Led by the Spartacists and the Independent Socialists, the revolutionary councils opposed the program of the majority Socialists and reformist unions calling for parliamentary democracy; they favored instead a more decentralized, shop-floor–oriented government of soviets. Although the revolutionary council movement was never very large, its strongholds in the Ruhr and in Berlin provided a firm base from which the movement's impact reverberated throughout Germany.

Employers' fear of the radical movement drove them into the arms of the reformist unions (Stern 1925:66). In this way, the revolutionary council movement inadvertently helped create the basis for the tentative truce between labor and capital in the early years of the Weimar Republic, embodied in the Stinnes-Legien Agreement of November 1918. Agreement on union representation in the plant was a part of this deal.[7] As Gerhard Braunthal points out: "Once the Revolution erupted the employers were ready to make major concessions to the unions which they viewed as a bulwark against the threat of anarchy, bolshevism, and the socialization of industry, and because they wanted to keep state intervention to a minimum" (1978:35). In the uncertain political climate of the period, employers viewed even major concessions to the unions as by far the lesser of two evils.

Germany's reformist unions and the majority Socialists also banded together against the revolutionary upheavals of 1918–19 to defeat the challenge from the left (see also Brigl-Matthiaβ 1926:15). The unions supported parliamentary democracy against the idea of a government of soviets; the majority Socialists came to the aid of the unions in resisting the revolutionary council movement's attempts to decentralize and radicalize the union movement.

---

6. Peter von Oertzen (1963) has written an especially thorough account of the revolutionary workers' councils. Various documents from this period relating to the council movement's program and its political battles with the reformist unions can be found in Crusius, Schiefelbein, and Wilke, 1978, volume 1. English sources on the council movement include Guillebaud 1928; Braunthal 1978; Moses 1982; Reich 1938; and Stern 1925.

7. The 1918 agreement was much broader and constituted a major breakthrough for the unions. Among other things, it granted the unions legal status and the right to bargain collectively, established an eight-hour working day, and created jointly managed arbitration committees for mediating disputes between labor and employers (Braunthal 1978:35).

The Works Council Act of 1920, which established works councils in plants with at least twenty workers, was pivotal in bolstering the position of the reformist unions against the more radic rents in the labor movement. The law made works councils   and subordinate organs of the Trade Unions" (Guillebaud   ti-cle 8 of the law states that "the right of economic manual workers and salaried employees to represen their members is in no way prejudiced by the provis (Bureau of Labor Statistics 1920:1251). Article 31 pro possibility of union representation in an advisory capacity on councils. Articles 66 and 78 bind works councils to uphold and enforce collective agreements concluded by trade unions. Finally, articles 62, 63 and 64 stipulate that under certain circumstances the form of labor representation in the plant specified in the Works Council Act could be replaced with another through (union) collective bargaining (Bureau of Labor Statistics 1920:1251–52; and Winschuh 1922:15–17; see also Hoffmann 1978: iii–iv). As Marcel Berthelot noted, "The prerogatives of the unions and the authority of the labour contract could not have been more energetically upheld" (1924:26).

Institutionalizing works councils in this way shored up the position of the free trade unions in two ways. First, it provided the unions with a stable legal foothold and greater influence on the shop floor (Brigl-Matthiaß 1926:55, 74–75, 244–46). Historically, the plant had been a weak link in Germany's highly centralized union organization, a factor that no doubt had contributed to the political vulnerability of the unions at that level (Winschuh 1922:74). And second, it helped neutralize works councils politically by anchoring them legally. While the law established new avenues for labor participation in plant decision-making, it also indirectly limited their activities to these prescribed functions.[9] In other words, with the assistance of the state, organized labor had been able both to establish a broad presence at the plant level and at the same time to buttress central union authority against more radical strains within the labor movement.

Despite this setback, the Communists[10] and Independent Socialists still hoped to capture and control the councils and promote them as a revolutionary force. Thus, the unions turned their attention to the political struggle over the "unionization" (Vergewerkschaftlichung) of the works councils against these proponents of a stronger and more autonomous, and more radical, council movement. From the end of 1920

8. As Winschuh points out, in the debates over the wording of the legislation, the unions were often motivated less by a desire to grant works councils extensive powers than to ensure their subordination to the unions (1922:24–25; see also Brigl-Matthiaß 1926:35–36).

9. I am indebted to Joshua Dienstag for this formulation.

10. In January 1919, the Spartacus Union became the Communist Party of Germany (KPD).

onward, there was a clear trend toward the integration of the councils into the reformist unions (Brigl-Matthiaβ 1926:29–30; Winschuh 1922:75; Hoffmann 1978:iv). Although the Communists maintained a strong presence in works council elections in certain outposts in the Ruhr and Berlin in the early 1920s, elsewhere syndicalist-Communist candidates faded into a small minority, though sometimes still an important and vocal one (Brigl-Matthiaβ 1926:41, 44–45; Berthelot 1924:59–60). As Adolf Brock puts it, "The independent works council movement was defeated and the works councils were unionized, i.e., incorporated into the union organization and ... at the same time integrated into capitalist plant politics" (1978:10).

The formal dualism of the system had little practical significance in this period because works councils became the primary representatives of the unions on the shop floor. The works council office often served as a union local for one or more unions (Winschuh 1923:280–81).[11] And while the works councils were relegated to a subsidiary role in wage and collective bargaining issues, they assumed basic union functions in a range of other areas at the plant level (Brigl-Matthiaβ 1926:56). Ernst Fraenkel described the incorporation of the councils by the unions over the course of the 1920s as the "social masterpiece of the German union movement in the postwar period. . . . The works councils have become ... the 'long arm' of the unions in the plant. . . . Nominated, trained, and controlled [by the union], they are the organization's shop stewards in the plant" (quoted in Koopmann 1981:16).

Although the unions were able to wrest control of the works councils from their challengers on the left, the relationship between works councils and employers remained somewhat more problematic throughout the Weimar period. Despite their 1918 agreement with the unions to create some form of representation for labor in the plant, by 1920 the German Employers' Association had recovered sufficiently from the initial shock of the revolution to oppose the Works Council Law in the form that it was adopted by the Reichstag. Even after the law passed, some employers resisted its application in their plants (Brigl-Matthiaβ 1926:76).

Furthermore, extreme economic conditions repeatedly rocked German industry and destabilized labor relations in the plant. When the great inflation hit in 1923–24, many employers moved aggressively to

11. Although the free trade unions dominated in the Weimar years, other reformist and religious unions also competed for members. This fragmentation within the union movement set limits on the extent to which the law could explicitly link works councils to the free trade unions. Conversely, however, the works council system fostered a tendency toward industrial unionism and away from craft and programmatic rivalries within the labor movement, although unity was not achieved until after World War II (Hoffmann 1978:xiii; Brigl-Matthiaβ 1926:52–54).

weaken works councils. Emboldened by the crisis as much as they were panicked by it, they purged their plants of uncooperative works councillors and undermined collective bargaining by striking deals with their own councils at the plant level (Guillebaud 1928:57–58; Brigl-Matthiaβ 1926:34–35).[12] Works councils generally capitulated in the face of employers' attacks. Guillebaud describes these developments: "[Employers] were in a position, of which they made full use, to eliminate individual Works Councillors who had shown what they considered to be an undue or misdirected vigour in the exercise of their duties.... A sufficient number of examples was made to intimidate the bulk of the Councils and to reduce them to a state of inglorious quiescence" (1928:225). The fragmentation of the labor movement at the national level, which was reproduced in divisions within works councils, only exacerbated their problems. It allowed employers to play different unions off against each other and to favor more moderate factions (Winschuh 1922:48–49).

The system of labor representation in the plant that had been so painstakingly built up in 1918–20 gradually deteriorated into the pre-1914 mold of patriarchal "Herr im Haus" plant relations (Maier 1975:446–50). The inflation of the early 1920s weakened, and the depression in 1929 ultimately destroyed, the already fragile basis of industry-labor cooperation in Weimar Germany, and with it German labor's first (limited) experience with codetermination. The economic upheavals of the 1920s and the political turmoil of the early 1930s rendered extraordinary the circumstances under which works councils attempted to operate.

The period of National Socialism constitutes a hiatus in the history of the works councils system.[13] Hitler destroyed the unions and dismantled the Weimar works councils as he consolidated central control in 1933. Industrial relations were recast in an explicitly patriarchal mold. Workers were denied the right to bargain collectively and to strike. In 1934, Hitler created the so-called Labor Front, an arm of the NSDAP (National-Sozialistische Deutsche Arbeiterpartei) which included both workers and their employers, whose purpose was "to create a true social and productive community of all Germans" (quoted in Shirer 1960:263). The National Socialist "Charter of Labor" denied workers all rights of consultation and participation, instead making employers the masters in their own plants and charging them with responsibility for the welfare of their workers, or "following" (*Gefolgschaft*). The latter, for

12. Since it required ongoing wage adjustments, hyperinflation necessarily undermined central bargaining and enhanced the role of works councils (Guillebaud 1928:107; Reich 1938:224).

13. Space does not permit a full discussion of organized labor's fate under National Socialism. On this period, see Neumann 1944; Craig 1980; Shirer 1960; and Deppe, Fülberth, and Harrer 1977.

their part, owed their employers loyalty and obedience (Shirer 1960:263).

German labor's first experience with works councils and codetermination during the Weimar period was important for the lessons the post–World War II leaders of the union movement drew from it. They concluded that labor's weakness in the Weimar years was in part a consequence of its own internal fragmentation and the ideological cleavages that had prevented a unified opposition to the reactionary tide of the early 1930s. They also decided that their first attempts to realize economic democracy had been in the right direction, and that "their real error lay in not pushing along that course far enough" (Schuchman 1957:91). These perceptions would inform German labor's program for the postwar period.

CODETERMINATION IN POSTWAR WEST GERMANY

When the banished leaders of the Weimar labor unions returned from exile to reconstruct Germany's labor movement, they agreed to emphasize organizational unity and centralization to avoid the ideological tensions that had plagued the labor movement in the Weimar Republic.[14] They also embraced a broad notion of codetermination and made this the centerpiece in the labor movement's postwar program for social and economic reform. As one of the new DGB's "Principles of Economic Policy" put it: "The experience of the years 1918–1938 has taught that formal political democracy does not suffice for the realization of a truly democratic organization of society. The democratization of political life must be supplemented by democratization of economic life" (quoted in Shuchman 1957:2). Thus, delegates to the confederation's founding convention in 1949 called for labor participation in economic decision making on all levels of the economy: national, industrial, and plant. German unions viewed (and still view) codetermination at each of these levels not as separate goals, but as parts of an overall program in which each component forms part of an "indivisible whole" (see Pirker 1979, 1:68–69).

As in Weimar, the prevailing political and economic climate influenced power relations in West German society, which in turn shaped the outcome of organized labor's attempts to implement its codetermination program. Labor won significant concessions on company-level representation in heavy industry during the occupation, partly as a result of the power vacuum created by the removal or discrediting of the previously powerful industrial magnates of the Ruhr. The unions

---

14. The most thorough account of the postwar history of the German labor movement is Pirker 1979. See also Borsdorf, Hemmer, and Martiny 1977. On the role of the occupying powers in actively shaping the structure of unionism in the Federal Republic, see especially Schmidt 1970.

also secured relatively favorable provisions for plant-level representation prior to the founding of the Federal Republic in 1949. But by the time the new West German legislature met to decide these issues, the business sector had recovered, and it was labor that was on the defensive.

Company-level codetermination in the coal and steel industries evolved almost unintentionally out of labor's and heavy industry's responses to events in the immediate postwar period. Faced with threats to dismantle their companies, employers in some firms formed alliances with labor against the occupation authorities. Where labor participated in such coalitions, employers granted them significant concessions, including equal representation on company supervisory boards (Markovits 1986:68). In other cases, labor won similar concessions from employers through industrial action or the threat of it. By 1947, labor had achieved equal representation on company supervisory boards in virtually all German steel firms, iron works, and coal mines in the British zone, though not in the French or American zones. Allied Law (*Kontrollratsgesetz*) Number 75 merely formalized this situation in 1948 in the British zone by recognizing parity codetermination at the company level in the coal and steel industries, at least for the duration of the occupation and until a new German government could decide the issue.

Meanwhile at the plant level, works councils had resurfaced in factories in a range of industries immediately after the war. In many cases, they provided crucial basic services in the first chaotic weeks after the country's defeat, organizing the provision of food, clothing, and shelter for scores of uprooted Germans. They also often played a key role in restarting production in many plants (Koopmann 1979, 1:338–40; Markovits 1986:63).

Thus, as early as 1945, works councils were already a political fact in search of a legal identity. Unlike the revolutionary councils of the early Weimar years, these works councillors harbored no radical intentions. They did not see themselves as an alternative to the central unions, but rather sought to rebuild the unions from the bottom up (Hoffmann 1978:IV). Among other things, they collected union dues, distributed the union newspaper, and recruited new union members (Koopmann 1981:27–28). Based on a study of the relationship between the unions and works councils in 1949–50, one observer found that "in many plants the relationship is so close that it makes the election of the union stewards superfluous. The works councils function as the union" (quoted in Koopmann 1981:27).

Early trade union congresses called for the legal anchoring of works councils, on the assumption that any new law would recognize and promote strong ties between them and the unions. And Allied Law Number 22, passed by the Western occupying powers in 1946, did just that.[15] It acknowledged the close relationship between the works coun-

---

15. For a text of the law, see Hemken n.d.

cils and the unions, and charged works councils not only with negotiating with employers over internal plant affairs but also with enforcing the unions' collective bargains in the plant. Article 7 explicitly bound works councils to discharge their duties in collaboration with the recognized unions (Koopmann 1981:64).

The modest momentum the unions had built up in realizing their codetermination goals under the occupation was interrupted in 1949 with the founding of the Federal Republic. The onset of the cold war contributed to the speedy rehabilitation of the moderate right. In the first election the Social Democrats, running on a platform that included the nationalization of key industries, lost to the conservatives, who were committed to a free market ideology. This shifting political climate provided the context in which employers and their political allies went on the offensive against codetermination.

In November 1950 the unions learned that the Ministry of Economics was working on a bill that would abolish codetermination in the coal, iron, and steel industries (Markovits 1986:77). Both of the affected unions, the IG Metall and the Miners' Union (IG Bergbau), reacted quickly to defend codetermination, organizing votes in which 96 percent of the metalworkers and 92 percent of the miners expressed their willingness to strike in defense of *Montanmitbestimmung* (Deppe 1977:337). The unions prevailed without a strike; on 10 April 1951, the CDU government passed a new German Montanmitbestimmung law that contained all the essential features of the model developed under British occupation and established parity codetermination in the coal, iron, and steel (Montan) industries (see Chapter 1).

While the ability of the unions to mobilize a strong demonstration of resolve no doubt contributed significantly to their victory, other factors also played a role. Chancellor Konrad Adenauer's intervention was decisive in mediating between labor and business on the codetermination issue (Pirker 1979, 1:197–98). Since the business community opposed the "renewal" of Mitbestimmung, the conservative Adenauer was a somewhat unlikely ally for labor. But Markovits points to several factors that helped push him toward a defense of codetermination. Among these was his genuine "respect and affection" for Hans Böckler, who led the DGB through most of the fight for the 1951 law (Markovits 1986:78–79). Despite his initial skepticism, Adenauer ultimately decided that a conflict with the unions over the issue of codetermination at that point "would have cost too much, politically, and economically" (*Handelsblatt*, 31 March 1987; see also Schmidt 1975: 39–46). The bill upholding Montanmitbestimmung passed in the legislature against only fifty votes, cast mostly by F.D.P. representatives (*Handelsblatt*, 31 March 1987).

Thus, the unions' defense of company-level codetermination in the coal and steel industries was successful, even if this model of labor participation in company decision making remained limited to the coal and steel industries. A year later the unions again struggled with employers and the government—but this time unsuccessfully—over extending the Montan model to other industries and institutionalizing labor representation at the plant level.

The Works Constitution Act of 1952

The contrast between the fight to defend codetermination in the coal and steel industries and that to extend it to the rest of German industry and to legislate labor's plant-level powers a year later is stark. If the reasons for the unions' victory in 1951 lay in their mobilization and in Adenauer's support, then the lack of both probably contributed to the unions' defeat in the Works Constitution Act of 1952 (Markovits 1986:80–82). The DGB's charismatic leader Hans Böckler died in 1951, and losing his leadership hurt the unions in two respects. First, it deprived them of the personal link to the chancellor's office that had proved so crucial in the Montanmitbestimmung battle. Second, the shift in power to his successor Christian Fette left the DGB in transition at a crucial juncture. Labor's strategy for mobilization was confused, and the unions mustered only weak resistance to the conservative Works Constitution Law that parliament passed in 1952 (Koopmann 1979, 1:436–39).

The unions' demand in 1952 was for an extension of parity codetermination to the rest of German industry, and for the institutionalization of works councils as the unions' representatives in the plant. The unions came up short on their demand for parity representation at the company level in all industries. Instead, the law provided for a watered-down type of codetermination, in which labor representatives would be present on the supervisory boards of large companies, but in a minority.[16]

The unions also lost on the issue of works councils. The 1952 legislation restricted labor's legal rights in the plant (compared to Allied Law Number 22 and some of the more progressive state laws it replaced). And although the law upheld the unions' collective bargaining monopoly, it redefined other aspects of works councils' relationship with employers and unions in ways that weakened their ties to the latter.

The new Works Constitution Act narrowed the range of rights works councils had previously enjoyed in part by specifying their responsibilities, rights, and obligations more precisely. Allied Law Number 22 had been briefer and less detailed. Its more general provisions had left much more room for interpretation, room that works councillors had been able to exploit by seeking influence in areas where their participa-

---

16. The 1952 law gave labor one-third of the seats in supervisory boards in companies employing over five hundred workers.

tion was not explicitly forbidden or circumscribed (interview with former IG Metall president Eugen Loderer, June 1989).

In addition, however, the provisions of the 1952 law fell short of those in some of the more progressive state laws that had supplemented the Kontrollratsgesetz 22. It narrowed the powers of works councils in personnel decisions such as hiring and firing, and defined more restrictively the range of "plant changes" that required consultation between the works council and employers (see *Metall*, 20 February 1952:3; *Die Quelle*, June 1952:284–85; and the IG Metall's *Geschäftsbericht 1952/53*:123). The new law's provisions for works council inspection of company records was also more modest than some of the state laws it replaced. The DGB executive board passed a resolution charging that the 1952 legislation not only would annul the better regulations provided by existing state laws, in some ways it was not even as favorable as the 1920 Works Council Law (*Die Quelle*, May 1952:225; see also the letter from DGB president Christian Fette to Adenauer in *Die Quelle*, June 1952:329–30).

More important, the 1952 law took a step back from the practice of recognizing and actively promoting close ties between the works councils and the unions. It did so both by emphasizing works councils' duties to foster the welfare of the company and by underscoring their autonomy from the unions. As Markovits puts it:

> The employers and their parliamentary allies hoped to restrict—even eliminate—labor's collective power on the shop floor by replacing the presence of unions with that of factory-oriented, syndicalist and highly particularistic works councils. Moreover, the representational power of these works councils would be further curtailed by an elaborate legal system which in essence tied them closer to the welfare of the company than to that of their ostensible clients, the workers. Indeed, these firm-oriented works councils were to become the only legal and official representatives of labor in its daily interaction with capital on the shop floors of West German plants. [1986:80–81]

In this respect, the tone of the new law deviated sharply from that of the Kontrollratsgesetz 22 and existing state laws, which had explicitly acknowledged close and ongoing links between works councils and the unions (Bührig 1952:130). But the 1952 legislation was arguably also more restrictive on this score than its Weimar predecessor.

Even though some of the language of the new Works Constitution Act paralleled that of the 1920 Works Council Law, a comparison of the two reveals a subtle but decisive shift on the issue of the relationship of the works councils to the unions.[17] While the 1920 law emphasized the subordination of the works councils to the unions in the ways cited

---

17. See Hoffmann 1978:xv–xvii, for a detailed comparison of the two laws. This paragraph and the next draw on his analysis.

above,[18] the 1952 law stressed the autonomy of the works councils and especially their countervailing loyalty to the welfare of the company (Hoffmann 1978:xv). The 1920 law bound works councils to protect workers' right of free association, but the Works Constitution Act of 1952 went somewhat further, charging them explicitly with guarding employees against discrimination on the basis of political or trade union activity (paragraph 75, part 1) (Hoffmann 1978:xvi). The new law conceded only specific, limited rights for the unions in the plant (e.g., union representatives' rights of access to the plant and their right to attend plant assemblies, both contingent on the works council's approval) (Hoffmann 1978:v–vi). Both laws obligate works councils to take the "welfare of the plant" into consideration in their actions, but this obligation is expressed more strongly in the 1952 law, which binds them to "work together with management in a spirit of mutual trust" (paragraph 2, part 1). Finally, while the 1920 law implied an obligation for the works council to help maintain peace in the plant, it did not contain an explicit ban on its right to strike, as the 1952 law did (Hoffmann 1978:xv–xvii).

More important than the nuances in the language of the legislation is what the law meant in the broader context of the 1950s. As Reinhard Hoffmann (1978) argues, the very different political and economic environment in 1952 put a whole new spin on the "legalism" and the "dualism" of the dual system. In the conservative political context of the 1950s, the issue of unionizing the formally autonomous works councils had a very different meaning: "In the Federal Republic, it was never a question of thwarting a revolutionary council movement in favor of the union organization" (Hoffmann 1978:iv). The task for the unions was much more to resist attempts by employers to exploit works council autonomy to keep the unions out of their plants, or to foster more conservative union-neutral or even antiunion factions on the shop floor.

This issue emerged with greatest clarity in the debate over election rules under the new Works Constitution Act. The conservative government and the employers insisted on election rules protecting plant minorities and encouraging separate elections for salaried workers. Their hope was presumably to promote union-neutral or even antiunion candidates in works council elections. The unions viewed the employers' defense of "minority rights" as "pure hypocrisy," a ploy to undermine the unions through "divide and conquer" strategies and to weaken the links between works councils and the unions and between the unions and the shop floor (*Die Quelle*, February 1952:61). They

18. Indeed, recall that the 1920 law stipulated that this form of plant labor representation could be superseded entirely by another collectively bargained by the union.

charged that these provisions would encourage plant egoism and (now conservative) syndicalist tendencies.[19]

The reaction of the unions to the new Works Constitution Act shows how the changed context of the 1950s reversed the logic of the original Works Council Law. While the 1920 legislation was the result of a collaboration between the government and the unions, designed in part to shore up the latter's position against a radical minority, the 1952 law was geared more toward protecting and promoting (conservative) minorities against union dominance in the plant. In a letter to Adenauer, DGB president Christian Fette accused the lawmakers of an attempt to "undermine the unified trade union movement" and of intent to "cause a split between the unions and the works councils" (*Die Quelle*, June 1952:329; see also *Die Quelle*, August 1952:442). After the bill passed, Fritz Strothmann, the IG Metall's executive board member in charge of shop stewards, summed it up in this way: "The law stands so to speak as a barrier between the plant and the union" (quoted in Koopmann 1979, 1:431).

Despite the unions' vehement opposition to the 1952 Works Constitution Act, the conservative government granted them only two minor concessions on the works council issue (*Die Quelle*, August 1952:397).[20] When it was enacted, the IG Metall condemned the law as an "open challenge for battle (*ein Akt offener Kampfansage*) by German employers and their political allies against the unions" (*Metall*, 23 July 1952:2). The German Trade Union Confederation called the occasion "a dark moment for democratic development in the Federal Republic" (Koopmann 1981:33; Markovits 1986:81). The DGB publication *Die Quelle* declared: "All reports that the Works Constitution Act is a compromise between the positions of the employers and the unions are false. This law has to be changed because it is clearly directly against workers" (*Die Quelle*, August 1952:398). Convinced that the new law showed the conservative government's "true face," the unions placed their hopes for its revision in the Social Democratic party. Under the motto "Elect a better parliament!" they withdrew their passive tolerance of the conservative government and vowed to work for its defeat in the next elections.

The political tide, however, was moving against labor. The SPD was stagnating in the polls, and the CDU was gaining strength. By 1953 it was clear that the political route to a new codetermination law would be a long and arduous one for the unions. In that year, the electorate returned the conservatives to office with 45.2 percent of the vote (up

19. See also Rundschreiben Nr. 2/52, IG Metall Vorstand, 22 January 1952 (IG Metall Archives); IG Metall *Gewerkschäftsbericht 1952/53*:115, 123; and *Metall*, 9 January 1952:3.

20. Regarding a worker's minimum age and the minimum number of years of seniority in the plant before he or she could run for works council office.

from 31.0 percent in 1949), as against 28.8 percent for the SPD (down slightly from 29.2 percent in 1949) (Edinger 1986:143).[21]

The Union Offensive on the Shop Floor

The IG Metall's immediate response to the 1952 defeat was twofold.[22] First, the union mounted a plant-level drive to create alongside the works councils an official *union* beachhead on the shop floor through its campaign to promote the establishment of shop steward committees on a broad basis. And second, the union campaigned actively to fill the works councils with its own members.

The union's goal in creating shop steward committees was to ensure a union presence in the plant as a check on the autonomous (and potentially rogue) works councils (Koopmann 1979, 1:442–48). In the same month that the Works Constitution Act went into effect, the IG Metall executive board issued a directive to all regional and local union offices to establish union shop steward committees in all plants. The union leadership explicitly linked this move to the problems that the law had created for the union (Koopmann 1981:34). The letter the locals received from union headquarters ends with the dictum: "No plant without union shop stewards!" (IG Metall 1952).

Among the most important trends propelling the IG Metall along this course was a marked drop in union membership in the years just following the Works Constitution Act. The overall organization level fell from 56.2 percent in 1952 to a low of 37.7 percent in 1963, when the trend was finally reversed (Schmidt 1974:130). Moreover, as Klaus Koopmann has noted, tendencies toward plant egoism and the isolation of works councils from the rank and file seemed to be growing in the years following 1952, causing great concern within the union (1979: 448–54).

Thus, in 1955 the union launched a major shop steward "offensive" in its plants (the Union Steward Action Program) under the auspices of the newly created department for shop stewards (headed by Otto Brenner, who would later become the union's president).[23] The main goals of the IG Metall's Action Program were (1) to increase the number of elected shop stewards in its plants, (2) to institutionalize regular shop steward meetings, (3) to increase collaboration between shop stewards and union locals, (4) to ensure collaboration between

21. The CDU formed a coalition with the F.D.P., which had received 9.5 percent of the vote in 1953 (down from 11.9 percent in 1949) (Edinger 1986:143). Indeed, it would not be until 1966 that the Social Democrats would enter the government, and then first as the conservatives' junior partner in the Grand Coalition of 1966–69.

22. The best treatment of these events can be found in Koopmann 1979, vol. 1. This section draws heavily on Koopmann's account.

23. This was followed a few years later by a second similar "offensive," in 1966–67 (Koopmann 1979: vol. 1:592–608).

works councils and shop stewards, and (5) to increase union membership levels and dues (Koopmann 1981:45).

In short, the union's plant-level campaigns in the 1950s and 1960s were intended to establish a strong union presence at that level to counteract the effects of the new Works Constitution Act. At the Fourth IG Metall Congress in 1956, executive board member Fritz Strothmann explicitly charged union stewards with controlling the works councils (IG Metall *Gewerkschaftstag 1956*:145; Koopmann 1981:38). The union's monthly publication for functionaries specified how this would be accomplished: "We can best fight [the isolation of works councils from the union] by setting up strong shop steward committees alongside them, which will simply make it impossible for them to forget that they belong to the IG Metall and what duties follow from that membership" (*Der Gewerkschafter*, December 1961:3).

The IG Metall's efforts did reverse the negative membership trend, as well as increase the number of plants with shop stewards and the ratio of stewards to workers. In just seven years (1960–67) the number of plants with shop steward committees more than doubled, and the union had nearly twice as many shop stewards in 1970 as it had in 1960 (see Table 10).

Table 10. IG Metall shop steward development

	Year of shop steward election			
	1960	1967	1970	1973
Plants with shop stewards	3,339	5,227	5,483	6,087
Plants with shop steward committees	1,641 (49%)	3,336 (63.8%)	3,703 (67.5%)	4,374 (71.9%)
Total Number of shop stewards	53,273	88,001	103,407	121,595
Workers per shop steward	n.a.	35.5	33.4	29.1

Source: Klaus Koopmann, *Vertrauensleute: Arbeitervertretung im Betrieb* (Frankfurt: Büchergilde Gutenberg, 1981), 49. Used by permission of the publisher.

One of the most important tasks for shop stewards was to draw up the candidate lists for works council elections. Indeed, this had been one of the primary motives for bolstering the union stewards in the first place. In a 1952 article entitled "The Works Constitution Act and Our Tasks," the union predicted the appearance of "anonymous" lists in works council elections and assigned to shop stewards the task of exposing the groups behind them and guarding against the fragmentation that would result from the election of candidates backed by employers and other non- or antiunion forces (*Metall*, 26 November

1952:1; see also *Der Gewerkschafter* no. 12, December 1961:3). In addition, of course, union stewards were to see to it that the best union representatives ran for office and were elected to the works councils (Koopmann 1981:39). In this respect, the union's shop steward campaigns dovetailed with its strategy to get union members elected to the new works councils.

Here too the union was very successful; the IG Metall dominated works council elections in the metalworking industries from very early on (see Table 11).[24]

Table 11. Percent of works councillors in the steel and metalworking industries belonging to each of the major unions, 1955–87

	IGM	DAG	CGB	Nonunionized
1955	78.1	(6.0)[a]		15.9
1957	81.7	—	—	13.5
1959	81.6	4.3	0.4	13.7
1961	82.2	4.4	0.5	12.9
1963	82.1	4.0	0.8	13.1
1965	82.6	3.6	0.9	12.9
1968	82.6	3.4	0.6	13.4
1972	81.3	2.6	0.4	15.7
1975	83.3	2.3	0.5	13.9
1978	84.5	2.0	0.6	12.7
1981	83.1	1.9	0.5	14.3
1984	83.3	1.9	0.6	14.0
1987	82.4	1.7	0.5	15.2

Source: IG Metall (1957) *Zusammenstellung der Ergebnisse der Betriebsrätewahlen 1957*; and IG Metall (1987) *Ergebnisse der Betriebsratwahlen, 1987*:3).
[a]Available data on the results of the first postwar works council election do not break down which unions received the votes that did not go to the IG Metall or to nonunion candidates (see IG Metall 1957).

The union's early—and continuing—dominance in works council elections no doubt has to do with the relative political vacuum that exists at the plant level. The IG Metall is the dominant if not the only real organized group in most of its plants, and its members have been able to win elections even in plants that have low overall unionization levels.

Despite these plant successes, however, the political setback of the early 1950s left the union predisposed to suspect works councils as a potential threat to union interests. Apart from its efforts to establish a separate union presence in the plant, and to "take over" the works councils with its own members, the union leadership concentrated on collective bargaining and centralized power within the organization at the national level.

24. A similar pattern obtains in other industries as well. Nationally, over 80 percent of all works councillors belong to the DGB-affiliated unions.

The Centralization of Bargaining in the 1950s

Although centralized and coordinated bargaining is now taken for granted in Germany, this arrangement is the outcome of intensive political wrangling in the 1950s and early 1960s. The IG Metall's collective bargaining rounds in the first years of the Federal Republic were organized along industrial lines, but fought on a regional basis. Regional union officers enjoyed great autonomy in formulating their own demands and strategies, and regional bargaining proceeded with little or no coordination by the central union. Many observers cite this lack of coordination among regions as the cause of several critical bargaining defeats in the early 1950s (see, for example, Markovits 1986:185–86, 188–89).

The structure of bargaining changed in 1956, when the IG Metall not only centralized negotiations within its own organizational domain, but in fact emerged as the leader in collective bargaining for the German labor movement as a whole.[25] In 1955, the DGB had adopted a new "Action Program" of union demands, in which the introduction of a forty-hour workweek was a high priority (Markovits 1986:86).[26] DGB leaders negotiated with the national Federation of German Employers (BDA) over working time reduction in 1956, but they failed to reach any agreement (Markovits 1986:190).

Instead, the IG Metall made the crucial breakthrough on the forty-hour workweek. National-level negotiations between the union's top leadership and the employers' association for the metalworking industries (Gesamtmetall) produced the Bremen Accord of 1956, the first in a series of agreements on working time reduction, which would serve as the pattern for other industries as well (Pirker 1979, 2:185). The agreement consolidated the IG Metall's leadership within the DGB. In addition, with the Bremen Accord, the top IG Metall leadership wrested control over collective bargaining from its own regional officers and established a degree of centralization in bargaining that would persist until 1969.

Auspicious economic conditions facilitated the union's collective bargaining victory, and with it the centralization of bargaining authority at the national union headquarters. The organization and strategy of German employers also facilitated the institutionalization of centralized bargaining. Business interests in Germany have a long tradition of organization and centralization (Shonfield 1969: chap. 11). And, once it had been established in the Bremen Accord, the employers became ardent defenders of centralized bargaining.

---

25. Pirker's analysis of the IG Metall's rise to dominance in the DGB is the most thorough account of these events, which can only be summarized here (see Pirker 1979: vol. 2, especially chap. 3).

26. At the time, a forty-eight-hour week was the norm.

The trend toward the centralization of bargaining in the 1950s had enormous consequences for the evolution of relations between works councils and the central union. Centralized bargaining necessarily produced wage deals that did not fully exhaust the ability of many employers to pay. And by the late 1950s, the "economic miracle" was in full swing. Shop-floor (and therefore, works council) politics in this period began to be characterized by informal "second rounds" of wage negotiations at the plant level (see especially Teschner 1977; also Schmidt 1973:185–86).

Although works councils cannot (by law) officially negotiate wage levels, in the 1950s and 1960s they bargained unofficially over what became a hefty "wage drift" factor, which in 1955 averaged 22.5 percent for men in the metalworking industries, but for some workers reached 70 percent.[27] They did so either in direct, albeit informal, negotiations with managers over "supplemental" wages and benefits (*übertarifliche Leistungen*) or in negotiations over wage determination methods (or their application) that indirectly boosted wage levels in the plant (Teschner 1977:9). In the 1950s and 1960s wage drift became an important component of workers' incomes, thus giving the works councils considerable (though again, informal) power. Between 1960 and 1970, collectively bargained wages increased at an average annual rate of 7.3 percent. Workers' effective wages in that period, however, rose at an average annual rate of 9.4 percent (Teschner 1977:4).

As Eberhard Schmidt points out, the function of works councils after World War II in the area of wages was quite different from that of the Weimar works councils. Weimar works councils did not have as much room for carving out a measure of power independent of the unions on the wage issue both because bargaining was less centralized and because economic conditions in the 1920s and 1930s did not leave room for longstanding, significant wage drift (Schmidt 1973:179–80). Works councils did negotiate wage adjustments during the inflation of the 1920s, but this was more an ad hoc response to the breakdown of centralized bargaining than a stable, ongoing supplement to it, as in the 1950s and 1960s.

In the context of the post–World War II economic miracle and of the centralization of bargaining, however, the growing importance of works councils did not clash with the central union's interests. Indeed, the works councils' informal role in negotiating wage drift served to shore

27. "Wage drift" is the difference between collectively bargained wage rates and the "effective" wage rate in the plant, i.e., that which employers actually pay. The figures reported here on the extent of wage drift come from a survey conducted by the IG Metall in 1955, the results of which appear in Zoll 1981:56–57. The average difference between collectively bargained and effective wage rates in the metalworking industries was 22.5 percent for men and 17.6 percent for women. In addition, wage drift varied widely for different workers: for men, between 3.6 and 58 percent, for women between 0 and 70.1 percent.

up centralized bargaining by stemming opposition to it in the plants (Streeck 1981:159; Zoll 1981:63). In the positive-sum wage game of the 1950s and 1960s, the ability of works councils to extract further concessions from employers in stronger plants complemented the union's interest in the centralization of bargaining.

Leading up to the late 1960s, then, the union had by and large made its peace with the works council system it had opposed a decade and a half before. The IG Metall had established its presence on the shop floor both through the expanded network of shop steward committees and within an overwhelming majority of works councils as well. Moreover, in the 1950s and 1960s, the works councils helped stabilize central bargaining by providing a wage "safety valve" (Streeck 1981:159). Leaner times, however, would test this division of labor between the central union and the shop floor.

CHAPTER FOUR

Tensions in the Dual System

The dual system of the 1950s was conceived and created when labor's political power was low. However, nearly two decades later when the union faced pressures from the rank and file to change the relationship between the central union and the shop floor, the IG Metall responded not by challenging the dual system but by reinforcing it. The union answered spontaneous strikes and calls for a decentralization of power within the union in the late 1960s and early 1970s by defending central authority in collective bargaining and redirecting the demands of the militants into channels that reinforced and expanded the authority of works councils in the plant. Plant militancy in this period and the union's response to it constitute the second "turning point" in the evolution of the dual system.

The events of the late 1960s have been the subject of several excellent analyses, some by participants in the debates and events of that period themselves (see, for example, Schmidt 1975; Zoll 1981; Koopmann 1979, 1981; Krusche and Pfeiffer 1975; and Bergmann, Jacobi, and Müller-Jentsch 1979). A dominant interpretation in the existing literature on the subject sees the turmoil of this period as an expression of the contradictions inherent in cooperative unionism. In this version, the economic downturn of the late 1960s revealed latent tensions between the conservative union hierarchy and local activists supported by an at least potentially more militant rank and file. The outcome is typically characterized as a rather straightforward defeat of rank-and-file militants at the hands of the central union "apparatus." In most existing analyses, the formal structure of dualism is the independent variable, that is, part of the explanation of how the unions were able to resist decentralization (and to preserve "social partnership").

My own analysis draws on these studies, and is in many respects not

84

incompatible with them; I emphasize, however, somewhat different aspects of the same story. In my account, what is important is how the conflicts of the late 1960s and early 1970s affected the dual system itself, how strategic maneuvering within the institutions of the dual system precipitated political conflicts, the outcomes of which in turn became institutionalized in ways that influenced the parameters of subsequent battles. In the context of the present study, recounting how the IG Metall coped with demands for decentralization from within its own left wing in the 1960s is important above all for understanding the institutional bases of the union's relative success in dealing with *employers'* demands for decentralization and flexibility two decades later.

Macroeconomic and political developments help explain both the tensions between the shop floor and the central union in the late 1960s and the union's changing interests in the dual system. The German economy, which had been steaming along in the 1950s and early 1960s, hit a bump in 1966. The recession in 1966–67 was Germany's first since reconstruction. Although it pales in comparison with the economic turmoil of the late 1970s and 1980s, the recession temporarily upset the positive-sum game (centralized bargaining but with substantial wage drift at the plant level) that had stabilized intraunion relations in the 1950s and 1960s.

Just as organized labor's market strength took a turn for the worse, however, its political situation took a turn for the better. When the Social Democrats came to power in the Grand Coalition of 1966, the IG Metall saw a chance to consolidate its own (and the Social Democrats') political position by cooperating with the government in a national incomes policy as part of the government's efforts to restart growth. Centralized bargaining and the union's policy of wage restraint set the scene for heightened tensions between the union leadership and the rank and file. Plant militants called for the decentralization of bargaining and other measures to increase intraunion democracy.

The IG Metall leadership defended its authority in collective bargaining and rechanneled rank-and-file militancy into legislative efforts to enhance the powers of works councils. It defused the criticism and resolved the crisis through a rebalancing of interests within the dual system.

Political maneuvering by the union leadership in response to strategic openings provided by changes in the economic and political context help explain this outcome. Germany's quick recovery from the recession allowed the union to deflect criticism of centralized bargaining through renewed aggressiveness on wages. The Social Democratic victory in the 1969 national election provided the union leadership with the political opening it needed to redefine demands for greater organizational democracy within the union into legislative efforts to strengthen works councils in the plant.

Markets and Politics in the Late 1960s

In retrospect, the recession in 1966–67 was mild, but it was sufficient to expose the fragility of the positive-sum wage game that had developed between the works councils and the central union. Since works councils are legally prohibited from negotiating over general wage levels, the second (plant-level) round of wage bargaining had always been informal. During the recession employers unilaterally cut wages and benefits above the collectively bargained minimum by simply refusing to negotiate informally (Teschner 1977:93; IG Metall *Geschäftsbericht, 1965–67*:123). Works councils watched wages drift back downward and were relatively helpless to stop it. Early in the recession, workers in a few scattered plants protested these reductions in plant wages and benefits in spontaneous strikes (Teschner 1977:93). Thus, although the recession was mild, it did drive home to workers that they could not count on the wages to which they had grown accustomed in the heyday of wage drift in the 1950s and early 1960s.

Meanwhile at the national level, the IG Metall saw the Social Democratic party's entry into the government—first in the "Grand Coalition" with the CDU in 1966, and then as majority partner with the F.D.P. in 1969—as a political opportunity. The union agreed to participate in an informal incomes policy to help shore up the new government and bolster the position of the Social Democrats within it in return for the SPD's assistance in implementing labor's political program, which had been put on hold over a decade earlier.

Economics minister Karl Schiller was the driving force behind the Konzertierte Aktion, the national-level discussions between business, labor, and the government. Schiller wanted the major economic actors to agree in advance of collective bargaining rounds on "orientation data" for wage settlements, in which the unions would agree to self-imposed wage restraint in order to encourage investment and help Germany out of the recession.

Although there was nothing formally binding about the orientation data, the IG Metall (which led wage bargaining for the other unions as well) cooperated in holding its wage demands to the levels discussed in peak negotiations in 1967, 1968, and into 1969. Indeed, settlements in the metalworking industries never exceeded the orientation figures in those years, and annual collective bargaining outcomes for the economy as a whole also followed the Konzertierte Aktion guidelines closely (see Table 12).

The erosion of effective wages at the plant level (a drop in wage drift) and central union wage restraint set the stage for rank-and-file revolt in 1969.

Table 12. Concerted Action orientation data and collectively bargained wage and salary increases, 1967–69

Year	Orientation data (%)	Collectively bargained wage and salary increases (%)
1967	3.5	3.5
1968	4.0–5.0	4.3
1969	5.5–6.5	6.0–7.5 (first ½ yr.)[a]

Source: Joachim Bergmann, Otto Jacobi, and Walther Müller-Jentsch, *Gewerkschaften in der Bundesrepublik* 3d ed. (Frankfurt: Campus Verlag, 1979:247). Used by permission of the publisher.

[a]The somewhat higher settlements are due to the fact that other unions (e.g., ÖTV and IG Chemie) settled somewhat higher than the orientation data. In 1968, the IG Metall had signed an eighteen-month contract, so it did not bargain in the first half of 1969.

RANK-AND-FILE MILITANCY AND PSEUDO-DECENTRALIZATION, 1969–1972

The shop-floor revolt against the union's central wage policy coalesced around two separate but related movements: a series of spontaneous strikes in the steel industry in 1969 and more general calls for a decentralization of bargaining that emanated especially from workers in the automobile industry. The demands for decentralization peaked at the union's 1968 and 1971 congresses.

Many factors played a role in Germany's spontaneous strike wave in 1969, but dissatisfaction with the IG Metall's performance in Concerted Action was certainly one of them (see especially Zoll 1981:115–16; Bergman, Jacobi, and Müller-Jentsch 1979: chap. 5). In light of the slow economic growth in 1967, in its 1968 bargaining round the IG Metall agreed to modest wage increases, and also to an eighteen-month rather than the usual twelve-month contract.[1] However, by early 1969, the German economy was well into recovery; indeed, business was experiencing an extraordinary boom. With industry reaping huge profits and the IG Metall still committed to the modest settlement of 1968, unrest grew on the shop floor. Labor representatives at the plant level called for "social symmetry" in distributing the benefits of the boom, arguing that workers who had agreed to sacrifices during the recession should share in the rewards during the recovery.

The IG Metall was able to push forward by a month negotiations for a new contract in the metalworking industries, settling for an 8 percent

1. The 1968 wage settlement called for a 4 percent increase in 1968 and a further 3 percent raise beginning on 1 January 1969 (Bergmann, Jacobi, and Müller-Jentsch 1979:249).

wage increase in August 1969 (Schmidt 1975:112). Although the outcome quelled some of the criticism from the rank and file, the process through which it had been achieved fueled widespread dissatisfaction with the union's methods and with the extreme centralization of wage negotiations in general. Not only were lower-level union functionaries not consulted in the negotiations, most were not even aware that negotiations were taking place. Informal discussions between top union leaders and representatives of the employers' organization were simply transformed at some point into formal negotiations, and a settlement was announced (Schmidt 1975:114).

The steel industry, which historically has bargained separately from the rest of the metalworking industry, was still bound by a previous agreement, which was not scheduled to expire until the end of November 1969 (Schmidt 1975:114). Steel employers rejected an appeal by the union to renegotiate that contract as well (IG Metall Geschäftsbericht, 1968–70:121). Their refusal only heightened tensions at the plant level. On 2 September, three thousand steelworkers at Hoesch in Dortmund walked off their jobs, setting off a wave of spontaneous strikes involving a total of ninety-eight thousand metalworkers (Schmidt 1975:81, 103).[2]

The strikes ultimately brought the employers back to the bargaining table before the contract's scheduled expiration, and a new settlement put an end to the episode. Importantly, however, it was the employers rather than the union leadership who bowed to the pressure of the strikes. The union's executive committee publicly expressed its sympathy with the strikers' demands. But union leaders, who were bound by the no-strike clause in the existing contract, repeatedly and summarily rejected all calls for official union support of the strike. Representatives of the striking workers made several visits to the union headquarters in Frankfurt demanding the union's support in the strike. They argued that the IG Metall had to respond; after all, tens of thousands of its members were out on the streets. Hans Mayr, then the union's secretary in charge of collective bargaining policy, describes union president Otto Brenner's cool reaction: "Na, und?" (So?) (interview, June 1989). These tens of thousands of workers constituted a very small percentage of the IG Metall's total membership. The executive board actively ignored the steelworkers' requests, since supporting this strike would create a precedent and only invite similar demands in the future. As Mayr put it, "Only such a big organization can hold out under that kind of political pressure" (interview, June 1989).

Tensions eased when employers and the union signed a new contract for the steel industry, but the entire episode left a legacy of lingering unrest. Many delegates to the 1969 conference for shop stewards and

---

2. Those involved were mostly iron- and steelworkers, but some workers from the shipyards in northern Germany participated also. Workers organized in some other industries joined in, though in much smaller numbers (Schmidt 1975:103).

works councillors criticized the union's bargaining methods as too centralized and even secretive (IG Metall *Vertrauensleute, 1969*:42, 84–85). Throughout the conference various delegates spoke out for a retreat from centralized negotiations and for greater shop steward involvement in collective bargaining.

BETRIEBSNAHE TARIFPOLITIK

A related though distinct threat to centralized collective bargaining originated in a movement within the union in favor of *betriebsnahe Tarifpolitik*, or plant-oriented collective bargaining.[3] Although it is often conflated with the events in the steel industry just described, the debate over betriebsnahe Tarifpolitik began before the spontaneous strikes of 1969 and also outlasted them. Its proponents often—though not always—shared the steelworkers' criticism of union participation in Concerted Action.[4]

Supporters of betriebsnahe Tarifpolitik found fault with both the process and the outcome of the union's collective bargaining policy. They criticized the highly centralized negotiations as exclusionary and even antidemocratic. More importantly, though, they criticized the results of centralized bargaining. They asserted that because central collective bargaining was geared toward establishing minimum standards for all metalworkers, it did not always exhaust the ability of each individual employer to pay. As pointed out above, plant negotiations could raise workers' "effective" incomes, but this wage drift was always vulnerable to renegotiation and unilateral cuts since the second wage round in the plants was informal and could not be defended through recourse to industrial conflict. Thus, the only part of a worker's income that was truly "safe" was that which was secured through collective bargaining. Betriebsnahe Tarifpolitik was meant to redress this gap between collectively bargained and "effective" wages.

Plant-oriented collective bargaining meant different things to different people, but the core demand was for a partial decentralization of wage negotiations. Most proponents foresaw the establishment of wage committees in individual plants, through which local labor representatives (especially shop stewards) would become more active in formulating demands and devising strategies—up to and including strikes—to achieve them (see especially Schmidt 1975:170–78). "Opening clauses" in centrally bargained agreements would solve the wage drift problem

---

3. Comprehensive treatments of this subject can be found in Zoll, 1981, and Schmidt, 1975.
    4. I say "not always" because some proponents of betriebsnahe Tarifpolitik supported union participation in the informal incomes policy. The most prominent of these was perhaps Hans Matthöfer (Matthöfer 1968e:5).

by allowing these plant-level representatives (together with local union authorities) to negotiate supplementary, binding wage agreements in a second, formal bargaining round at the plant or company level.[5]

There was a time, the late 1950s and early 1960s, when betriebsnahe Tarifpolitik enjoyed some support in the upper echelons of the union (see especially Zoll 1981:56–64; Krusche and Pfeiffer 1975:118–19). Fritz Salm, Mayr's predecessor as secretary in charge of the IG Metall's collective bargaining, vigorously promoted the idea at union congresses in the 1950s. Salm argued on both economic and organizational grounds. First, betriebsnahe Tarifpolitik was necessary to secure contractually the wage drift that was rampant in the heyday of the economic miracle. Second, such decentralization would revitalize union activity at the regional and local levels (Zoll 1981:59). In the end, however, Salm never translated his ideas—which were always formulated in highly abstract terms—into concrete proposals for action.[6] He retired in 1963 without having realized, nor even really seriously fought for, the practical implementation of a plan for betriebsnahe Tarifpolitik.

Moreover, as time went on, and especially as the union consolidated its central bargaining authority in national-level negotiations with employers over working-time reduction (the last agreement on the forty-hour week was reached in 1965), the union leadership increasingly distanced itself from all proposals for betriebsnahe Tarifpolitik that involved the decentralization of bargaining authority within the union.

A closed session (*Klausurtagung*) of the union's executive board in 1965 decided the issue formally.[7] The critical decision made at that meeting was that the union would not throw its power behind a strike to obtain opening clauses in collective bargaining contracts. This decision was tantamount to rejecting betriebsnahe Tarifpolitik outright. Since employers were adamantly opposed to opening clauses in central

5. This kind of "opening clause" would have allowed for a second round of negotiations between union representatives and employers, in which the union could use strikes as a form of pressure. They are thus different from other sorts of "opening clauses" (which are not uncommon), which delegate responsibility to works councils (who are bound by the no-strike obligation under the Works Constitution Act) to negotiate "plant agreements" with employers over certain issues (see Streeck 1981:160).

6. An exception to this was Salm's conception of new wage determination methods, which he sometimes included in the broad package of ideas he had regarding plant-oriented collective bargaining (see, for example, his articles in *Der Gewerkschafter*, August 1958 and December 1959). Certain wage "framework agreements" of the late 1960s did address some of these issues (IG Metall, *Geschäftsbericht 1968–1970*:123ff; IG Metall, *Geschäftsbericht 1965–1967*:121ff). However, these (central) agreements are quite different from other proposals that implied real decentralization.

7. The following account is based on an interview in June 1989 with Hans Mayr, at that time the union secretary in charge of collective bargaining (as Salm's successor) and later president of the union. For a summary of the results of the meeting, see "Zusammenfassung des Diskussionsergebnisses der Klausurtagung des Vorstandes der IG Metall am 6/7. Januar 1965," in Radke, 1969:28.

agreements, readiness to strike on the part of the union would have been necessary to pursue the demand.

The decision not to strike for plant-oriented collective bargaining made the issue academic. However, this should not obscure the fact that the union leadership also opposed the measure for its own reasons. The consensus that emerged within the executive board at the 1965 meeting was that collective bargaining should remain centralized, focusing on setting minimum standards for the entire industry and not on securing maximum gains in individual plants or companies. Union leaders decided that delegating to plant-level representatives substantial powers on wage issues would fragment and weaken the union. And institutionalizing a second formal round of wage negotiations would undermine central union authority and power in collective bargaining. Stronger plants would have less incentive to fight for a high minimum wage level for all in the first round if they could be sure of obtaining a higher wage deal for themselves in subsequent plant-level bargaining. In short, and as Salm's successor Hans Mayr put it, if the union were to push for betriebsnahe Tarifpolitik through "opening clauses" in central contracts, then the whole system of organized interests (*Verbandsstruktur*) would come apart.

The language the executive board adopted in its official policy statement on betriebsnahe Tarifpolitik was nuanced in important ways (Mayr: "raffiniert formuliert"). To reject the concept outright would have been tantamount to sanctioning wage drift. Thus, the union committed itself to conduct its collective bargaining policy "in as plant-oriented a way as possible" (*so betriebsnah wie möglich*). By adopting the subtle wording it did, the executive board "absorbed" the demand at a conceptual level, at the same time that its decision not to strike reflected the deeper opposition to the demand by rejecting the practical measures that would have been required to realize it. The carefully crafted language is important, for it makes sense of what appears to be a curious doublespeak in subsequent union documents on betriebsnahe Tarifpolitik, and explains as well why the union appeared to embrace the concept at a rhetorical level.[8]

The recession of 1966–67 and the entry of the Social Democrats into government in 1966 only str~~~~~~~~~~~~~~ ~~~~~~~~~~~ officials to centralized barga political power by helping s crats by cooperating in Sc decentralization in bargaining was ou hopelessly complicate the union's participa~~~~ in ~~~~ incomes policy Schiller advocated.

8. See especially the 1969 brochure by Olaf Radke, who headed the union's collective bargaining department under Mayr (Radke 1969).

Thus, when "plant-oriented collective bargaining" emerged again as a theme in 1968–69, the issue was long since closed within the executive board. Its proponents consisted of a minority left wing within the union and local union functionaries, especially from the automobile industry, where wage drift was particularly high. The recession of 1966–67 and the accompanying cuts in wage drift and other plant benefits had taught plant-level representatives how vulnerable local agreements were to renegotiation and unilateral management cuts. Once the recession was over, wage drift rose again sharply because of the central union's wage restraint under Concerted Action, and labor representatives at the plant level were eager to secure these gains contractually.

Betriebsnahe Tarifpolitik thus became a leitmotif and the subject of ongoing debate at union conventions in the late 1960s and early 1970s. At the 1968 congress in Munich, several delegates spoke out in favor of betriebsnahe Tarifpolitik, some invoking the name of the now deceased Fritz Salm (IG Metall, *Gewerkschaftstag, 1968*:153–55, 177–82, 190–93). Proposals for plant-oriented collective bargaining were also introduced at the 1969 national conference for shop stewards and works councillors (where the resolution actually carried) and at the union's 1971 congress.[9] By 1971 proponents of betriebsnahe Tarifpolitik were especially infuriated by what they considered the executive board's duplicity: full of rhetorical support for the demand, but unwilling to act on it. As a delegate from the Ford plant in Cologne put it: "For fifteen years the IG Metall Congress has had a resolution that says we will pursue plant-oriented collective bargaining. Why hasn't that resolution ever been realized?" (IG Metall, *Gewerkschaftstag, 1971*:182).

The union leadership ignored thinly veiled threats by some plant representatives from the powerful automobile industry to form a separate union, staying with its policy of unified, centralized bargaining. Hans Mayr, who as head of collective bargaining was the target of much of the criticism of the plant militants, echoed Otto Brenner's reaction to the steel workers two years earlier: "You have to stay cool in the face of such political pressure" (interview, June 1989). Most importantly, the union leadership carried the day at the union congresses. All proposals for betriebsnahe Tarifpolitik were defeated.[10]

In sum, the leadership continued to emphasize its commitment to a collective bargaining policy that was "as plant-oriented as possible." As a practical matter, however, the only "opening clauses" the union would actively support were those mandating negotiations between works councils and employers, which by law could not directly compete with

9. Koopmann (1979, 2:635–41) covers these debates.
10. The executive board recommended that some of the proposals at the 1971 congress be considered "taken care of" (*erledigt*) by the board's own collective bargaining resolution, which, however, did not really address the demands of the plant militants.

union collective bargaining outcomes, were not subject to strike, and had to be carried out according to the stipulations of the Works Constitution Act.[11] The IG Metall's leaders were united against all attempts to decentralize and fragment wage bargaining through strikeable opening clauses negotiated between local union representatives and employers. Throughout the conflict over betriebsnahe Tarifpolitik the executive board acted to preserve what Mayr calls "the IG Metall's secret" in collective bargaining, namely "to allow no one to break out of solidarity, and in this way to bound the boundless egoism" of the union's various parts (interview, June 1989).

MITBESTIMMUNG AM ARBEITSPLATZ

A second debate of the late 1960s overlapped with and drew on the same themes as the controversy over plant-oriented collective bargaining. This debate revolved around demands for "on-the-job codetermination" (*Mitbestimmung am Arbeitsplatz*).[12]

In 1968, the Social Democratic party created a commission to review existing codetermination legislation and to make recommendations to the Social Democratic faction in the "Grand Coalition" government. For the unions, SPD participation in government opened up new possibilities to achieve the codetermination demands they had been forced to shelve in 1952. When the Social Democrats became the majority coalition partner (with the F.D.P.) in 1969, revising the Works Constitution Act was high on labor's policy agenda.

In the debate over the revision of the Works Constitution Act—and against the backdrop of the 1969 strikes and the conflict over plant-oriented collective bargaining—the concept of "on-the-job codetermination" became a part of the democratization debate in the union. Hans Matthöfer, head of the IG Metall's education department and SPD member of parliament was the foremost proponent of Mitbestimmung am Arbeitsplatz. Matthöfer's idea was that in plants employing more than five hundred workers, "work groups" should be formed in various divisions of the plant. Workers in each division would elect group representatives to promote the interests of the work group vis-à-vis their immediate supervisors either directly or in collaboration with the works council (Matthöfer 1968c; Matthöfer 1968d:5; and Schmidt

11. Union president Otto Brenner later suggested that the IG Metall leadership's conception of betriebsnahe Tarifpolitik was fulfilled through negotiations between works councils and employers. Referring to works council bargaining over the application of the 1968 Rationalization Protection Agreement and over wage classifications, he said, "That is what we call plant-oriented collective bargaining" (IG Metall, *Gewerkschaftstag, 1968*:264–65).

12. The most detailed account of these events can be found in Koopmann 1979, 2:703–63. See also the accounts by Zoll, 1981:87–89, and Schmidt, 1975:183–92, both of whom were themselves advocates of Mitbestimmung am Arbeitsplatz.

1975:187). Matthöfer advocated that those questions directly affecting a given group of workers (e.g., changes in production organization, jobs, material delivery, or wages) be dealt with in work group meetings headed by these group representatives (Schmidt 1975:187–88). Influenced by the American model of industrial relations,[13] Matthöfer's proposal in essence called for bolstering the grievance rights of group representatives on issues affecting their areas of immediate jurisdiction (interview, June 1989; Matthöfer 1968d:5).[14]

Other proponents of Mitbestimmung am Arbeitsplatz discussed variations on Matthöfer's concept, but all of them called for the establishment of work groups below the works council level and for the election of group representatives who would be empowered to represent the group's interests in direct negotiations with their immediate supervisors.[15] What made Mitbestimmung am Arbeitsplatz attractive for some was the desire to increase the participatory rights of individual workers and to fight tendencies toward the "professionalization" and "isolation" of works councils from the membership. Others hoped that the measure would strengthen the position of union stewards in the plant, who were virtually eclipsed by the works councils.

Strategically located in the union's education and press departments, the main proponents of Mitbestimmung am Arbeitsplatz skillfully used the union press and especially union seminars to disseminate and promote their idea among union functionaries at the plant level. Even Matthöfer's most strident critic, Eugen Loderer (the union's vice president until 1972, thereafter its president), admitted that Matthöfer had promoted his idea "with a degree of effectiveness that really was remarkable" (interview, June 1989). Numerous proposals at both the 1968 and, especially, the 1971 union congresses testified to the growing support for the idea within the organization, even if all such proposals were ultimately defeated.

Mitbestimmung am Arbeitsplatz was controversial within the union for a number of reasons.[16] Some critics felt that the legal recognition of group leaders would create a platform for nonunion or even antiunion factions within the plant, and their suspicions were fueled by the relative receptiveness of employers to the idea of work groups. Others

13. Matthöfer studied under Selig Perlman at the University of Wisconsin in Madison in the 1950s (interview, June 1989).

14. Matthöfer also developed proposals for union education policy (*Bildungsarbeit*) that would complement and support Mitbestimmung am Arbeitsplatz in the plants (see for example, Matthöfer 1968a).

15. See, for example, Schmidt 1968; Vilmar 1968, 1971; Hoffmann 1968; and Schumann 1969.

16. For the views of two critics, see Radke, 1968, and Pinther, 1970. But see also Koopmann, 1979, 2:712–26, for a very comprehensive discussion of the union critique of Mitbestimmung am Arbeitsplatz. Koopman also provides a full account of debates on this issue at union congresses.

argued that even if union stewards dominated the work groups, their new legal status as group leaders would circumscribe their political activities in the plant (Koopmann 1979:715–16).

In general, however, union officials seemed most troubled by the idea that work groups with independent legal status could pose a threat to the authority of the works council in the plant. A statement issued by the IG Metall executive board asserted that this kind of "immediate and 'direct' representation of interests through small circles of workers" could "result in the formation of an opposing base of power in the plant (*Gegenpol*) to the works council" (quoted in Schmidt 1975:190). Nor were union leaders' concerns assuaged by the arguments of the left-wing proponents of the measure who pointed out that those workers who would be most inclined to become group leaders would most likely be unionists (and indeed union activists).[17] Although the union leadership cited the threat of nonunion factions, in the broader context of the period it seems clear that union officials were also concerned about left-wing union activists using work groups as a platform to further politicize plant relations.

On 14 April 1970, the union advisory board unanimously approved a resolution rejecting initiatives for Mitbestimmung am Arbeitsplatz that involved the establishment of work groups and work group representatives. A letter from the executive board to all union locals and district offices justified the decision, citing many of the criticisms enumerated above (IG Metall 1970). Among other things, the executive board argued that the tasks foreseen for work group leaders were in fact no different from those that union shop stewards should already be performing. In a twist that played on the rhetoric of the militants themselves, the executive board argued that "collective bargaining has to be as plant-oriented as possible; but shop steward work has to be as union-oriented as possible" (IG Metall 1970:4). But in an unmistakable allusion to the leadership's fears of encouraging factionalism within the union, and especially of creating a platform for more militant factions, the document argues that proponents of Mitbestimmung am Arbeitsplatz wrongly juxtapose "organization" and "movement" as mutually exclusive and contradictory. Using the French case as an example, the letter suggests that too much spontaneity and "movement" at the expense of strong organization leads to union weakness (IG Metall 1970:4–5).

The Social Democrats had been willing to include a provision for some form of Mitbestimmung am Arbeitsplatz in their draft legislation for a revised Works Constitution Act (Koopmann 1979:713; Zoll 1981:88). Indeed, Matthöfer presented his proposal at an SPD strategy session at the party's invitation. Afterwards, however, union president Otto Brenner

17. As supporters pointed out, works council elections verified this assumption: though only 30 percent of all workers were organized, union members accounted for 80 to 90 percent of all works councillors (Vilmar 1970:140).

made it clear to Chancellor Willy Brandt that he and the rest of the top union leadership opposed the measure, and the idea quickly disappeared from the SPD proposal (interview with Matthöfer, June 1989).

Stymied at this level, the proponents of Mitbestimmung am Arbeitsplatz and of the whole package of reforms aimed at "democratizing" the union (betriebsnahe Tarifpolitik, protection for shop stewards, and plant-oriented education policy) took their case to the full union congress in 1971. The leaders of the movement orchestrated the presentation of various proposals to the congress and held numerous strategy sessions in the course of the convention. However, just as proposals for betriebsnahe Tarifpolitik were neutralized, those for Mitbestimmung am Arbeitsplatz were defeated, though in some cases by rather slim majorities.

In sum, where the union had itself once actively encouraged a counterweight to the works councils (in the shop steward "offensives" of the 1950s and 1960s), in 1968–69 the IG Metall leadership found itself defending the authority of the works councils against potential rivals who could operate independently of them. As Matthöfer puts it, by the late 1960s and early 1970s, the union had "learned to live with works councils, and recognized that they were a stabilizing force, not a threat" (interview, June 1989). Union leaders couched their arguments in terms of a defense of union solidarity, but their position on this question was clearly a response as well to growing criticisms by plant militants of centralized collective bargaining and calls for plant-oriented collective bargaining. The union leadership feared giving plant militants a new legal foothold by endorsing Mitbestimmung am Arbeitsplatz (Schmidt 1975:183–92).

The Union Responds

The IG Metall's response to the challenges of the 1969 strikes and debates over plant-oriented collective bargaining and "on-the-job codetermination" represented a delicate balancing act in which the union ultimately consolidated central authority over the shop floor while addressing demands for increased plant-level powers by redirecting them into channels the union could control. The union distanced itself from Concerted Action discussions and pursued greater wage aggressiveness, which defused the issue of plant-oriented collective bargaining. At the same time, the IG Metall lobbied for legislative reform of the Works Constitution Act and recast the issue of intra-union democracy into greater rights for works councils (and also killed the Mitbestimmung am Arbeitsplatz initiative). Thus, the IG Metall's response to plant militancy in the late 1960s reinforced the dual system.

In central wage bargaining the union beat a timely retreat from the

Concerted Action guidelines (Flanagan, Soskice, and Ulman 1983:281–82).[18] In response to the steel strikes, the union and employers reopened bargaining before the eighteen-month (1968–69) contract expired, and negotiated longer vacations and an 8 percent increase in wages. As a concession to its restless plant representatives, the union also secured contractual protection for union stewards against arbitrary dismissal (Zoll 1981:116). Concerning the related problem of wage drift that had fueled the demand for betriebsnahe Tarifpolitik, the union in 1970 negotiated a substantial increase in base wages (on which percent increases are then calculated). This adjustment (*Vorweganhebung*) contractually secured a larger percentage of workers' wages, and it accounts for how the union achieved a total wage rise of 15.3 percent in that year when the percent increase it originally sought had been 15 percent (interview with Hans Mayr, June 1989; see also IG Metall 1987a:14).

Rapid economic growth between 1969 and 1973 facilitated this aggressive collective bargaining strategy and allowed the union to score a series of rather substantial wage gains (see Table 13). Indeed, in this period real wages in the economy as a whole outpaced productivity gains for the first time since 1963 (Flanagan, Soskice, and Ulman 1983:224). These dramatic gains served to defuse rank-and-file militancy and neutralize the advocates of more decentralized wage bargaining.

Table 13. Wage increases in collective bargaining rounds in the metalworking and steel industries, 1969–73

Date	Metalworking	Date	Steel
(from)		(from)	
1 Sept. 1969 (13 mon.)	8.0%	1 Sept. 1969 (13 mon.)	11.0%
1 Oct. 1970 (15 mon.)	15.3%[a]	1 Oct. 1970 (12 mon.)	10.0%
1 Jan. 1972 (12 mon.)	7.5%	1 Oct. 1971 (15 mon.)	10.5%[b]
1 Jan. 1973 (12 mon.)	8.5%	1 Jan. 1973 (11 mon.)	9.2%[c]
1 Jan. 1974 (12 mon.)	11.6%	1 Dec. 1973 (10.5 mon.)	11.0%

Source: IG Metall (1987) *Daten, Fakten, Informationen:*14–17.
[a]Averaged across all bargaining districts, includes Vorweganhebungen.
[b]DM 200 flat payment and a 4.5% increase starting 1 October 1971, with an additional 6.0% increase starting 1 February 1972.
[c]Plus a DM 100 flat payment.

The events of the late 1960s did lead to a partial decentralization of contract negotiations, as the union's ten bargaining districts were given more leeway to formulate their own demands (IG Metall, *Geschäftsbericht 1968–1970*:121).[19] A system of pattern bargaining developed, in which

18. It was after the 1969 outburst that Concerted Action became little more than a forum for discussion, and the "orientation data" for wage rounds became more vague and were largely ignored by the union.

19. Top union leaders also adopted a new policy of avoiding wage and salary contracts exceeding twelve months.

demands were raised and fought in one district and the settlement was carried over to the others. But IG Metall headquarters still called the final shots: the central union had sole control over strike funds, which made it impossible for bargaining districts to strike without its approval. Union leaders thus resolved the question of decentralization in the crucial area of wages in favor of the central union. On balance, then, the events of the late 1960s did not fundamentally transform central union relations with the shop floor, since the locus of power in wage negotiations never got anywhere near the plant.[20]

The union's response to the more general question of intraunion democracy and Mitbestimmung am Arbeitsplatz was more complicated, but the gist was to vigorously defend the authority of the works councils in the plants and at the same time push for an extension of their rights vis-à-vis management through what became the revised Works Constitution Act of 1972.

The union's defense of works council authority in the plant was accomplished in part through a semantical sleight of hand by the union leadership. As mentioned above, the union was wary of granting separate legal status to small work groups who might challenge the works council and even use their plant base to cause trouble for the central union. But again, rather than speaking out directly against Mitbestimmung am Arbeitsplatz, union leaders focused on defining the concept in a way that the union could live with, even if that meant ignoring its proponents' core demands.

In his address to the Seventh Conference of Shop Stewards in Braunschweig in 1969, Fritz Strothmann, IG Metall executive board member in charge of shop stewards, defined the terms on which the union leadership could endorse Mitbestimmung am Arbeitsplatz:

> That plant codetermination should also involve "on-the-job codetermination" is not contested in union circles. But what form this should take, that is where we have different conceptions. One conception is to create a new legal institution alongside the works council in the form of work groups.... In contrast, the DGB proposal for Mitbestimmung am Arbeitsplatz is that this form of codetermination, like all other forms of plant codetermination, should be practiced through the works council. That [the latter conception] is the IG Metall executive board's conception as well. [IG Metall, *Vertrauensleute, 1969*:35–36.]

20. The question of betriebsnahe Tarifpolitik resurfaced briefly in 1977 when a small number of works councillors and shop stewards in the (again thriving) automobile industry introduced a proposal to the IG Metall congress to allow them to bargain separately. By this time, however, the macroeconomic situation was quite different. Shipbuilding, steel, and other industries were in decline. Representatives from these sectors were not anxious to lose the clout their counterparts in the then-booming automobile industry could wield. Stronger counterpressures to the auto workers' initiative existed, therefore, not only within the ranks of central union officials, but among shop-floor representatives in other industries. The opponents handily defeated the proposal.

Thus, as far as the central union leadership was concerned, Mitbestimmung am Arbeitsplatz could not mean new legal rights for work groups or group leaders below the level of the works council. Moreover, top union officials insisted on defining Mitbestimmung am Arbeitsplatz in terms of the already existing division of labor between shop stewards (who would transmit workers' demands to the works council) and works councillors (who would negotiate with managers over these demands). Strothmann added, "And that, dear colleagues, is how it should stay" (IG Metall, *Vertrauensleute, 1969*:38).

Somewhat less finesse was used in dealing with the leading proponents of Mitbestimmung am Arbeitsplatz, who soon found themselves somewhat marginalized within the union. Matthöfer, for example, was relieved of his responsibilities as head of the education department and assigned to an obscure department (without a staff) handling "international" issues. He became in effect "a department head without a department" (interview, June 1989). He left the union soon afterward.

Moreover, while the union continually underscored the importance of shop stewards in the Mitbestimmung am Arbeitsplatz debate, in fact its leaders moved to limit their authority in the plant and to subordinate them to the works councils.[21] The role and function of union stewards was a constant topic of debate in the late 1960s and early 1970s. After all, proponents of betriebsnahe Tarifpolitik sought to enhance the influence of shop stewards in annual wage negotiations, and the advocates of Mitbestimmung am Arbeitsplatz hoped to increase their influence through the position of group leaders. These and related issues of greater protections for shop stewards were debated at the 1968 and 1971 union conventions.

However, apart from a new agreement with employers in 1969 protecting shop stewards from dismissal for political actions,[22] subsequent union policy toward shop stewards worked in the other direction: to limit the scope of their influence and to subordinate their position to that of the works council. For example, new guidelines (*Richtlinien*) for shop stewards, drawn up in 1973, bind stewards more closely to the union locals and to the plant works councils (Schmidt 1974:138–39). And new principles (*Leitsätze*) to guide their work made them responsible to support and cooperate with the works council (Schmidt 1974:139–40).

These changes, prompted by the increasing vocalness of the shop stewards within the union, seemed to reverse the logic behind the union's original shop steward campaigns in the 1950s and 1960s. Now the union was trying to dampen the political influence of the shop

21. See especially Schmidt, 1974:130–45, on which this paragraph and the next draw.
22. And at the 1969 convention for shop stewards and the 1971 union congress even this measure was widely criticized as insufficient.

stewards in the plant. The union was encouraging works councils to act as a check on the stewards, rather than the other way around.

Redefining Mitbestimmung am Arbeitsplatz and downplaying the role of the shop steward committees it had so painstakingly built up a decade earlier were only part of the IG Metall's answer to the demands for more power from the shop floor. The other part of the union's response was to rechannel the demands of those who sought more power within the union into legislative efforts to enhance the rights of works councils in the plant. The Social Democratic party helped the union achieve this goal in the revised Works Constitution Act of 1972 (Betriebsverfassungsgesetz).

The 1972 Betriebsverfassungsgesetz

The political situation in the early 1970s was propitious for labor to reopen the codetermination question. The Grand Coalition of the CDU/CSU and SPD ended with the election of 1969, which gave the Social Democratic party enough votes to form a governing coalition with the small Free Democratic party. The electoral victory of the Social Democrats in 1969 ushered in an era of "reform euphoria" for the unions (see especially Markovits 1986:117). The revised Works Constitution Act of 1972 was a part of their agenda, and one of the fruits of the unions' newfound political clout.

Two features of the new law governing works councils are of special importance for their impact on the structure and subsequent operation of the dual system. First, the law expanded significantly works council rights at the plant level. Second, it explicitly acknowledged and strengthened the link between works councils and the unions (Streeck 1983:14; Markovits 1986:49).[23]

The Works Constitution Act of 1972 strengthened the rights of works councils in a number of areas.[24] In addition to enhancing their general rights to information from management, the new law gave works councils extensive powers in the area of personnel policy. For example, it granted them full codetermination rights on issues such as working time arrangements in the plant, short-time work, overtime, work breaks, the establishment of vacation times, plant wage systems,

23. Although a significant breakthrough for the union in both respects, the law was nonetheless a political compromise. The SPD's junior coalition partner, the F.D.P., was able to secure some concessions in negotiations with the SPD that weakened the law (Farthman 1972; Muhr 1972). Among other things, they vetoed a proposal authored by SPD labor minister Walter Arendt allowing for the possibility that the codetermination rights of works councils be extended through collective bargaining between the unions and employers' organizations (Farthman 1972:5; interview with Hans Matthöfer, June 1989; interview with Eugen Loderer, June 1989).

24. For a full text of the law with commentary, see Kittner 1984:426–502.

and the setting of piece rates (paragraph 87). According to the new law, managers must inform and consult the works councils on planned changes in jobs or production systems, on the introduction of new technologies, and on other alterations in the work environment (paragraph 90). They must secure (in advance) the consent of the works council on a range of personnel decisions affecting individual workers, including job assignments, classifications and reclassifications, and transfers (paragraph 99) (see also Farthmann 1972; Rose 1973).

The new law put more force behind the codetermination rights of works councils by providing for conciliation and arbitration procedures in the event that management and labor fail to reach an agreement (Muhr 1972:3). This provision gives works councils, which are forbidden from initiating strikes, additional leverage in negotiations with management. Conciliation board decisions can go either way, of course, so both parties have a certain interest in avoiding them. However, employers pay for the proceedings, which gives them an additional incentive to agree to concessions, even if only to avoid lengthy and frequent use of such procedures.

Another clause in the new law expanded the role works councils can play in the event of "major changes" in the plant, including major layoffs. According to paragraphs 111 and 112, employers must inform works councils "comprehensively and in a timely fashion" of any plans that may involve the closing of the plant or parts of it, or any other changes that could involve major layoffs. In such cases, employers must bargain with the works council over measures to protect workers' interests (*Interessenausgleich*) or, in the event of layoffs, over compensation for the affected workers (*Sozialplan*) (paragraphs 111–12).

The significance of this provision may not have been fully apparent in 1972, but it has come to play a central role in Germany's negotiated adjustment (interviews with Eugen Loderer and Hans Matthöfer, June 1989). Although works councils in the steel industry had previously negotiated such "social plans" on a more informal basis (and because of their political strength and institutional powers through parity codetermination), the 1972 law codified and mandated the practice for the first time. More importantly, the new legislation extended the social plan requirement to other industries where works councils lacked the political clout typical of steel.

The 1972 law also alleviated some of the damage done by the 1952 Works Constitution Act by codifying stronger and more explicit links between the unions and the works councils (see especially Gester 1972). Throughout negotiations over the revision of the law, the DGB demanded a strengthening of union rights in the plant and the explicit acknowledgment of the unions' support role vis-à-vis the works councils (Gester 1972:20). The most important such provisions in the new law include those which made it easier for union representatives to gain access to plants, enhanced the rights of the union in works council elections, made it possible for the union to require the works council to call a plant assembly, and required the works councils to inform the union of the times and agendas of plant assemblies they call on their own (Gester 1972:21). Most importantly, perhaps, the 1972 Works Constitution Act promoted stronger ties between works councils and unions by protecting the rights of works councillors to perform functions and activities in the plant on behalf of the union, as well as by allowing them to participate in union seminars at the company's expense and on paid leave (Streeck 1983:14).

The new law thus reinforced links between the unions and the works councils in numerous ways, even if the formal obligation of works councils to remain neutral (paragraph 75) remained on the books (Gester 1972:22).

THE CREATION AND "MATURING" OF THE DUAL SYSTEM: A SUMMARY

When the dual system was created under conservative auspices in 1952, the IG Metall protested vehemently against what it saw as the government's attempt to drive a wedge between the union and the shop floor and looked forward to changing the system. But in the fourteen years it waited for the Social Democrats to get to Bonn, the union learned to live with dualism. Its leaders answered a challenge from below in the late 1960s with a vigorous defense of central authority in collective bargaining and of works council authority in the plant. The central union was able to seize the initiative and maintain its authority in collective bargaining through a timely retreat from the Concerted Action orientation data and a series of highly successful wage rounds. At the same time, the union channeled demands for a decentralization of power within the union into the struggle to extend the rights of works councils vis-à-vis management.

Central unions in many West European countries faced a similar challenge from the rank and file in the late 1960s (see especially Crouch and Pizzorno 1978). As in Germany, shop-floor militancy was in many cases precipitated by central union cooperation in state incomes policies. Yet once the dust had settled, it became clear that the organizational consequences of the unrest in this period varied widely across countries. Italy's "Hot Autumn" of 1969 had a significant and lasting impact on the structure of power within the unions, while in Germany these events did not provoke the same kind of decentralization (Zoll 1981). In some respects, however, events within the IG Metall parallel those in Sweden, where as Andrew Martin (1977) points out, the LO's codetermination initiatives of the 1970s emerged in part in response to the unions' internal organizational problems.

These episodes in the evolution of the dual system illustrate the dynamic interaction of political strategies and institutional constraints within a changing political and economic context. Changes in the political and economic context set in motion new conflicts within the dual system, but they also provided new openings for the union to cope with them. The dual system of industrial relations in some ways may have exacerbated tensions within the union; however, it also provided a framework within which the IG Metall could address the demands of its more militant plant representatives in a way that enhanced labor's plant-level powers without directly undercutting its own central authority. The union transformed the tension of an absolute struggle over central versus decentralized authority into separate battles over various substantive worker interests and found ways to resolve these at different levels.

The combination of labor's relative market weakness and the promise of greater political strength when the Social Democrats first entered the government in 1966 contributed to the rise in tensions within the union. After all, the IG Metall's cooperation in restraining wages to help Germany out of the recession was one factor that precipitated the 1969 outburst. However, economic recovery and the Social Democratic victory in 1969 showed the union a way out of this bind. Economic recovery provided an auspicious context for the IG Metall to reassert itself in wage bargaining. And, the "reform euphoria" that the Social Democratic victory in 1969 ushered in gave the union a golden opportunity to channel calls for greater shop-floor power into the debate over new legislation to extend the rights of works councils. The revised Works Constitution Act strengthened works councils even as it subordinated them and bound them more closely to the union.

The union's defense of centralized collective bargaining in this period was important, and some theorists have stressed that the dual system has helped stabilize centralized bargaining (Streeck 1979). The legal restrictions on works councils from calling strikes and their legal obligation to uphold centrally negotiated contracts in the plant helped stabilize centralized bargaining in the tense 1966–69 period.

However, the battles of the late 1960s and early 1970s are significant not just in how the outcomes circumscribed plant powers. The other, equally important, result of the political struggles of this period was the revised Works Constitution Act, which redefined and expanded the role of the works councils. The maturing of the dual system in this period consisted of more than just the defense of central union authority. An equally important outcome of the struggles of this period was the extension of the rights of works councils, though the significance of the plant-level rights labor won was obscured at the time by economic prosperity.

The importance of these rights was revealed in the course of the 1970s. Economic growth and "reform euphoria" gave way to economic crisis and political stalemate. Germany's negotiated adjustment came increasingly to rely on the plant-level rights labor had won in 1972 as relations at a national level between labor and the government and between the union and employers deteriorated in the 1970s. Moreover, the rights of works councils have become even more important to central union strategies as labor confronts the problem of unemployment and the increasingly urgent challenge of technological change since the mid-1970s.

Part III

WEST GERMAN LABOR IN THE CRISIS

CHAPTER FIVE

Markets and Politics in Transition, 1973–1978

The maturing of the dual system can be summarized in terms of three developments: (1) the consolidation of central union authority in collective bargaining, but (2) the development of a strong (de facto) link between the central union and the works councils, and (3) the strengthening of labor's plant rights under the revised Works Constitution Act.

When the government passed the revised Works Constitution Act in 1972, the German economy was booming. The importance of works councils' rights on issues such as working time, hiring, layoffs, transfers, and the introduction of new technologies was not fully apparent. After all, hirings and not layoffs were the order of the day in 1972, and technology was still a welcome contributor to productivity gains from which workers also benefited in the form of rising real wages.

This chapter is about the end of easy growth in West Germany. It traces the tensions that emerged between labor and the Social Democratic government and between labor and employers as growth slowed and as full employment ceased to be something the unions could take for granted. It is in this context that the dual system came to be a crucial component of Germany's negotiated adjustment and an asset for German labor in two ways. First, decentralized bargaining between employers and plant labor representatives allowed for continued stability in labor relations despite a gradual but unmistakable deterioration of the national-level cooperation between the IG Metall and employers, and between the unions and the Social Democratic government after 1974. Second, works councils' rights at the plant level gave the IG Metall a crucial lever in the defense of worker interests as non-wage issues such as employment and technological change came to dominate labor politics in a period of structural adjustment.

The dual system shored up central bargaining by accommodating the demands of employers for the flexibility they needed to compete in increasingly volatile international markets. In addition, the dual system gave the union a stable second avenue for participating in adjustment at the subnational level.

Upheaval in the International Economy

The economic turmoil that followed the 1973 oil crisis is well known and need not be described here at length. Throughout the advanced industrial world, governments confronted slow growth, rising inflation, and growing unemployment. Competition in international markets became intense as countries clamored to cover their rising energy bills.

The immediate impact of the oil crisis, however, turned out to be only a part of the problem. What became clear in the years following 1973 was that the economic turbulence the advanced countries were experiencing was only partly cyclical in nature. The international economy underwent profound structural shifts in the 1970s and 1980s. The maturing of Japanese manufacturing increased competition both at home and abroad for companies in many sectors. Likewise, industrialization in countries like Taiwan, South Korea, and Brazil has made these NICs serious competitors in a range of traditional industries (e.g., shipbuilding, steel, and textiles) long dominated by the advanced countries. Traditionally stable mass markets (in the automobile industry, for example) became less stable and more "fragmented" (Piore and Sabel 1984).

Technological change, while always a potential problem for labor, rose to the top of union agendas as the cost of programmable automation dropped to levels that made it possible for employers in a range of industries to begin introducing it on a broader scale. The variety of industries in which microelectronics could be applied contributed to the breadth and scope of its economic impact, and thus its political impact as well. By the late 1970s, observers began to talk about the "revolution in production" (Cohen and Zysman 1987), the "crisis of mass production" (Piore and Sabel 1984) and the "end of the division of labor" (Kern and Schumann 1984). Technology became an especially urgent concern for unions in countries where rapid technological change was taking place in the context of high unemployment.

In West Germany, the aftermath of the oil crisis gradually undermined the collaborative relations among business, labor, and the Social Democratic government that had characterized the late 1960s and early 1970s. Katzenstein (1987) has argued that the character of politics and institutions in Germany encourages incremental change and is biased against abrupt policy shifts. The events of the mid-1970s corroborate this. Characteristically for Germany, national-level corporatism did not break down dramatically. Rather, it began to deteriorate over the period from 1975 to 1978.

The end of "easy growth" in Germany made the politics of accommodation more difficult and national-level relations between the IG Metall, employers, and the government more strained. In the late 1970s, the IG Metall found itself caught in a squeeze: the union's market strength waned with rising unemployment at the same time that it watched the prospects for a political solution to labor's problems (especially unemployment) grow increasingly dim. Markovits and Allen's important analysis of the politics of the late 1970s documents the growing tensions in German labor relations and traces the IG Metall's strategic shift toward a policy of "self-reliance" through collective bargaining and industrial action (Markovits and Allen 1984: especially 166–73).

These developments seemed to signal the end of collaborative labor relations in Germany; however, what the national-level focus of most analyses of this period obscures is how works councils picked up the slack in Germany's negotiated adjustment. As relations between labor and capital grew more acrimonious at the national level, plant bargaining by works councils channeled conflicts as they presented themselves at the plant and company levels. Moreover, the works councils gradually moved toward center stage in the union's relations with employers over precisely those issues—employment and technology—that had begun to dominate labor politics in this period of structural economic change. In a sense, the "balance" within the dual system began to shift in the 1970s as works councils began to bear a greater share of the burden in Germany's negotiated adjustment.

The Response of the German Government to the Crisis

Overall, Germany has adjusted relatively well to the economic changes of the 1970s and 1980s. But it has done better on certain dimensions than others. For example, German inflation was lower than that of any other OECD country in the 1970s (see Table 7 in Chapter 2). However, beginning in 1975, unemployment in Germany began to rise steadily, and by the 1980s reached levels unprecedented in the postwar period.

The imbalance in the German economy's performance on these dimensions is what contributed most to the growing tensions between the Social Democratic government and organized labor, especially the IG Metall. In the "classic" corporatist democracies such as Austria and Sweden, government policy assigned high priority to maintaining near-full employment. In Germany, in contrast, the government sought first and foremost to maintain a stable currency and hold inflation in check, even if it meant higher unemployment.[1] Politics within the social-liberal coalition and institutional features of the German political economy explain why policy priorities in Germany differed from those in the corporatist countries in ways that led to a "cooling" of relations between organized labor and the German state.

Keynesianism was an early casualty in the government's response to the economic events of the mid-1970s. As Werner Sengenberger (1984) points out, neoliberal economics began gaining momentum in Germany as early as 1974–75. The Social Democratic government answered the crisis not with stimulative measures, but instead with fiscal austerity, the centerpiece of which was the 1975 Budget Structure Law (Haushalts-strukturgesetz). This measure called for cutbacks in a number of areas, but it came as a particular blow to labor, since it rolled back significantly many of the gains that labor had won in the reforms of the late 1960s.[2]

A critical *political* actor in the government cutbacks in this period was the Social Democrats' junior coalition partner, the Free Democratic Party. The SPD and the F.D.P. had come together in 1969, a period of relative economic stability, if not prosperity. At that time, foreign policy questions dominated the political agenda in Germany, and the F.D.P.'s support for Brandt's *Ostpolitik* helped forge the SPD–F.D.P. coalition in the first place. But the Free Democrats have always had strong ties to the German business community, and when economic issues pushed their way back on the agenda in the mid-1970s, longstanding policy differences between them and the SPD resurfaced (Markovits 1986:130). While the F.D.P. had been willing to go along with the Social Democrats on the social and economic reforms of the late 1960s and early 1970s, the party's "accommodating posture began to evaporate in the mid-seventies, as growth declined and unemployment rose to levels unprecedented since the fifties. Neocapitalist forces grew stronger in the F.D.P." (Sengenberger 1984:326).

The Free Democrats' turn toward what Sengenberger calls "market liberalism" was prompted in part by a shift within the F.D.P. itself. From the late 1960s until the crisis, the party's "social-liberal" wing had held sway within the party, and its liberal positions on civil rights and many social issues meshed with those of the Social Democratic Party under Brandt (Katzenstein 1987:39). But the economic downturn of the mid-1970s strengthened the F.D.P.'s "market-liberal" wing, which opposed strong government intervention in the economy and favored market-led solutions to adjustment.

Thus, the F.D.P. increasingly advocated fiscal restraint and austerity as the appropriate response to the crisis. Its spokesmen argued that:

1. The most complete account of economic policy in this period can be found in Riemer 1983.
2. Active labor market policies had been greatly expanded in the 1969 Work Promotion Law (*Arbeitsförderungsgesetz*), and the 1975 Budget Structure Law's cutbacks in this area were especially severe.

Germany had gone too far in the direction of developing a "social net." Wages and the level of social benefits and social services had become too high.... Excessive social spending would burden the state budgets, hamper the profitable use of resources, strain capital markets, and take too much revenue away from private investments. In short, the neocapitalists [in the F.D.P.] argued that the received level of wages, benefits, and services was not merely no longer affordable, but was becoming counterproductive. [Sengenberger 1984:326]

The F.D.P.'s political power on economic issues was enhanced in part by the party's pivotal position in German politics as the "coalition maker or breaker."[3] In addition, a reshuffling of the cabinet in 1974 had given the F.D.P. control of the Economics ministry (Allen and Riemer 1985:8).

The outcome of political infighting within the Social Democratic party pointed as well toward fiscal restraint. While the party's left-wing faction sided with the unions in advocating stimulative measures, Chancellor Helmut Schmidt himself leaned toward the Free Democrats' market-oriented prescription. Schmidt was then able to justify the government's deflationary strategy in terms of the "exigencies of the coalition" (*Koalitionszwang*) (Markovits 1986:131–32; Allen and Riemer 1985:8).

Another factor that pushed Germany toward the deflationary policy that aggravated relations between the unions and the government was institutional. The German Central Bank (Bundesbank) is more autonomous than any of its European counterparts (Katzenstein 1987:60–61). Fritz Scharpf (1984) lays much of the blame for Germany's poorer employment record (when compared to those of Sweden and Austria) at the door of the Bundesbank. While Austrian monetary policy between 1973 and 1977 accommodated fiscal expansion, "the steep rise in German unemployment in 1975 can be attributed to the continuation of a sharply deflationary monetary policy even after the onset of the world wide recession" (Scharpf 1984:281).

According to Scharpf, the Bundesbank's restrictive monetary policy in this period was related both to its "subjective view of the world" and to its institutional autonomy within the German government, which insulated it sufficiently from political pressures to allow it to act on this view. The Bundesbank has traditionally considered inflation to be the German economy's number one enemy, and seen wage-push inflation as the major threat to price stability.[4] In the wake of the oil crisis, the Bundesbank abandoned the Keynesian countercyclical course it had

---

3. Since the "Grand Coalition" of 1966–69, neither the CDU/CSU nor the SPD has been able to form a government without the F.D.P.

4. The irony for Scharpf is that "macroeconomic policy in West Germany was less exposed to the pressures of wage-push inflation in the mid-1970s than in any other Western European country. Objectively, at least, the Bundesbank would seem to have been entirely free to pursue a less restrictive monetary policy without having to fear accelerating rates of inflation" (1984:281).

pursued in the early 1970s in favor of an explicitly monetarist strategy. Scharpf dates this shift to the summer of 1974 (1984:284), and argues that with it "the tenuous co-ordination between monetary policy and incomes policy disintegrated under circumstances which can be explained by a lack of communication and mutual trust between the central bank and the unions" (1984:286).

These two developments–the Social-Liberal coalition's move toward fiscal austerity and the Bundesbank's turn toward a restrictive monetary policy—distinguish the German case rather sharply from the classic corporatist countries and explain the growing tensions between the unions and the government in this period. Rising unemployment hurt labor's market power, and the government's policies, which emphasized monetary and price stability over employment, exacerbated rather than alleviated the unions' problems.

In this sense, corporatism as it had emerged in the late 1960s and early 1970s in Germany had indeed proved to be a fair-weather system. Some cross-national studies of corporatism stress that even after the government cutbacks on social and active labor market policies in 1975, Germany was still spending more than other countries in both areas (Wilensky and Turner 1987). While this is true, it must be remembered that German unions were not making such cross-national comparisons, but were instead evaluating their situation against the previous period in Germany. Thus, the unions experienced the mid-1970s as a period of cutbacks and of Social Democratic betrayal. Understanding the unions' perception of these developments is crucial to understanding how relations between labor and the government and between labor and business deteriorated in the late 1970s and into the 1980s.

UNION POLITICS AFTER 1975

The IG Metall was caught off guard by these market and political changes. When unemployment rose sharply in 1975, the unions believed that the problem was largely cyclical. This perception helps explain why the IG Metall's wage demands remained moderate from 1975 to 1977, despite the fact that the political trade-offs for restraint (demand-stimulative fiscal policy and active labor market policies) were no longer forthcoming (Markovits and Allen 1984:152). Table 14 documents the IG Metall's continued commitment to wage restraint even after the government launched its 1975 austerity program.

However, by 1977, and with unemployment still on the rise, the union grew more vocal in its criticism of the government. The IG Metall advocated strong countercyclical spending, but by now it also recognized that unemployment had a strong structural component. Thus, the IG Metall demanded that the government intervene to

Table 14. Wage settlements in the metalworking and steel industries, 1974–78

Year	Wage settlement (%)	
	Metalworking	Steel
1974	11.6	9.0
1975	6.8	5.0
1976	5.4	6.0
1977	6.9	4.0
1978	5.0	4.0

Source: IG Metall (1987) *Daten, Fakten,
Informationen*: 15, 17.

alleviate unemployment in the hardest-hit regions (like the Ruhr) and among those groups of workers who had proved most vulnerable in the crisis. At the union's national congress in 1977, IG Metall president Eugen Loderer criticized the government's emphasis on inflation and its lack of clear action on the employment front: "We have nothing against price stability, nor even against profits; we just want an employment policy that is independent of these goals. The macroeconomic policies of the 1960s are no longer sufficient today. We need an economic policy that is structurally oriented and linked to the goal of full employment" (*Der Gewerkschafter*, October 1977:6). The union called for targeted employment-promotion measures, especially for particular sectors, such as steel and shipbuilding, and regions (IG Metall 1977a). Hans Mayr, who was in charge of the union's collective bargaining division in 1977, demanded "an economic policy that gives first priority to full employment...[and] coordinated regional and sectoral policies that give priority to the creation of stable jobs" (IG Metall 1977b:127).

The union's criticism of government policy in this period may have seemed an overreaction to some. After all, unemployment in Germany was still only 3.7 percent in 1978, higher than in other Social Democratic countries such as Sweden, but still much lower than neighboring countries such as France, Britain, and Italy. And yet, on closer examination, the cause for the union's alarm was very real and pressing.

In an important analysis of labor market developments in the 1970s, Fritz Scharpf (1980) argued that Germany's employment record in the 1973–77 period was in fact much worse than the unemployment figures suggested. He shows how the country's record on job creation and employment maintenance lagged far behind the eight other OECD countries he studied (see Table 15).

Between 1973 and 1977, unemployment grew in virtually all the advanced industrial countries. However, in most of these countries the overall participation rate in the labor market (total employment) remained stable or very nearly so (France, the United Kingdom, Denmark, the Netherlands, Belgium, and Japan). In some countries, the level of

Table 15. Index of civilian employment 1967–77 in various OECD countries (1973 = 100)

Year	W. Germany	France	U.K.	U.S.	Italy	Denmark	Netherlands	Belgium	Japan
1967	97.2	94.3	99.8	88.1	101.9	94.9	96.1	94.3	93.6
1968	97.3	94.3	99.3	89.9	101.6	95.3	97.1	94.3	95.1
1969	98.7	96.0	99.4	92.3	100.6	95.7	98.9	96.1	95.8
1970	99.9	97.4	99.0	93.2	101.1	97.1	100.2	97.9	96.0
1971	100.1	98.0	97.7	93.7	100.8	98.0	100.8	98.9	97.4
1972	99.7	98.7	97.6	96.8	99.1	98.8	99.8	98.7	97.5
1973	100.0	100.0	100.0	100.0	100.0	100.0	100.0	100.0	100.0
1974	98.0	100.8	100.4	101.8	102.2	98.7	100.0	101.5	99.6
1975	94.6	98.9	99.9	100.4	102.8	97.8	99.5	100.1	99.3
1976	93.7	99.4	99.3	103.6	103.4	100.3	99.3	99.3	100.2
1977	93.5	100.1	99.8	107.3	108.4	101.2	99.5	99.1	101.6

Source: Fritz Scharpf, "Beschäftigungsorientierte Strukturpolitik," IIM-LMP *Discussion Paper* 80–42 (Berlin International Institute of Management, Wissenschaftszentrum Berlin, 1980), 21. Used by permission of the author.

employment even grew significantly (the United States and Italy). In Germany, in contrast, the overall rate of employment dropped by 6.5 percent between 1973 and 1977. Had some groups (women and foreigners especially) not dropped out of the labor market, and hence also out of the unemployment statistics, Germany's unemployment rates would have been much higher. And, Scharpf's prediction in 1980 that "prognoses that predict a doubling of unemployment by the mid-1980s are not at all unrealistic, so long as Germany's employment policies do not change dramatically" (1980:2) in fact came true.[5]

Like the unions, Scharpf argued that government policy in the mid-1970s had if anything aggravated rather than alleviated the employment problem. In effect, Scharpf documented in 1980 what the unions had suspected since 1977, namely that the investment policies the government was promoting had had negative employment effects:

> While the proportion of expansionary investments dropped from 55 to 18 percent between 1970 and 1976, the proportion of replacement investments rose in the same period from 12 to 25 percent, and rationalization investments rose from 33 to 57 percent. Thus, to the extent that state investment promotion was effective at all, it was overwhelmingly for investment that did not create additional jobs, but rather, on balance, reduced employment further. [Scharpf 1980:5]

Scharpf argued in 1980 in favor of a structural policy oriented toward "human capital formation" and (selective) demand stimulation. But he

---

5. A later study by Scharpf (1984) indicates that this trend toward lower labor market participation rates continued into the 1980s. In 1982, total employment in Germany was 4.8 percent lower than it had been in 1973. In Austria, by way of contrast, employment in 1981 was up by 4.4 percent over the 1973 level; and in Sweden in 1982 it was up by 8.8 percent over the 1973 level (Scharpf 1984:265). Nor would updating these figures change the picture significantly. Civilian employment in Germany dropped in 1982 by 1.7

notes that in the industrial policy debates in the late 1970s, demand-side policies had become largely "taboo" in Germany (Scharpf 1980:14).

Thus the union's criticisms of the Social Democratic government's economic policies and employment record were largely legitimate, even if the Social Democrats continued to point to Germany's still moderate unemployment rate. But through the late 1970s, the union's demands for stimulative intervention and measures to ease structural unemployment still largely fell on the ears of policymakers who cherished monetary stability over all else.[6]

Significantly, one of the ways the SPD chose to attempt to appease the unions on the eve of the 1976 elections was to reopen the debate on company-level codetermination.[7] The fact that the SPD was willing to take up the unions' cause on this issue may seem somewhat inconsistent. As noted above, on matters of government spending, the SPD often invoked Koalitionszwang (pressure from the F.D.P.) in order to justify their policies to the unions. But nothing was more sure to lead them into a direct conflict with their coalition partner than to initiate a renegotiation of union rights under company codetermination.

One possible explanation lies with the politics and predilections of the chancellor himself. As Markovits has noted, Schmidt was only a lukewarm Keynesian. He actually sided with the Free Democrats on fiscal matters, but he also enjoyed very close relations with the unions (at least early in his tenure) and saw codetermination as a way of rewarding them for their restraint in wage bargaining in 1975 (Markovits 1986:131, 132).

A less idiosyncratic explanation is that renegotiating the legal framework of industrial relations was both preferable from a political standpoint and easier from an institutional one than pursuing more directly prolabor policies through the state. Viewed in this light, the episode is entirely consistent with the general pattern of state intervention in Germany, in which the government relies more heavily on Rahmenbedingungen rather than direct intervention in the market (see Chapter 2). The idea of renegotiating codetermination at this time seemed to be to arm the unions with stronger rights to do battle with employers *for themselves*, but in a market still more or less unfettered by strong state guidance.

---

percent from the previous year, and again by 1.5 percent in 1983, before it rose again slightly (by 0.1 percent) in 1984 (OECD 1986b:27).

6. In 1977 and 1978, Schmidt did "reluctantly" respond to pressures for increased spending with two long-term investment programs totalling DM 29.3 billion (Allen 1989d:279; see also *Soziale Sicherheit* 3, 1981). However, many unions, and especially the IG Metall, viewed these measures as "too little, too late" (Markovits 1986:135, 137).

7. Recall that the existing law allowed labor one-third of the seats on supervisory boards of companies outside the coal and steel industries employing over five hundred workers. In the coal and steel industries the stronger Montanmitbestimmung legislation (parity codetermination) applies.

In the debates over the new codetermination legislation, the unions favored the extension of the Montan (parity codetermination) model to German industry as a whole. Employers vehemently opposed entertaining any revision of company-level codetermination. This fundamental conflict was reproduced within the coalition, where the debates were often quite intense. The Free Democrats (who after all had cast many of the opposing votes in the 1951 Montanmitbestimmung legislation) allied with the business community on the issue, while the Social Democrats favored an extension of labor's company-level representation (Streeck 1983: especially 13–19).

In the end, the 1976 codetermination legislation that emerged from the struggle was a compromise that pleased almost no one. The new law enhanced labor representation on the supervisory boards of companies (outside the coal and steel industries) employing over two thousand workers. However, the unions did not get the parity representation they had sought. Under the new legislation, labor representation on supervisory boards was increased to half the total seats, but with the stipulation that one of the labor representatives be from middle management (and thus inclined to vote with the shareholders). The law also ensured that the supervisory board chairman (who casts the deciding vote in the event of ties) would be a representative of capital. Finally, and again unlike the Montanmitbestimmung model, the 1976 Codetermination Law stipulated that the labor director on company executive boards could be elected against the votes of labor representatives on the supervisory board.[8]

The unions were profoundly disappointed with their minority position in company decision making under the new law. Employers, who felt that the law went too far, also condemned the outcome and in fact challenged its constitutionality. The courts ultimately ruled that the law did not constitute a violation of property rights as the employers had charged. However, the employers' legal challenge was sufficient to prompt the unions—led by the IG Metall—to withdraw from the national-level Concerted Action discussions in 1977.

The unions' withdrawal from Konzertierte Aktion was mostly symbolic, since its meetings had become very infrequent and never resulted in concrete and binding agreements. As Flanagan, Soskice, and Ulman point out, these meetings were "largely ceremonial and informal—too short, sometimes lasting less than a full day, too infrequent, held only two or three times a year, too unwieldy, sometimes attended by more than a hundred people, and too understaffed, having no permanent secretariat—to function as policy-making sessions" (1983:285). Nonetheless, the end of Konzertierte Aktion did mark the end of the IG Metall's "wait and see" attitude, and the coming years would be charac-

8. A complete text of the law appears in Kittner 1984:749–79.

terized by more acrimonious relations between the union and employers at the national level.

In sum, the IG Metall faced a significantly different political and economic landscape by the late 1970s. Slow growth had ended the positive-sum game of the late 1960s and early 1970s. Unemployment was rising, with no political solution on the horizon. Indeed, the government's emphasis on monetary stability and fiscal austerity if anything exacerbated the union's problems. Labor's share of GDP was dropping; by 1979, it had reached its lowest level since the late 1960s (Markovits 1986:127). The codetermination battle had not produced the results the unions sought. In this context, relations between the union and the government, and between the union and employers, were at a new low. The national-level trade-offs that had existed before 1975 seemed to the union to be growing increasingly one-sided.

MOBILIZATION AND THE RETURN TO "SELF-RELIANCE," 1978

Markovits and Allen characterize the union's response to these developments in terms of a "return to self-reliance" on the part of Germany's activist unions, led by the IG Metall (Markovits and Allen 1984: especially 169–73). The union, which had not waged a major strike since 1973, fought *two* in 1978—first in the metalworking industry in Baden-Württemberg and later in the steel industry.

Understanding these two battles is enormously important for understanding labor politics in Germany since that time. The 1978 strikes are important because they mark a shift in the union's agenda from the dominance of wages to the growing importance of non-wage demands (Markovits and Allen 1979; Markovits and Allen 1984:166–69; and Thelen 1986). They foreshadow the conflicts over "qualitative" issues that have become central since the 1980s.[9] Unemployment and the negative effects on workers of production rationalization lay at the heart of the two strikes in 1978.

The key demand in the union's first strike in 1978 (in Baden-Württemberg) was the protection of workers' skills and incomes against downgrading in the course of production rationalization. In the 1970s, and in the context of rising unemployment, the union had grown

9. Although I think the distinction between "qualitative" (non-wage) and "quantitative" (wage) issues is a useful one, it cannot be pushed too far since "qualitative" demands almost always have a "quantitative" component (e.g., working-time reduction *with full pay*). In addition, it should be noted that the IG Metall's concern with non-wage issues is not entirely new. In 1973, for example, the union called a strike in Baden-Württemberg over "humanization of work" issues. But the changed economic context and the more defensive nature of these non-wage demands did give the 1978 conflicts a decidedly different character from this earlier confrontation.

increasingly concerned about the employment and income effects of computer-based technologies, which were being introduced into production at an accelerating pace.[10] In the 1978 conflict the union demanded income guarantees for individual workers in the event of transfer or job reclassification, and also a freeze on *plant* wage levels.

For the union, protection against the downgrading of workers' skills and incomes meant more than individual income guarantees. It also meant that the average wage of the plant as a whole should be maintained over time. Collective income security would mean that if the average wage for the plant fell, employers would be required to raise it again, either by hiring new (higher-paid and more highly skilled) workers, or by reclassifying (upward) the lowest-paid wage groups in the plant.[11]

The steel strike the union waged later in the same year revolved around the problem of unemployment.[12] As discussed above, the union had consistently demanded that the government intervene with policies designed to stimulate employment in those sectors which had been especially hard hit by the crisis. Impatient with the government's lackluster efforts on the employment front, the IG Metall decided to take the matter of structural unemployment into its own hands. The union demanded a reduction of the regular workweek to thirty-five hours for workers in the steel industry as a way of alleviating the high unemployment in Germany's steel-producing regions.

The outcomes of both conflicts were mixed. In Baden-Württemberg, the union secured eighteen-month income guarantees for individual workers in the event of transfer or job reclassification. But Gesamtmetall sharply rejected the idea of a collective income guarantee. The union's attempt to generalize the Baden-Württemberg agreement to other bargaining districts foundered on employer resistance.[13] In the steel industry, the union won an increase in paid annual vacation time to six weeks (which would later become the norm for the metalworking industries as well) and secured extra paid working days for night-shift and older workers, but it made no progress on reducing the regular workweek.

---

10. In 1977, for example, the union had hosted a conference on technology entitled: "Structural Unemployment through Technological Change?" (IG Metall 1977b). For a more detailed treatment of the union's changing views on technology, see Chapter 8.

11. For a text and explanation of the IG Metall's demands in this strike, see IG Metall 1978.

12. For a more complete account of the steel strike, see Thimm, 1980: chap. 3, or Markovits and Allen, 1979.

13. The outcome of this strike in this sense resembles that of another in 1973, when the union had won important concessions on "humanization of work" goals, but the outcome applied only to Baden-Württemberg.

THE MEANING OF 1978

More than in the classic corporatist democracies, the continued strength of German unions hinges on periodic mobilizations of their membership, and in this sense the 1978 strikes fit a general pattern in German labor relations.[14] What distinguished these conflicts from those in the past was the unusual intensity with which they were fought. Not only did the IG Metall wage two major strikes in a single year; the union underscored the links between its political and industrial struggles by having the steelworkers walk off their jobs on the same day that the Constitutional Court convened to consider the employers' challenge to the 1976 Codetermination Act (Thimm 1980:81). Employers' aggressive use of lockouts—affecting a larger number of workers than ever before—was an indication of great resolve on their part as well (Markovits and Allen 1979).

The intensity of the 1978 strikes was partly related to the fact that economic conditions had simply narrowed the room for compromise between labor and capital. However, it was also related to the changing content of the union's demands (Markovits and Allen 1984). What became clear in this period was not so much just that employers were in a stronger market position than before, but that they would systematically resist being hemmed in by central contracts on issues they saw as crucial to maintaining managerial control over qualitative aspects of the labor process and the organization of production (see also Silvia 1988). While employers and the union traditionally have been (and still are) able to reach peaceful compromises on wages, the IG Metall came up against stiffer resistance in central bargaining when it came to demands that would narrow the parameters within which managers would have to maneuver at the plant level.

The importance employers attached to such issues is reflected in a BDA document published in early 1979 during the steel strike. This "List of Wage and Collective Bargaining Issues to be Centrally Coordinated" itemizes a range of issues on which the employers' organization sought central coordination among its members in their negotiations with the unions. Because the document lists items on which the BDA opposed any further concessions to labor, the unions dubbed it the employers' "Tabu-Katalog" (Degen, Siebert, and Stöhr 1979).[15]

Among the issues that figure most prominently in the catalogue are those that would circumscribe managerial freedoms concerning the organization of work, production scheduling, and other qualitative

14. I am grateful to Wolfgang Streeck for this observation.
15. See also Markovits, 1986:146–47, on the Tabu-Katalog. The important excerpts from the document appear in *Die Zeit*, 2 February 1979:11.

aspects of the labor process (Markovits 1986:146–47). The "taboos" include collective bargains that have the effect of extending the codetermination rights of labor representatives at the plant or company levels, regulations on overtime that would limit working times below ten hours per day or fifty hours per week, and contracts containing (strikable) "opening clauses" (along the lines of betriebsnahe Tarifpolitik). The Katalog recommends strongly against income guarantee contracts other than those that redefine the lowest wage group in the plant. The most notorious "taboo" of them all was weekly working-time reduction (*Die Zeit*, 2 February 1979:11).

Although not the "secret document" the unions claimed it was, the Tabu-Katalog is illuminating because it clarifies the connection between employers' determined resistance in the 1978 strikes and the changing content of the union's demands as it confronted the challenges of technological change and unemployment. Subsequent events have of course demonstrated that taboos can be broken, but what is also true is that such breakthroughs have come at the price of new flexibility in central contracts themselves (see Chapter 7). Negotiations over such issues were to play an important role in the shifting balance between central and decentralized bargaining in the dual system. In 1978, however, all that seemed clear was that as the IG Metall's concerns shifted toward "qualitative" demands concerning technology and working time, it increasingly bumped up against issues that employers considered non-negotiable.

At the time, observers of the events of 1978 were struck by the dramatic increase in conflict between labor and capital at the national level and by the new "militancy" shown by the IG Metall. While some feared for the end of social harmony in West Germany (e.g., Thimm 1980:60), critics of "social partnership" applauded the union's strategic reorientation and newfound mettle. However one evaluates these developments, the conflicts of 1978 seemed to signal a decisive "change in the political discourse and social climate of the Federal Republic," an end to the "honeymoon" and with it the "much-admired *Burgfrieden* (social peace) between labour and capital" (Markovits and Allen 1980:83).

With the benefit of hindsight, we can now see that neither the hopes nor the fears of these observers were fulfilled. Collaborative, negotiated adjustment survived even the "hardening of positions" (Markovits 1986:146) that characterized collective bargaining in the late 1970s. The pattern that ultimately prevailed was characterized more by continuity than crisis in German labor relations.

On the national level, what stands out in this period is how the union's relations with employers in collective bargaining became more acrimonious and how the outcomes for the union became more ambiguous. However, a national-level focus obscures the subnational bargaining through codetermination that assumed greater importance in Germany's system of negotiated adjustment. As labor's political and market power at the national level began to wane, the (somewhat) less market-sensitive *legal* rights works councils possess through codetermination helped stabilize labor's position at the plant and company levels. In addition, works councils became increasingly important actors on precisely those "qualitative" issues that have come to dominate labor politics since the late 1970s.

Thus, despite the tensions at the national level, labor relations in Germany did not deteriorate into open industrial warfare. What filled the void as negotiated adjustment became more difficult at the national level was the stability of negotiated adjustment through codetermination. The resilience of the dual system in this sense shored up collaborative labor-capital relations in Germany. Even as employers and the union stepped up their war of words (and deeds) at the national level toward the end of the 1970s, labor representatives and managers were seeking— and largely finding—modes of accommodation and peaceful routes to adjustment at the plant level.

CHAPTER SIX

Works Council Politics in the Crisis

Collaborative labor relations in Germany by and large survived at the plant level despite the tensions between the union and employers at the national level. Employers have not used the opportunity of the union's declining market and political power to launch an attack on labor's position and prerogatives in the plant. German managers have come to terms with labor participation in plant decision making, despite the fact that labor's plant rights constrain management in important ways. The Works Constitution Act provides stable, institutionalized channels that routinize and channel labor conflict. The advantage for employers is predictability in plant labor relations, and this they value as they negotiate today's volatile international markets.

From the perspective of labor, the legal basis for plant negotiations puts works councils in a curious and paradoxical situation (see also Kotthoff 1981; Höland 1985). On the one hand, the Works Constitution Act gives them a lever for influencing managerial decision making to defend the interests of their constituents. On the other hand, being plant based gives works councils an equally strong incentive to cooperate with managers in the interests of the firm, which of course dovetails with their longer-term interest in the job security of the workers they have been elected to represent (Streeck 1984c).

This constellation of rights and interests has produced a pattern of plant politics that is characterized by a careful mix of conflict and cooperation between labor and capital at the plant level. Employers, unable to ignore or defeat labor head on, are forced to consider the social consequences of their economic decisions. Works councils, for their part, share management's concern for the long-term viability of

122

the firm and adapt their strategies to fit both the demands of their constituents and the exigencies of the market.[1]

Plant politics in the dual system is thus best characterized in terms of ongoing political jockeying for position in the context of a stable institutional framework that neither employers nor labor is seriously trying to dismantle. Except in the most extreme circumstances (e.g., plant closure), both managers and works councils are predisposed to compromise. Managers do so in part because the smooth operation of production depends on a modicum (at least) of works council cooperation and in part for fear that an assault on labor in the plant will bring on the plague of a new and more radical works council leadership in the next election. Works councils tread a fine line between defending the interests of workers and taking account of the market situation and economic interests of the firm. The outcome is a balance of conflict and cooperation that varies across plants.

There is a substantial body of opinion that questions the continued stability of the dual system in periods of economic crisis. These contemporary theories of the behavior of works councils in crisis are characterized by some curious inconsistencies. Two prominent but competing perspectives hold works councils responsible for the growing instability of the dual system under conditions of economic downturn and high unemployment. Both see works councils as the "weak link" in the German labor movement, yet their explanations of why this is so point in different—indeed contradictory—directions.

One view sees works councils as the "Achilles heel" of the German labor movement because they are simply too weak to defend the interests of workers at the plant level (Erd 1978; Bergmann, Jacobi, and Müller-Jentsch 1979; Bergmann and Müller-Jentsch 1983; and Hoffmann 1978). Economic prosperity had masked this weakness by providing room for concessions and accommodation between labor and capital (*Konzessionsspielraum*) in shop-floor negotiations. But according to this view works councils are *kampfunfähig* (literally: incapable of fighting) so when the Konzessionsspielraum evaporates, the underlying weakness of the works councils is exposed. Economic downturn generates a crisis both in cooperative unionism and in the dual system of interest representation itself (Erd 1978:23; Bergmann, Jacobi, and Müller-Jentsch 1979:395).

Analysts in this camp attribute works council weakness to the legal restrictions the Works Constitution Act imposes on plant labor representatives. They typically cite three specific paragraphs in the Works

---

1. Again, the similarity between this characterization and the logic of national corporatism as defined, for example, by Harold Wilensky, 1983:53, is obvious.

Constitution Act that they argue prevent works councils from effectively defending worker interests. These three limitations are (1) the inability of works councils to strike (paragraphs 2 and 74, Works Constitution Act); (2) the legal obligation of works councils to "work together in trustful cooperation with management in the interests of employees *and of the firm*" (paragraph 2, my emphasis); and (3) legal sanctions against works councils revealing company secrets to outsiders, including their own union representatives at a local, regional, or national level. According to these authors, legal limitations on works council behavior (and these paragraphs in particular) render plant labor representation ineffective because they are biased against the active (and, if necessary, militant) defense of worker interests.

The second perspective reaches similar conclusions, but from a strikingly different starting point. A number of analyses suggest that works councils may be the Achilles heel of the German labor movement not because they are weak, but because they are *strong*, but "plant-egoistic" (see Streeck 1984c: Windolf and Hohn 1984; and especially Hohn 1988). "Plant egoism" means that works councils use their plant powers in order to defend the particularistic interests of the existing plant work force. For example, they participate in plant "productivity coalitions," in which they actively collaborate with plant management to raise firm productivity in exchange for job and income security for the presently employed.

Far from stressing works councils' weaknesses, these authors suggest that the very success with which works councils are able to defend their own parochial interests translates into problems of fragmentation for the national union. Wolfgang Streeck's 1984 article was a point of departure for those emphasizing how an "emergent enterprise unionism" can threaten central union authority and labor solidarity by fragmenting labor interests along plant and company lines (1984c:306). Streeck's own treatment of the issue is more subtle, but Hohn (1988), perhaps the most ardent proponent of this perspective, even points to a trend away from "unitary unionism" toward "plant syndicalism" in Germany.

Relatively few empirical studies are available to assess the general validity of either perspective.[2] Moreover, existing analyses that attempt to classify different patterns of plant relations in Germany tend to conceptualize works council behavior across plants in terms of two opposing and dichotomous categories (either social partnership vs. class conflict or cooperative vs. conflictual).[3] The problem with such characterizations is that they conceptually rule out the *coexistence* of conflict

2. Many are case studies of a single plant or firm. Among the comparative studies that do exist are Höland 1985; Kotthoff 1981; Dybowski-Johannson 1980; Kern and Schumann 1984; and Windolf and Hohn 1984.

3. Many of the articles on works councils in the *Kritische Gewerkschaftsjahrbücher* in particular characterize works council behavior in terms of such distinctions.

and cooperation as a defining feature of plant politics in Germany.

Even more refined studies do not escape this essentially dichotomous construction. Kotthoff (1981), for example, develops a sixfold typology to characterize relations between works councils and plant managers.[4] But while Kotthoff's typology formally goes beyond dichotomous characterization, it does not entirely abandon it. In the end, Kotthoff lumps his six types into two broad categories that correspond more or less to the old conflict/cooperation models.[5] Having rejected dichotomous characterizations in favor of a more discriminating typology, in the end Kotthoff cannot avoid slipping back into the well-worn tracks of these earlier works.

The trouble with any dichotomous construction is that it fails to come to terms with the very ambiguity that is built into the dual system. Plant politics in Germany are characterized (simultaneously, not dichotomously) by both cooperation and conflict, by weakness and strength.

This chapter will attempt to shed light on this debate by examining both the question of works councils' weakness and work councils' tendencies toward "plant egoism." To preview my conclusions, the analysis suggests that both literatures fail to capture the complexity of plant relations in the dual system. The emphasis in the "works council weakness" literature on the inability of works councils to strike misses the more important sources of works council power. Because managers rely on works council approval on some of the most routine plant decisions, the power of the councils depends much less on their ability to disrupt production through conventional tactics than it does on their power over the smooth daily operation of production.

The "plant egoism" theory, I will argue, draws too sharp a line between labor's interests at the plant level and those of national unions. My own evidence supports the assertions of these authors that works council influence in personnel decisions has made internal plant labor markets less permeable to outsiders, and on this point works councils' interest in job security for their plant constituents clashes with the union's interest in increasing employment. However, on myriad other issues, the interests and behavior of works councils (and even their egoistic interests and behavior) complement and support central union policy.

So much can be said generally for the works council system. The fact that plant negotiations have picked up much of the slack in Germany's

4. His six types are the ignored works council, the isolated works council, the works council as organ of plant management, the respected and split works council, the respected and stand-pat works council, and the works council as cooperative counterforce within the plant.

5. His first three types, the ignored, the isolated, and the works council as organ of management, are "less effective" at representing labor interests than the other three types: the respected and split, the respected and stand-pat, and the cooperative counterforce works councils.

negotiated adjustment as relations between labor and capital grew more tense at the national level does not mean that works councils in all plants have dealt with adjustment pressures in the same way, or even equally well. Indeed, an examination of plant politics in Germany exposes substantial variation in how works councils interact with management: variation in what they seek to accomplish through plant bargaining, in how conflicts are played out, and in the outcomes for labor. The following sections of this Chapter develop and elaborate a typology of works council behavior in the crisis. They draw on information collected in the course of interviews in thirteen plants in three industries—steel, automobiles, and consumer electronics.[6]

All three of these industries faced mounting difficulties in the 1980s. All have suffered from increased competition in international markets from Third World and Japanese producers. In all three industries, employers have undertaken extensive rationalization measures to upgrade productivity and reduce costs, which have also affected the size and composition of the work force. The interviews reveal different patterns of bargaining over changes in personnel (including layoffs and transfers) and in production organization (including the introduction of new technologies and changes in workers' jobs and skills) in the three industries I selected for study.

A TYPOLOGY OF WORKS COUNCIL BEHAVIOR IN THE CRISIS

I distinguish three distinct plant types: *social partnership, politicized legalism,* and *depoliticized legalism.* The "type" of bargaining pattern that characterizes a given plant depends on two factors: the level of union presence in the plant (measured in terms of union organization) and the type of formal rights possessed by labor.[7] Plants characterized by

6. The size of this sample of course limits my ability to derive general conclusions. However, I opted for a restricted number of cases rather than a broad survey because I was interested in the character of works council–management interactions, in addition to the outcomes of plant conflicts that might be more easily quantified for comparative purposes. The cases are all plants employing over one thousand workers; a study of plant politics in smaller firms could produce significantly different results. In addition to these thirteen cases, my results also draw on shorter and more informal interviews I conducted with between fifty and seventy shop stewards and works councillors at union seminars and conferences and on case study material available in the literature on works councils.

7. Only in the coal and steel industries are works council rights at a plant level augmented by the stronger version of company-level codetermination (Montanmitbestimmung). The much weaker rights of labor at that level in all other industries (1976 Codetermination Law) do not affect plant negotiations to the same extent as in the Montan industries. Thus, the base rights enjoyed by works councils in all the plants derive from the Works Constitution Act. Those cases in which these plant rights are supplemented by the stronger *company-level* rights fall in the "stronger legal rights" category in this typology.

social partnership have a strong union presence and strong legal rights; those characterized by politicized legalism have a strong union presence, but weaker rights; in plants with depoliticized legalism works councils are weak on both the organizational and legal dimensions. These three variations are ideal typical, and any single plant will only approach a given type. As general patterns of plant bargaining, however, the three types correspond roughly to the three industries I studied: steel, automobile, and consumer electronics. I will use these three industries as references in my exposition of each plant type. The three types are summarized in Figure 1.

Figure 1. Typology of works council behavior

		Union presence (level of plant organization)	
		Strong	Weak
Legal rights of works council	Stronger	"social partnership" (example: steel industry)	NONE[a]
	Weaker	"politicized legalism" (example: auto industry)	"depoliticized legalism" (example: consumer electronics industry)

[a]There are no cases of "stronger" legal rights and weak union presence because only in the Montan industries are works councils' plant rights augmented by full parity codetermination at the company level (making them cases of "stronger" legal rights in my classification), and the Montan industries are all well organized.

What all these types of plant labor-management relations share is labor participation in plant decision making within the framework of a routine and channeled form of conflict resolution. In terms of outcomes, the types vary in (1) the channels through which conflicts are pursued, whether legal, political, or a combination of the two; and (2) the scope and effectiveness of labor participation in plant decision making, from broad and effective to narrow and less effective.

I elaborate and illustrate each of these types, but the results of my analysis support the following general propositions:

Channels of conflict. Where union presence is strong, conflicts regularly flow outside the strict legal institutions of the Works Constitution Act. This does not mean that they are uncontrolled; merely that they routinely contain an important noninstitutional element. Unions and management in social partnership, for example, have especially well developed practices for resolving their differences on an ongoing basis and rarely need to take their battles to court.[8] Negotiations in plants

8. The Works Constitution Act allows for conciliation or arbitration on certain issues, should labor and management fail to reach an agreement.

where union presence is high but works councils' legal rights are more limited (politicized legalism) are more likely to be politicized and hence contain an important nonlegal dimension, but breakdowns in negotiations are usually resolved through formal channels. In contrast, where union presence is weak (depoliticized legalism), conflicts—from start to finish—follow the rules of the game more narrowly defined, as laid out in the law, though works councils more often stop short of appealing unfavorable outcomes to a conciliation board.

Scope and effectiveness of labor participation in plant decision making. In general, a strong union presence is associated with a more aggressive use of works council rights across a broader range of issues. Stronger legal rights under Montanmitbestimmung and the greater political power associated with high unionization are sources of strength for labor in its dealings with employers. Where union presence is low as in depoliticized legalism, works councils are neither as likely to challenge management, nor are they as successful in doing so as in plants where union presence is higher.

The following sections elaborate each of these plant types, and the character of bargaining in each of these three industries. In each case, I will describe the institutional and political factors that produce three different patterns of labor-management interaction, then show how plant labor representatives in these industries have coped with the particular challenges of change and crisis in the workplace. The final two sections of this chapter connect my findings to the theoretical issues sketched out at the beginning.

Social Partnership in the Steel Industry

Those searching for instances of class conflict needn't study the German steel industry, for it is here that the concept of social partnership best describes relations between labor and capital. Works councillors in the German steel industry are a powerful and privileged group.[9] The defining feature of social partnership in the steel industry is that labor representatives wield considerable power in plant decision making, but with a deep sense that their ability to codetermine outcomes implies as well shared responsibility for the firm's success. The political and institutional strength labor commands means that virtually nothing happens in the steel industry without labor's assent. This is the crucial element in the social partnership model of plant relations.

The political source of works council strength is related to the

9. At one plant I visited, the company had provided the head of the works council with a company car (Mercedes) and driver. This works councillor's counterpart on the management side (the plant personnel director), by way of contrast, drives a VW Golf, himself.

composition and character of the work force. Steelworkers are highly organized. In the plants that I studied, over 90 percent of all workers belonged to the IG Metall. The political potential to create havoc in the plant is a powerful (though as I will show, little-used) tool in the hands of works councils in their negotiations with management. As one works councillor put it, "We can call the guys out any time, and count on them. They don't ask any questions, they just go" (interview, 1985).

However, the potential to disrupt production remains largely latent in the steel industry. Works councils occasionally orchestrate a show of force, for example by organizing a demonstration against planned rationalization measures. But such demonstrations are more often demonstrative than truly disruptive. They are almost always planned with management's prior knowledge. Indeed, both works councils and management see it as part of the works councils' job to maintain order in the plant. The key to social partnership, and the reason for such a low level of political conflict, is the other resource labor commands in the steel industry, a strong institutional position in the firm through Montanmitbestimmung.

The institutional basis for labor participation in managerial decision making is nowhere stronger than in the coal and steel industries.[10] Here, labor's plant rights (under the Works Constitution Act) are augmented by strong labor participation at a company level. Codetermination in the coal and steel industries, known as Montanmitbestimmung, is distinguished from the weaker form of codetermination that applies to companies in other industries (under the 1976 Codetermination Law) in two ways.

First, it allows for parity representation for labor and capital on company supervisory boards, which meets three or four times a year and decide on issues such as long-term investment and rationalization measures. A tie-breaking "neutral" member chairs these meetings. This neutral member can be appointed only with the approval of both labor and shareholder representatives on the supervisory board and literally alternates from one side of the negotiating table to the other at consecutive meetings (interview, 1985).

Second, the board of directors in steel companies, which is responsible for the daily operation of the firm, includes a labor director who cannot be appointed without the approval of the labor representatives on the supervisory board. For this reason, and unlike in other industries, labor directors in steel generally come from the ranks of organized labor, and they are typically nominated by the union. Although there are many routes to becoming the union candidate for labor director, these candidates are often drawn from the works council of

10. The coal industry is organized by the Miners' Union (IG Bergbau und Energie).

one of the plants, or from the company works council (*Gesamtbetriebsrat*). In some cases, labor directors come from union headquarters.[11]

As members of the board of directors, labor directors are intimately involved with the company's long-term investment, rationalization, and production plans, as well as the day-to-day operation of the firm. Labor directors are specifically charged with supervising plant personnel departments and company-level industrial relations.

The Works Constitution Act of 1972 calls for mutual trust and cooperation between management and labor representatives. The general atmosphere of social partnership makes this somewhat superfluous in steel. Labor's strong institutional presence in decision making at both the plant and company levels encourages cooperation and a strong sense of shared responsibility for the smooth operation of the company. Indeed, because of the structure of labor representation under Montanmitbestimmung, relations between labor and capital sometimes take on a certain "fun-house" quality, in that it is sometimes hard to distinguish the managers from the managed.

First, since works councillors from individual plants often sit on the company supervisory board, they themselves are involved in the very investment and rationalization decisions that will affect their own plant.

Second, Montanmitbestimmung gives labor representatives a voice in choosing the managers with whom they will have to deal on an ongoing basis in plant negotiations. Personnel directors in steel plants can only be appointed with the approval of labor representatives on the company supervisory board. As a result, relations between labor and plant managers are informal, even very friendly.[12] Occasionally this has even given rise to curious role and career reversals. For example, the head of the works council at Krupp's Rheinhausen plant went on to become the plant personnel director (interview, 1985).

Third, and in terms of plant relations, strong labor presence on supervisory boards means that the incentives for both works councillors and managers to reach a consensus in plant-level conflicts is very high. Because of the parity between labor and management under Montanmitbestimmung, managers cannot simply let plant negotiations fail and know that if the decision gets "kicked upstairs" their dominance in the supervisory board ensures them victory (interviews, 1985).

Fourth, if parity codetermination tends to produce a certain "blurring" of the line between managers and the managed at a plant level, it produces something bordering on schizophrenia at the company board level. Labor directors in the steel industry occupy an unenviable posi-

11. In one case that I studied, for example, the labor director had been the assistant to the president of the IG Metall, and was nominated for labor director of the steel company after he lost a bid for a spot on the *union's* executive board.

12. Labor representatives and managers in the steel industry—unlike in virtually any other industry—address each other using the informal *du*.

tion between worker interests and company interests. The fact that labor directors in steel are simultaneously managers and labor representatives puts them in a very ambivalent position. However, statements by labor directors suggest that they take their position as managers very seriously. The words of one labor director are typical:

> Although the labor director depends on the confidence of the union and the works councils, it would be wrong to expect him to be able to take into account the work force's every petition and request. Whoever does not see this expects too much and strains [*strapaziert*] the institution of labor director by failing to recognize that as a member of the board of directors, the labor director by law counts as part of the management side... and thus has to represent the interests of the company as a whole. [Ludwig 1979:67]

Labor directors in steel command considerable power to influence *how* rationalization occurs, but they rarely question whether it should occur. Their position within the company fosters a sense of shared responsibility for the company's success in the market, and they typically emphasize the link between power and responsibility, between codetermination (Mitbestimmung) and coresponsibility (*Mitverantwortung*).

Sometimes plant works councils will vent criticism on the labor director and tell the work force how the labor director has "sold out" the workers' interests behind the scenes on particular decisions. Yet behind the politicking, the same notion of codetermination *and* coresponsibility—the essence of social partnership—runs deep at the plant level as well.

Because they are involved in virtually all stages of decision making, plant labor representatives also bear a part of the responsibility for decisions that are taken. For instance, when asked about the consistently high levels of overtime worked in his plant, one works councillor replied, "The workers do not always like it, but we cannot turn down overtime—somebody else would just do it. As works councillors we have to make decisions that are right *in the long run*, and try to explain to the workers why we do what we do" (interview, 1985). Another works councillor put it this way:

> Codetermination means that we have to stand behind the decisions we help make. In the case of rationalization measures, for example, the workers come to us and ask why we agreed to them. We have to explain to them that there was no other way to go. We have to assume a broader perspective. We have to explain that in order to maintain jobs in the longer run, it often makes no sense to fight for a few in the short run. In other words, when the workers ask why we could not prevent it, we're stuck with part of the responsibility for the decision. We cannot say that it was the nasty boss who did it. We carry responsibility for the decision, and because of that we have to look at the whole and not just particular jobs in particular decisions. [Interview, 1985]

In their interactions with managers, works councils in the German steel industry wield formidable power but with a deep sense of shared responsibility for the firm's economic health.

Although labor's rights constrain management considerably, the advantage for employers is stability and predictability in plant labor relations. As one plant manager put it:

> Mitbestimmung in fact has a lot of advantages. Negotiations take longer, but the point is that the whole thing doesn't grind to a halt. Nothing goes around here against the will of the works council. But what we can do is anticipate conflicts.... We simply negotiate until we reach a compromise. It is worth it in the end, because then the works council shares responsibility for the decision. Mitbestimmung means more than just codetermination; it also means shared responsibility. When we both [management and labor] go before the work force [for example, at a plant assembly] to report that from an original plan involving say, four hundred redundancies, three hundred jobs are still going to have to go, then I can say this decision represents an agreement we have reached with the works council. The workers still whistle and boo, but I can present it as a compromise that their own representatives have agreed to. The works council can then sell the one hundred jobs it saved as a success. [Interview, 1985]

As a type of plant labor relations, social partnership describes a situation in which labor wields considerable (latent) political and (active) institutional power, but sees its job as crucial intermediary—softening rationalization for the workers in the short run, and cooperating with management in the long run interests of the firm. The continuous flow of information between labor representatives and managers, the fuzziness of the line between managers and the managed, and labor's strength and pervasive presence at all levels of company decision making produce in the German steel industry a form of labor relations that epitomizes the concept of social partnership.

The Politics of Industrial Decline

The pattern of plant relations discussed above helps explain the low levels of conflict the German steel industry has experienced over the last decade, despite prolonged economic crisis.[13] Labor representatives and managers in the steel industry largely agree on the problems the industry faces. Neither side, by and large, blames the other. Instead, both agree that the problem for German steel is competition from lower-wage producers in the newly industrializing countries, the subsidies and protectionism of other European Community member states, and increased competition from Japan (interviews, 1985).

Given this broad consensus on the source of their competitive diffi-

13. On the relative success of the German steel industry to adapt to the crisis of the 1970s and 1980s see also Thelen, 1987a, and Esser and Fach, 1989.

culties, both sides also largely concur on what the German industry has to do to compete. Not whether, but how, to rationalize production is the question in steel. Indeed, works councils themselves are often great proponents of rationalization measures that elsewhere instill fear in the hearts of labor representatives. At one plant I studied, for example, the works council was a prime mover in a campaign to rationalize steel casting operations. The works council demanded that the company abandon its outdated ingot-casting equipment and invest in continuous casting. One works councillor estimated that 280 of the 400 jobs in the steel works would be lost with the introduction of continuous casting.[14] Despite this enormous employment effect, he described the decision as a necessary step in maintaining the viability of the company, and ultimately in keeping the plant in operation (interview, 1985).

In fact, works councils in different plants often actively *compete against each other* for new equipment, whatever the short-term employment effects might be. The goal in steel is to modernize and rationalize production as far as possible, in order to make one's own plant indispensable to the firm. In the face of capacity reductions, the most modern plants are least vulnerable to the threat of closure. For this reason, competition among individual works councils is fierce when it comes to new investment.

Thus, one reason works councils are so pro-modernization is that it is better to rationalize now than to get closed down later. But the other reason *steel* works councils in particular cooperate in rationalization measures with fewer reservations than in other industries is that the way work-force reductions are accomplished is politically easier for them to sell to the work force.

Think steel in Germany and one immediately thinks as well of social plans (*Sozialpläne*). Social plans are agreements between works councils and firm management that regulate the number and terms of layoffs. The steel industry pioneered the use of social plans, though they are not unique to that industry.[15] But social plans in steel are different from those in other industries. For one thing, steel works councils have been extremely effective in preventing involuntary layoffs. The industry as a whole has lost over one hundred thousand jobs in the past twenty years (Esser and Fach 1989:223), but this was largely accomplished without layoffs.

The centerpiece of social plans in steel is early retirement, though this measure is sometimes combined with others such as voluntary

14. But see below: such employment reductions are not accomplished through layoffs.
15. The Works Constitution Act of 1972 introduced social plans on a broad basis. The law stipulates that in the event of "fundamental changes" in production that affect workers, management is obligated to negotiate an "interest-accommodation" agreement, and if the changes result in redundancies, to negotiate with the works council a "social plan" that addresses the number of workers affected and the compensation they will receive beyond state unemployment benefits.

severance agreements between individual workers and management. Early-retirement schemes in the steel industry are uniformly generous, though the particulars vary from case to case. In the companies I studied, workers who retired (usually at age fifty-nine or sixty) received between 90 and 100 percent of their previous pay in the first two years, between 85 and 95 percent in the next two years, and no less than 80 percent until they reach retirement age and become eligible for pension payments.[16]

Because the provisions of social plans in steel are so generous, and because work in the steel industry is so physically taxing, volunteers for early retirement are not hard to find. Indeed, one major role the works council sometimes plays in all of this is to lobby management to "fire" particular workers so as to enable them to take advantage of the early retirement scheme (interview, 1985). Sometimes this produces conflicts between works councils and management, in cases for example of the worker whose age makes him or her a candidate for early retirement, but whose skills or experience management is unwilling to lose.

The politics of social plans set in motion complex personnel maneuvers—again negotiated with the works council—that transfer workers across production units within the plant (interviews, 1985).[17] Particular rationalization measures affect individual production areas, in which not all of the workers will be eligible for early retirement. Older workers from throughout the plant retire via the social plan, and they are then replaced by those workers whose jobs have been eliminated or changed through rationalization. This complicated system of transfers occurs not only within particular plants, but across plants within a company. In the latter case, the firm-level works council (Gesamtbetriebsrat), which is composed of works councillors from the company's various plants, orchestrates and negotiates inter-plant transfers.

The politics of social plans have contributed significantly to the relatively smooth and conflict-free industrial restructuring that distinguishes the case of German steel from many other countries.[18] Works councils tolerate—indeed they encourage—rationalization investment, which they see as their only hope of making the remaining jobs "krisensicher" (crisis-proof). Labor's influence on supervisory boards ensures that investment goes toward this end. This has meant, among other things, that industrial adjustment in the German steel industry has been adjustment more *within* as opposed to *out of* steel than for example in the United States.

16. The company supplements state unemployment benefits up to these levels until workers become eligible for retirement pensions.

17. This procedure is known as a "Ringtausch," or rotation exchange. See also Windolf and Hohn 1984.

18. Tony Daley (1988) describes the high levels of social violence that have accompanied the restructuring of the French steel industry. See also Thelen 1987a.

Labor's quid pro quo for its cooperation in industrial restructuring and in maintaining industrial peace in a period of decline is a virtual no-layoff clause and a comparatively generous package of benefits for those workers who are eased out of the industry. The result is industrial adjustment premised on continuous rationalization and the constant rejuvenation of the work force. In sum, social partnership in the German steel industry has contributed significantly to maintaining peaceful and collaborative labor relations in a period of industrial restructuring and decline.

Depoliticized Legalism in the Consumer Electronics Industry

The adjustment pressures the consumer electronics industry faces are different from those of the steel industry, a traditional industry in decline. With the maturing of the Japanese electronics industry and a growing number of lower-wage producers entering the market, the key competitive challenge, and the trend in consumer electronics, is the adoption and application of new technologies, both in production and in final products. The income and employment effects of these product and production changes constitute the most important challenges labor faces in this industry.

The resources labor brings with it to plant negotiations in electronics contrast starkly with those that works councils in the steel industry command. As in steel, most works councillors in the electronics industry are members of the IG Metall; often they are also active in the union local as well. But unlike their counterparts in steel, the political and institutional resources they control are much more modest.

The meager political resources works councils in the electronics industry command are related to the character and structure of the work force. Electronics employs far more white-collar workers than does steel, and these are more likely to belong to the IG Metall's more conservative white-collar rival, the DAG (Deutscher Angestellten Gewerkschaftsbund). Moreover, the overall level of unionization in consumer electronics is well below that in steel. The average for the plants I studied was 30 to 40 percent, as compared to over 90 percent in steel. The industry employs a large number of unskilled female workers in production. Not only have these workers proved more difficult to organize; in general they also have a looser and more instrumental connection to the union than their counterparts in the steel industry do. This adds up to a largely unorganized and depoliticized work force, which complicates the works council's job even where the works councillors are themselves active union members.

The works council's position is also institutionally weak. Unlike in the steel industry (but like in the automobile industry) the rules governing labor participation at a company level are not those laid down in the Montanmitbestimmung law of 1951 but rather in the Codetermination Law of 1976.[19] Labor participation at a company level gives labor access to information about what the firm's management is planning, but not the authority to veto or even significantly influence those plans in the way labor representatives in the steel industry can.

For these reasons, works councils in the electronics industry are the mirror image of the strong and self-confident but "responsible" steel works councils. Works councils in the consumer electronics industry know full well that the character of the work force prohibits strategies of strong *political* resistance to management. Indeed, they have a keen sense that the only thing that lies between them and managerial arbitrariness is the Works Constitution Act. In the words of one works councillor at a major consumer electronics firm, "The only tools we've got to work with here are a few paragraphs [in the WCA] and we're constantly running up against the limits of the law" (interview, 1985). This comment captures the essence of depoliticized legalism.

As in the steel industry, the fact that management needs works council approval on a range of routine plant decisions (overtime, shift work, and wage payment systems) encourages regular communication between labor and management. In the case of conflicting objectives, informal negotiations produce ongoing compromise. However, in the electronics industry, managers are occasionally bolder in their interactions with the works council. One plant manager put it this way: "I do what I feel is necessary, even if it means bending the rules. If they [the works councillors] don't like it they can take me to court."[20] This kind of "testing" of works councils is unheard of in steel. Under normal circumstances, however, works council–management relations in the consumer electronics industry are run "by the book."

Adjustment and Personnel Policy in the Electronics Industry

The feeling of shared responsibility for the firm's success in the market does not run as deep on the labor side in the electronics industry as in steel. Relations between works councils and management in the crisis can nonetheless be characterized in terms of negotiated trade-offs between the economic interests of management and the interests of labor, though the scope and effectiveness of labor participation in plant decision making are narrower.

The two most pressing problems with which works councils in the electronics industry have been confronted over the last decade are

---

19. In companies employing over two thousand workers.
20. Either the works council or management can call in a conciliation board in the event of conflicts on certain issues.

employment reductions and the effects of technological change on workers' incomes.

As in many large German enterprises, employers in the electronics industry initiate large-scale layoffs under extreme circumstances, but tend to rely as far as possible on other measures—attrition, inter- and intra-plant transfers, reduction of overtime, and short-time work (*Kurzarbeit*) (interviews, 1985).[21] The structure of the work force in the electronics industry (a high proportion of unskilled, female workers) would appear to make it a likely candidate for a less conservative personnel policy—more hiring and firing, less concern for employment stability—since the low skill requirements for production work in electronics make it relatively easy for management to find replacements in the labor market.

Unlike in the steel and automobile industries, management's reluctance to pursue aggressively a "hire and fire" policy has little to do with the works councils' political clout. Indeed, one of the defining characteristics of depoliticized legalism is that works councils generally lack the political resources to avoid layoffs. What encourages managers nonetheless to attempt to stabilize the work force is the provision in the Works Constitution Act that requires them to negotiate a social plan with the works council prior to large-scale layoffs (interviews, 1985).

Social plans in the electronics industry on average work out not to be as expensive for managers as in other industries. But layoffs also do not come free, and employers are legally obligated to negotiate with works councils over the number of layoffs and the terms of compensation. Indeed, they must reach agreement with their works councils on these issues before anyone can be laid off. These provisions provide strong incentives for employers to avoid large-scale personnel reductions if possible.

Depoliticized legalism means that the constraints on management posed by the works council system are those laid down in the law itself, and little more. Works councils generally lack the political strength to use the legal provisions of the law as a lever to extract further concessions from management, as in the case of the automobile industry described below.

Negotiations over layoffs in the mid-1980s at Grundig, a major German consumer electronics firm, illustrate some of the possibilities, but ultimately also the limitations of plant politics in the electronics industry. In 1984, Grundig management presented the works council with plans for extensive rationalization measures involving 2,530 re-

21. Short-time work is when workers' hours are cut back and they are compensated for a part of the income loss by state subsidies and employer contributions. Short-time work must be approved by the works council, though when it is introduced as an alternative to layoffs, such approval is of course readily forthcoming.

dundancies at five domestic plants (*Handelsblatt* and *Nürnberger Nachrichten*, 13 February 1985). By law, of course, management was obliged to negotiate with the works councils at Grundig over a "balancing of interests" (Interessenausgleich) and a "social plan" (Sozialplan). "Balancing-of-interest" agreements explore alternatives to layoffs such as inter- and intra-plant transfers, while "social plans" cover the number of layoffs and compensation.

Working together with the Nürnberg local of the IG Metall, the Grundig works council responded by rejecting the usual social plan negotiations and demanding instead an "employment plan" ("Beschäftigungsplan statt Sozialplan"). Rather than focus on the level of compensation for laid-off workers, the works councils demanded that Grundig instead provide laid-off workers with retraining. In view of the high unemployment in the Nürnberg area and the relatively low skills of the affected workers, labor representatives stressed that the chances of these workers finding alternative employment were low without appropriate skills.

Grundig management initially rejected the demand outright and insisted instead on negotiating the usual social plan compensation levels. However, shop stewards and works councils mobilized and backed up their demand with short work stoppages. The Works Constitution Act of course prohibits works councils from initiating strikes. But the Grundig works council exploited a legal loophole in the law that allows individual workers to leave their jobs to go to the works council office for information or consultation. One Grundig works council, with the assistance of the shop steward committee, organized workers to take advantage of this individual right collectively and simultaneously. Two thousand out of a total of six thousand workers participated in this demonstration (interviews, 1985). In addition, the works council organized a local campaign to publicize the issue of regional unemployment, which ultimately drew the local labor office into negotiations over the employment plan.

The agreement the firm and the works council reached provides workers made redundant by the rationalization measures with the right to two years of retraining, to be financed by Grundig and subsidized by the local employment office. Other important provisions included severance pay for voluntary quits and a "senior plan" providing an early retirement option for workers over fifty-five. Finally, the agreement contained a provision for the formation of two boards, composed of equal numbers of firm labor and management representatives. One committee, on "new product lines," would review possibilities for alternative products that the company could manufacture using existing facilities and the existing work force. The idea was to diversify production and move into more stable markets. The other joint labor-management committee was to administer the training program called for in the employment plan (*Betriebsvereinbarung* of 24 April 1985; see also *Der Gewerkschafter*, June 1985:40–41).

The Grundig employment plan was heralded in union circles as a great victory. IG Metall headquarters declared it a "model" for the entire consumer electronics industry (IG Metall 1985b). Stressing the importance of going beyond compensation for layoffs, unionists saw the Grundig solution as an important contribution to addressing the longer-term problems of skill acquisition for workers in this industry.

Implementing the plan, however, turned out to be much more difficult than the union had anticipated, as those involved in the process began to emphasize (Lobodda 1988; see also *Frankfurter Neue Presse*, 17 January 1987). Wrangling between the union and management over the training program was particularly intense, with the result that very few workers (especially unskilled workers) were retrained under the employment plan's provision. Grundig was still contractually bound to offer fired workers such training, but the firm got around this expense by reducing the work force through other avenues, especially early retirement and attrition (interviews, 1988).

The Grundig employment plan was in many ways exceptional, but in the end this case also highlights the limits of plant politics that characterize the electronics industry. The degree of political mobilization and the stipulations of the agreement were extraordinary for this industry, in which labor's resistance to employer initiatives is typically more passive. However, in the end, as soon as the agreement pushed beyond the legal minimums set down in the Works Constitution Act (for example, going beyond the traditional "social plan" obligation and instituting a joint labor-management retraining committee), the works council was on less solid footing and ultimately was not able to force Grundig to comply fully with the spirit of the agreement.

In sum, the works council was unable to avoid personnel reductions, and largely unsuccessful in achieving its goals for worker retraining. Nonetheless, it was able to forestall the massive layoffs that Grundig had planned and soften the blow for workers affected by them. The crucial lever for doing so was the social plan requirement in the Works Constitution Act. One need only compare this outcome with similar events in the U.S. electronics industry (in Silicon Valley, for instance) to appreciate how these legal levers bolster the powers of labor representatives even in poorly organized sectors. But the Grundig case also illustrates the limits labor faces in plants and industries characterized by depoliticized legalism.

Politicized Legalism in the Automobile Industry

Plant politics in the automobile industry illustrate the third ideal-typical pattern of plant relations: "politicized legalism." Both the automobile and electronics industries fall under the weaker company-level codetermination legislation, so automobile works councils enjoy no greater formal rights than their counterparts in electronics. Not legal parameters, but political factors distinguish "politicized legalism" in the automobile industry from "depoliticized legalism" in consumer electronics.

First, the character and composition of the work force give automobile works councils an edge over their counterparts in electronics. As in the steel industry, auto workers are predominantly male, though the average skill level in the industry is lower because of the larger number of assembly jobs. And again like steelworkers, workers in the auto industry are highly organized. This is particularly true for production workers, but it also applies to the white-collar workers, who are more likely to belong to the IG Metall than to the rival DAG as in the electronics industry. In addition, shop steward committees are in general both stronger and more active in autos than in electronics, a factor which both reinforces and is reinforced by higher levels of organization and political mobilization within the work force.[22]

Auto workers possess a higher degree of union (if not class) consciousness than workers in the electronics industry. They are in general extremely loyal to the IG Metall, even if they are critical of union policy at times. The higher degree of attention to (if not active engagement in) union politics among automobile workers is reinforced by the high profile the industry enjoys in national union politics. Because of its importance to the IG Metall, this industry gets disproportionate attention from union headquarters, a factor which also contributes to a higher level of training and professionalism among plant-level representatives in the automobile industry (see also Kern and Schumann 1984:117–21). Automobile workers have frequently played a vanguard role in annual collective bargaining rounds, going out on strike in support of demands the union hopes to push through for the entire metalworking industry. The IG Metall's strategy of "target strikes" (*Schwerpunktstreik*) in the 1970s, and its more recent "mini-max" strike strategy both rely heavily on the auto workers to shoulder the burden of fighting battles for the union as a whole.[23] The same is true for the "warning strikes" the union has come to use more frequently since 1980.

22. Shop stewards from the automobile industry are generally more vocal and active in national union politics as well. Recall, for example, the role they played in debates over betriebsnahe Tarifpolitik.

23. The "mini-max" strategy calls very few workers out in a few key plants whose position is so vital to production in other plants that the small number of plants directly involved has a "maximum" impact on production elsewhere. In 1984, for example, the union called out a very few plants that supply particular parts for virtually the whole German automobile industry. This strategy capitalizes on German managers' relatively recent adoption of Japanese "just-in-time" production methods. Low inventories in automobile assembly plants means that striking the suppliers quickly brings production in the industry to a halt (Silvia 1988).

High organization levels and higher mobilization within the automobile work force create a pattern of labor-management relations in auto plants that is very different from that in consumer electronics, even though works councils in both are subject to the same legal framework and command the same rights. What distinguishes depoliticized legalism in the electronics industry from politicized legalism in the auto industry is that works councils in the auto industry can back up their demands with the threat of political mobilization and potential disruption.

In some ways related to this, "politicized legalism" means that plant politics are themselves more highly charged, and this creates a dynamic within works councils themselves (and in their relations with shop stewards) that can translate into works council power in negotiations with management. The more politicized nature of plant politics in the automobile industry is reflected in (and reinforced by) more active and vocal shop steward committees, but it can also take the form of factional politics within works councils themselves. The political dynamic this situation creates on the labor side in turn can make it unwise for mangers to "test" labor by pursuing a policy of intransigence, and under certain circumstances it can even prompt them to greater concessions in negotiations with the works council, for if management were to adopt a purely confrontational strategy, it could politicize plant politics further and strengthen more militant factions on the labor side.

In extreme cases, factional politics can take the form of "alternative" IG Metall lists in works council elections. The classic, almost legendary case of factional politics in the automobile industry is the group formed in 1975 under the leadership of Richard Heller at Opel in Rüsselsheim.[24] In 1978 Heller's "alternative" list succeeded in winning a majority of seats on the works council, which it has controlled ever since (see Britscho 1978). The case of Opel demonstrates that such a minority faction can in fact come to power. But there is also a cyclical and somewhat self-sustaining feature to factional politics in the automobile industry. Heller's own "alternative" faction is currently being challenged by another left "alternative" list.

Opel is a somewhat extreme example; more often different political "strains" coexist more or less peacefully within the shop steward committee or works council itself. But related to this, and even where no official "alternative" list exists, works council elections and plant politics in the automobile industry in general tend to be more visible and politicized than in consumer electronics. Extreme factionalism can of course be paralyzing. However, higher mobilization among the work force, more active shop steward committees, and strong competition in works council elections can also create "positive loops" in labor repre-

---

24. A different—and far more extreme—case is Daimler Benz, where a much more militant alternative "*Plakat*" group formed in 1968 and has been a vocal minority in the firm ever since (Grohmann and Sachstetter 1979).

sentation and in the works council's relations with management that are absent in cases of depoliticized legalism.

To the extent that plant negotiations are politicized they are *open*. The policies of the works council are the subject of intense scrutiny and discussion, both in shop steward committees and more broadly among the work force.[25] A works council that concedes too much to management without a fight, or that is viewed as excessively cooperative, can be called on the carpet by the plant "activists," either a faction in the shop steward committee or in the works council itself. Works councils in the automobile industry that do not have major successes to campaign on at election time subject themselves to criticism and possible opposition from more activist groups. Thus, unlike the more timid politics of works councils under depoliticized legalism, works councils in cases of politicized legalism have both the political resources (a mobilized or at least mobilizable work force) and the incentive (due to the dynamics of competition in plant politics) to be more aggressive in their dealings with management.

The existence of a more politicized work force (and possibly the presence of a vocal, more militant opposition) can influence management's dealings with labor. Employers have a great interest in maintaining smooth and predictable relations with the works council. One way to keep the peace is to inform labor of upcoming changes rather than try to circumvent works council influence through secrecy. Although the Works Constitution Act stipulates that management must inform the works council "fully and in a comprehensive fashion" of all planned changes that will affect the work force, there is considerable variation in how this rule is interpreted and applied. Unlike their counterparts in electronics, works councils in automobiles are almost never surprised; indeed, managers are often more generous with information than the strict legal minimum requires.

Maintaining stable relations with labor can also mean keeping plant activists at bay. Where a "moderate" majority controls the works council, it is in management's short-term interest to shore up the position of this majority faction by granting strategic concessions that the latter can then present to the work force as the fruits of their diligent efforts in negotiations. And in the longer run, of course, if managers are intransigent in plant negotiations, they can bring a plague on themselves when the next works council election rolls around. The majority faction

25. Again, these are ideal types. One can also find works councils in automobile plants that are controlled by so-called *Betriebsfürsten*, who have a leadership style that discourages political debate and relies on informal arrangements with management. But even the existence of such Betriebsfürsten appears to be more contentious in the auto industry than in electronics. Moreover, I would also argue that even where the works council is controlled by such a character, one of his sources of power under conditions of politicized legalism is management's interest in strengthening his position against critics advocating more "open" (read: politicized) plant politics.

will have to run on its record, and if they have no major victories to boast, then the more radical appeals of left factions in the plant are more likely to fall on receptive ears. To the extent that management has an interest in plant stability, dealing with a new works council every three years (beginning in 1990, every four years) is something it is eager to avoid.[26]

In sum, "politicized legalism" describes a pattern of labor-management accommodation in which works councils almost never fail to exploit fully the legal leverage the Works Constitution Act provides, and where the dynamics of competition on the labor side can even prompt management to concede more than the minimum the law requires. Relations between works councils and management in the automobile industry are generally more contentious than those in the steel industry. But unlike those in the electronics industry, works councils in the auto industry bargain from a position of considerable political strength. Thus, management has a stronger interest in being open with the works council in order to keep labor conflicts channeled and, to the extent possible, depoliticized.

Personnel Policy and Technological Change in the Automobile Industry

By virtue of their strong political position and, related to this, their high degree of training and professionalism, works councils in the automobile industry are a force to be reckoned with when it comes to rationalization measures; and, consequently, they have been more successful than their counterparts in electronics in influencing the process of adjustment. As Horst Kern and Michael Schumann put it, in terms of modernization policies in the automobile industry, "There is no getting around the works council" (1984:117).[27]

The two most pressing problems confronting works councils in the automobile industry are the instability of employment (related to the highly cyclical nature of the automobile market) and rapid technological change. As in the consumer electronics industry, the costs associated with firing workers has encouraged managers in the auto industry to pursue a fairly conservative personnel policy. But, even when the depth of the crisis in the two industries is taken into account, arguably works councils in automobiles have been more successful in avoiding layoffs and stabilizing employment. In some companies such policies have even been formalized in negotiations between labor and management.

The best-known example of such an explicit deal is Volkswagen's

26. Until 1990, works council elections were held every three years. But in 1988 the CDU/CSU government lengthened the terms of works councillors to four years (*Wirtschaftswoche*, 9 September 1990:26).

27. "Am Betriebsrat vorbei gibt es keine Modernisierungspolitik."

"middle-line employment policy" (Streeck 1984b; Brumlop and Jürgens 1983). The core of this policy (which came out of negotiations with the works council over the approval of overtime) is a general commitment by management not to "let production and employment be determined by short-term market conditions, but rather to orient policy in terms of a middle prognosis of market developments" (Brumlop and Jürgens 1983:33). Specifically, the works councils extracted two concessions from management: (1) a commitment not to resort to short-time work (which cuts into workers' incomes) for a three-month period after the last overtime; and (2) a ban on dismissals for six months after the last overtime (Streeck 1984b:115). In exchange, the works council promised flexibility in the approval of overtime and extra shifts (Streeck 1984b:115–16).

Volkswagen's "middle-line employment policy" entails on the one hand a commitment by management to maintain employment in a cyclical downturn, for example by putting workers in training programs. Volkswagen has an on-site training facility at its plant in Wolfsburg, and even under normal market circumstances, 2 percent of the work force is involved—on a rotating basis—in retraining (interviews, 1985). But on the other hand, it also means that the company hires very conservatively in an upturn, even if that means falling behind on orders (Streeck 1984b:115, 117). The "middle-line employment policy" is often cited as a prime example of "plant egoism," for the core of the trade-off is works council cooperation in adjusting working times to changes in demand, in exchange for job and income security for the work force (Streeck 1984b:115). Eva Brumlop and Ulrich Jürgens summarize the employment policy practiced at VW:

> On the one side [the middle-line employment policy] increased employment security for a core labour force; on the other side [it] supported the willingness of the labour force and its representatives to accept increased work flexibility with respect to working time (overtime and special shifts), the location of work (transfers within the plant or between plants), and finally job content (transfer to different work operations, readiness to undergo retraining).[1983:35]

Similar deals between labor and management (though not as explicit) attempt to stabilize employment against cyclical swings in other automobile plants as well, which helps explain the occasionally very high levels of overtime worked in this industry (see also Kern and Schumann 1984:120–21).

The second major problem with which works councils in the automobile industry have been confronted is the income effect of new technologies. As is well known, the automobile industry is at the forefront of the widespread application of microelectronics-based production automation. The income problems this raises for workers derive in part from a dominant form of wage determination in Germany, the so-called analytic method. In the analytic system, a worker's wage rate is calculated according to a formula based on the physical characteristics of the job he or she performs. Physical strain and environmental factors are weighted heavily in the analysis. Since new technologies often reduce the physical strain of work and increase other responsibilities such as intervention in the case of machine breakdown (which are not heavily compensated in the analytic method), job reevaluation with the introduction of new technologies can mean income loss for workers.

Works councils in the automobile industry have been relatively successful in minimizing these negative income effects, either through their participation in the reclassification of the jobs, or by concluding agreements on income guarantees. In one plant, for instance, the works council secured a four-year income guarantee for persons whose jobs had been reclassified with the reorganization of production (interview, 1985). While this is a far cry from long-term income security, such plant agreements often exceed the provisions of existing collective bargains.[28]

Other plant agreements in the automobile industry go further toward providing the basis for a longer-term solution to the income effects of new technologies. The VW (Salzgitter) works council, for example, was able to participate actively in designing the layout of production in an area targeted by management for rationalization such that (1) the number of workers originally planned to operate the facility was increased;[29] (2) a system of job rotation was instituted and all workers received the training necessary to perform the most difficult job in the production area; and (3) as a consequence, almost all jobs on the facility were reclassified upward, which meant an increase in income not only for those workers directly affected in the reorganization, but also the same higher wage and skill level for workers who might subsequently fill those jobs (interviews, 1985).

This aggressive approach to the technology problem is more prevalent in the automobile industry than in virtually any other. Indeed, the central union's "handbook" on works council participation in production reorganization (*Das Zehn-Schritte-Programm*), as well as many of the union's initiatives and demands concerning group work and job rotation, were developed on the basis of experiences in the automobile industry (interviews, 1985). The automobile industry's vanguard role is explained in part by the fact that the problem of technological change is more pressing in this industry, but it also reflects the more auspicious

28. The union has concluded income guarantee contracts for older workers. Also, and as mentioned above, the union secured eighteen-month income guarantees for all workers in Baden-Württemberg.

29. Though the number of jobs in the production area still dropped; the affected workers were transferred to other areas in the plant.

conditions in automobiles for union politics, including the active engagement of plant labor representatives, characteristic of politicized legalism. In the Salzgitter case, the result was to go beyond traditional demands for job and income security for the affected workers (a onetime, short-term measure) to actively shape the organization of production itself. In another case, that of VW at Braunschweig, the works council successfully pressured management to allow labor representatives a voice in the choice of the technology (hardware) for a new production line, in addition to a say in how work would be organized with the technology's introduction (presentation at union technology workshop, 1989).

In sum, on the most pressing questions they have faced in the crisis—employment security and technological change—works councils in the automobile industry have been relatively successful in finding compromise solutions that protect the interests of their constituents and make for relatively smooth and conflict-free adjustment. Politicized legalism is the pattern of plant labor politics that has facilitated these outcomes.

THE "WORKS COUNCIL WEAKNESS" THESIS REVISITED

It should be obvious by now that the question of how and how much works councils are constrained by the Works Constitution Act is a question for which there is no single answer. Analyses that simply extrapolate works council behavior from the legal dictums that ostensibly limit their room for maneuver ignore the extent to which politics still govern labor relations in the plant. In this sense, the "works council weakness" thesis suffers from the same underlying determinism characteristic of many institutional analyses. But what the analysis above demonstrates is how different patterns of political maneuvering within institutional constraints can produce different outcomes. Works councils in the automobile and electronics industries are subject to the same legal constraints, and yet differences in the political resources they command produce very different patterns of plant relations. In short, what is important is the *interaction* of political strategies and institutional constraints.

Works councils in the automobile industry have on balance been more successful than those in the electronics industry in exploiting the possibilities of the Works Constitution Act (e.g., by insisting more aggressively on a quid pro quo for approval of overtime), and sometimes even in extracting concessions above and beyond the minimum requirements of the law. Works councils in electronics are less aggressive in wielding their rights and often either do not demand or do not receive such a quid pro quo. In light of these differences, the "works council weakness" theorists may have it exactly backwards: it is not that the law determines political possibilities in the plant; instead, the political strength and savvy of works councils determine how the law operates.

The effects of the legal stipulations that prohibit works councils from initiating work stoppages are usually overstated. The Grundig case demonstrates that a determined (and somewhat creative) works council can indeed create brief havoc in the plant. The Grundig case is in part so extraordinary because this is a work force (largely unorganized and unskilled) where one might least expect such a demonstration. The same thing goes on regularly (on a smaller scale) in other industries (Brumlop and Jürgens 1983:10). In other instances works councils have openly tolerated and even encouraged (although they may not actively direct) smaller-scale protests among groups of workers dissatisfied with particular management policies considered unfair (interviews, 1985). Works councils can use such (relatively spontaneous) disruptions as a lever in their negotiations with managers.

But the "works council weakness" thesis is flawed in a more fundamental sense; it fails to recognize sources of works council power other than its capacity to disrupt production. The routinized and ongoing character of plant negotiations under the Works Constitution Act, and indeed management's dependence on works council approval on routine matters such as overtime, mean that a works council can complicate the smooth functioning of production in more subtle ways. For example, on certain plant issues managers must have works council approval before they can proceed.[30] In such cases, simply stalling can be a works council's most effective weapon. Or, the more litigious works council might exercise its right to take conflicts over such issues to a conciliation board. Since employers pay for conciliation proceedings (the mediator's fees, for example), ongoing conflict with the works council can become expensive.

The more general point, then, is that one crucial source of works council power is the withdrawal of (or the threat to withdraw) its active (or even passive) cooperation in day-to-day decision making. This distinction—between the threat to disrupt production (which works councils do not have) and the threat to make routine plant decision making more cumbersome and possibly expensive—is analogous to Alessandro Pizzorno's (1978) distinction between "market exchange" and "political exchange." In a collective bargaining situation (an instance of a market exchange), "the weapon of the organized worker is the strike, or other forms of interruption of production. What the employer is paying for is the assurance of continuity of work" (1978:278).

30. Overtime is the one that comes up most frequently, but this applies as well to working time issues more generally, and other changes in the flow of production that affect workers.

In contrast, the resource labor commands in a situation of "political exchange" is its ability to generate or withdraw consensus. According to Pizzorno, labor power in a situation of political exchange "bears no necessary relation to the demand for the product of these workers" but derives rather from labor's ability to "threaten social order or social consensus" (1978:279).

Pizzorno emphasizes how the political resources of national labor organizations may affect their interactions with political parties, business, and the state, but in Germany the concept of political exchange describes labor-capital relations at the plant level as well. In the "strong labor" cases of politicized legalism and social partnership especially, what often prompts managers to concessions is their interest in predictability and stability in their relations with labor. Managers pay a price for the cooperation of work councils (in the form of greater job security for workers, for example), but in exchange the works council performs a crucial mediating function between plant management and the work force. This mediating role is particularly important under conditions of great market uncertainty, for it dampens conflicts over restructuring and rationalization and ensures the smooth operation of production.

Thus, Pizzorno's "withdrawal of cooperation" seems to be a source of works council power in comparison to which their legal inability to strike pales. The "works council weakness" argument is, in short, too narrowly construed, for it ignores the myriad ways works councils can routinely complicate managerial decision making by withdrawing support for the smooth operation of production. Maintaining order rather than the ability to create disorder through industrial action is the key to the relative *strength* of works councils. This ongoing political exchange is arguably much more important in Germany than in unionized firms in a country like the United States. Because plant conflicts in Germany are resolved through negotiation rather than through the application of rules (such as seniority), managers are more constrained by the need to work together with their works councils on an ongoing basis.

THE "PLANT EGOISM" THESIS REVISITED

The interests of plant management and works councils—as different as they are on many other dimensions—converge when it comes to a shared interest in the viability and competiveness of the firm. This observation is the basis for another argument that in many ways is the mirror image of the "works council weakness" hypothesis discussed above.

A number of authors claim that under conditions of high unemployment, the works council system in Germany promotes "plant egoism," which can undermine organized labor's strength (Hohn 1988; Streeck

1984a, 1984c; Windolf and Hohn 1984; and Tokunaga and Bergmann 1984). In contrast to the "works council weakness" theorists, "plant egoism" theorists argue that the problem is not that works councils are too weak to defend labor's interests. Rather, they maintain that works councils' very success in representing the interests of their plant constituencies has a strong centrifugal effect on the working class as a whole and exacerbates central unions' problems of maintaining organizational unity and solidarity on which, after all, the strength of national labor organizations depends. Hans-Willy Hohn, for example, argues that "cooperative syndicalism" at the plant level has contributed to a decline in the significance of central collective bargains, and to a growing tendency for works councils to view the union as simply a "service organization" (1988:15, 162).

The core of the plant egoism thesis hinges on the way the constraints of codetermination affect capital's and labor's interests. For managers, "co-determination has imposed organizational rigidities...that have turned labour, within limits, from a relatively fluid into a more fixed, or even constant factor [of production]" (Streeck 1983:30). But, argues Streeck, if codetermination has posed this problem for management, it has also offered a solution, namely for employers to incorporate works councils into "plant productivity coalitions" in which they concede job and income security to a lean, "core" work force in exchange for the active participation and cooperation of works councils in increasing the firm's productivity and managing highly fluid internal labor markets (Streeck 1983, 1984a; Windolf and Hohn 1984).

The rigidities codetermination imposes on plant- and firm-level personnel policy is confirmed in Rainer Schultz-Wild's (1978) study. Schultz-Wild found that in the wake of the 1973–74 oil crisis, employers let their work forces shrink to a minimum level. In the recovery of the mid-1970s German employers did not restore plant employment to the pre-1973 levels, but instead hired only enough workers to cover production at the low point in the firm's demand cycle. In periods of cyclical upswing, they maintained these "lean" work forces and resorted to extensive use of overtime, extra shifts, subcontracting, and similar measures in order to avoid possible redundancies later.

Paul Windolf and Hans-Willy Hohn's (1984) study confirms this phenomenon from a different perspective. In an analysis of works council–management bargaining over personnel policy, these authors document works councils' active participation in the "closure" of internal labor markets to plant outsiders. Personnel policy adjusts to upswings in demand through extensive use of overtime, subcontracting, and other short-term measures. For these authors, this policy of protecting the firm's core work force comes at the expense of other (non-core) workers (*Randbelegschaften*). This tendency is clear in the example of VW's "middle-line employment policy" cited above, in which the trade-off was the job and income security of the present work force for an implicit "no-layoff" policy.

This situation has led some authors to draw comparisons between the German and Japanese systems of industrial relations (see especially Tokunaga and Bergmann 1984). They cite a similarity between personnel policy in German firms and the explicit or implicit "lifetime employment guarantees" in the Japanese "core" economy. Both are characterized by high internal labor market flexibility and labor's active cooperation in rationalizing production in the interests of raising plant productivity. As in the Japanese "core" firms, the relative job security German workers enjoy makes them relatively receptive to the introduction of new technologies and rationalization measures. It is this fundamental agreement between German managers and works councils on the need to constantly rationalize production but in a way that is compatible with the job and income security of the present work force that lies at the heart of the plant "productivity coalitions" to which plant egoism theorists point.

The foregoing analysis confirms one of the central points on which the "plant egoism" thesis rests. Plant personnel policy under codetermination is indeed characterized by a strong tendency toward conservative personnel policies. And, works councils are not unreceptive to technological change so long as the interests of the work force are not damaged by it.

However, the broader conclusions some plant egoism theorists want to draw from these tendencies call for more careful examination. Before we can hold works councils responsible for West German unions' alleged "loss of internal sovereignty" and "political paralysis" (Hohn 1988:168), we must place the conservatism of works councils on personnel policy into the broader context of the dual system.[31]

First, plant egoism, defined as a preference on the part of labor for job and income security, is not unique to Germany. Workers in firms in all countries always, to some extent, share an interest with management in the viability of the firm in which they are employed. What does of course differ cross-nationally is how this is expressed in labor's and employers' behavior. In the United States, for example, this plant egoism can take the form of coalitions between labor and management for protectionism. The U.S. steel industry is a case in point. Another expression of the same phenomenon is concession bargaining. In the Chrysler bailout, for example, the UAW made major wage and pension concessions to management in order to save the jobs of some Chrysler workers.

31. Such broad conclusions about the weakness of German labor also do not stand up to comparative analysis. In Chapters 7 and 9 I demonstrate that German unions are in fact holding up much better in the crisis, and are far less paralyzed politically, than their counterparts in most of the other advanced capitalist countries.

That plant egoism does not (generally) find expression in protectionism or in wage concessions in Germany is explained by the larger structure of interest representation in which codetermination is embedded. The dual system in fact poses structural barriers to these options. In Chapter 1 I argue that part of the stability of the dual system has to do with its rigidities, and this is a case in point. Protectionism plays a much smaller role in adjustment in Germany in part because—plant egoism or no—the overarching system of multi-industrial unionism makes it hard for protectionist pleas from particular firms and even industries to find political expression. The IG Metall cannot (and will not) intervene to save particular plants or industries in this way because it is not in the interest of a multi-industrial union in an export-dependent country to do so.[32]

Wage concessions are another expression of plant egoism that runs up against structural barriers in Germany. Although works councils may concede firm-specific benefits (pensions, for example) in plant negotiations, they legally cannot (even if they wanted to) concede wage gains and other benefits that are binding for the entire industry.[33] In the episode that perhaps most closely resembles the Chrysler case, AEG-Telefunken's near-bankruptcy in the early 1980s, the works council was forced to accept cutbacks in the firm's pension benefits, but wage gains negotiated by the central union still stuck. Again, the rigidities of the dual system stabilize it in this way.

My point is that plant egoism is not unique to Germany, but the way it is expressed there (because of the rigidities of the dual system) is more compatible with negotiated adjustment than in other countries. It is compatible with *adjustment* because, unlike protectionism, it does not hinder the more efficient reallocation of resources (though it does affect how this is accomplished). And it is more compatible with *negotiated* adjustment because unlike in concession bargaining, nationally defined minimum standards (wage and employment standards

32. This raises another point that the plant egoism theory—which stresses plant productivity coalitions and labor *cooperation*—obscures, namely that other, *noncooperative* examples of the plant egoism phenomenon can also be found in Germany. Plant occupations in the face of the threat of plant closure are perhaps the most extreme expression of plant egoism imaginable. Yet such acts of labor militancy have little to do with the phenomenon that plant egoism theorists stress, for they represent the opposite of collaborative labor-management relations. Plant occupations are still a relative rarity in Germany, but they have increased in number in the crisis of the 1970s and 1980s (Ziegenfuß, Heseler, and Kröger 1984; König, Ostertag, and Schultz 1985; Blank and Unterhinninghofen 1983; and Hautsch and Semmler 1983). However, despite repeated calls for the national union to sanction and support these (plant-egoistic) acts of defense, the IG Metall has held firm to a position that the union will not financially support plant occupations, though of course expressions of solidarity flow freely. See the "Stellungnahme des Vorstandes zum Initiativantrag Nr. 4" of the Fourteenth IG Metall National Congress (Frankfurt: IG Metall Vorstandsverwaltung).

33. Unless the firm withdraws from the employers' organization and bargains separately with the union, but this is quite rare.

achieved in central collective bargaining) and relatively more generous social and unemployment benefits (achieved in part through labor's national political strength) still apply to the affected workers.

The second limitation of the plant egoism thesis is its virtually exclusive emphasis on the employment question. It is certainly true that the IG Metall would prefer works councils to pressure employers to hire new workers, and the union has criticized them for agreeing to excessive overtime, especially in Germany's high unemployment regions. However, a one-sided emphasis on plant employment policy obscures the many other areas in which the interests of the central union and plant works councils (even egoistic ones) converge.

The concept of plant egoism is too broadly construed for the empirical observation on which it is based. Understanding the interplay between central and plant-level labor representation in the dual system requires that we break down the concept into its component assumptions and systematically distinguish those points on which the interests of the two converge and diverge. On the employment question there is evidence of divergence (although of course the IG Metall is not in favor of employment and income *in*security). However, on other issues the central union's interests are identical with those of plant works councils.

This is in fact the point at which not the rigidities of the dual system, but its *flexibilities* are important. Codetermination has given the union an alternative, second avenue for pursuing labor's interests in *particular* plants and industries. The Grundig case cited above is an example of the way a works council, in its own "egoistic" interest perhaps, strove for a solution to the *particular* skill and employment problems that plague consumer electronics. Indeed, the union adopted the "employment plan" option as a model for the entire industry. In this case, the goals of the central union and the works council did not compete with, but complemented each other. The examples from the automobile industry of agreements works councils have achieved to alleviate the negative skill and income effects of new technologies are further examples of this point.

On other issues as well, works councils' behavior coincides with the union's interests. For instance, works councils generally fight tenaciously to get firms to offer apprentices permanent positions after their training period expires. In addition, they recruit new members for the union, and this is facilitated by the fact that one of the first places a newly hired employee is sent is to the works council office (interviews, 1985). Finally, on the many other issues where the works council intervenes on behalf of a worker or group of workers (on plant-specific, even trivial issues), these workers view it as the union representing their interests. As one union official put it: "When a works councillor does something for a worker, like get his son a job, that worker sees it as something the union did for him, personally. That strengthens his connection to the union; it is the small things that often count" (interview, 1987). As pointed out above, the IG Metall dominates works councils even in little-organized plants. Thus, by performing these functions, the works council system helps maintain a union presence even where the union itself is not particularly strong.

In sum, the "plant egoism" thesis is often premised on a very zero-sum conception of the relationship between central union and shop-floor strength (see especially Hohn 1988:162–67), and obscures the many ways in which works council strength itself helps sustain central union power. This point echoes a more general conclusion in organization theory. Martin Landau and Eva Eagle (1981) argue that decentralization in an organization need not necessarily imply a weakening of central authority. Indeed, where the upper and lower levels of an organization have complementary interests, delegation of authority and strong decentralized powers can enhance rather than detract from central power. The emphasis in the plant egoism theory on employment obscures the many areas in which such a harmony of interests between the central union and works councils exists. More concretely, the areas of converging interests cited above help explain why the IG Metall would rather live with works councils (even egoistic ones) than do without them.

A final point is in order regarding the so-called Japanization of German industrial relations.[34] Some scholars have drawn parallels between the tendency in Germany toward the closure of plant labor markets and lifetime employment in the Japanese core economy. This analogy is in itself not altogether misplaced; my criticism again is that it takes German codetermination out of its broader context. Whatever similarities may exist at a plant level, German and Japanese labor relations are worlds apart at almost every other level.

What of course fundamentally distinguishes the two is that organized labor in Japan lacks the strong structure of national unionism that is an essential feature (indeed the other half) of Germany's dual system. One of the enduring features of the German political economy is its strong tradition of centralization, and such historically entrenched structures are highly resistant to sudden change (Shonfield 1969; see also Katzenstein 1987). More specifically, there may be plant egoism in Germany, but so is there a strong overarching "superego" in the country's national unions, led by the IG Metall. Works councillors are not unaware of this and openly admit, in the words of one, that "we are nothing without the IG Metall" (interview, 1985).

Christoph Deutschmann (1988) makes a complementary argument, which however, unlike mine, has an important cultural component. Japan's less legalistic system of shop-floor relations is premised on what

---

34. See especially Tokunaga and Bergmann, 1984, where this is a recurring theme.

he calls "generalized social exchange within unequal and hierarchical power relationships" (1988:6). Although Deutschmann avoids the term paternalism, he describes shop-floor relationships as involving a degree of "personal commitment" on the part of employees and "benevolence" on the part of employers (1988:7). Relations between labor and capital at the plant level are thus very different from those in Germany, which are based on a highly elaborated, though general, body of (universally binding) rules.[35] Deutschmann thus reaches similar conclusions via a somewhat different route. For him, the "cultural incompatibility [in Germany, and the "West" generally] of generalized exchange with unequal power relationships" (which is in turn embedded in the institutions of labor relations) accounts for why the "Japanisation of management and industrial relations is not on the agenda in West Germany" (1988:20, 22).

Thus, in the end, the institutional and the cultural explanations point in the same direction. But what I wish to emphasize here is that analogies between Germany and Japan that stop at the plant level distort the German picture by overlooking those forces that hold the dual system together *as a system*. The resemblance between the two countries ends as soon as one considers that Germany's works councils move in a political economy in which there is a strong national leadership capable of defining a national agenda for labor. The IG Metall may currently be on the defensive, but the union is still a formidable political force in Germany, and a powerful opponent as well in national collective bargaining. Plant egoism accounts for some centrifugal tensions in the dual system, but strong centripetal forces are present as well in the overarching structure of national unionism and centralized bargaining. How the "center" continues to hold in Germany—even in a period when labor's market and political strength have reached a postwar nadir—is the subject of the next chapter.

35. Deutschmann cites telling examples of Japanese subsidiaries in West Germany that have been taken to court by the union or works council for violating codetermination or collective bargaining regulations, or for failing to adhere to national laws governing employment relations (Deutschmann 1988:21–22).

CHAPTER SEVEN

Contemporary Trends in Central Bargaining

The previous chapter described how an important role fell to plant works councils in Germany's "negotiated adjustment" as tensions grew between the IG Metall and employers at the national level in the late 1970s. This chapter and the next will document how subsequent conflicts between the union and employers have been resolved within the dual system. The discussion will focus on two issues that have risen to the top of the union's agenda in recent years, unemployment and technological change. I will demonstrate how the changing content of conflict between labor and capital has influenced the bargaining process and the locus of conflict and cooperation within the dual system.

The balance within the dual system is shifting toward plant-level bargaining. This change, while significant, has been gradual. Like the evolution of the dual system itself, it has taken place as a result of ongoing adjustments as employers and the union maneuver for position in response to changes in the external context. The resilience of the dual system lies in the way it has accommodated these changes in the face of the new challenges of the 1980s and 1990s.

NEOLIBERALISM AND THE POLITICS OF
WORKING-TIME REDUCTION

The IG Metall's strategic response to the persistent problem of unemployment was the union's now famous demand for a thirty-five-hour workweek. Negotiations between the IG Metall and Gesamtmetall over weekly working-time reduction provide a window on how macropolitical and macroeconomic changes have transformed central collective bargaining and redefined relations within the dual system.

The union's struggle for a shorter workweek shows the strains central-ized bargaining between labor and capital is likely to undergo in the face of high structural unemployment and a political shift toward the ascendance of neoliberalism and a market-led model of economic adjustment. It shows as well how strong the institutions of central bargaining in Germany are.

By 1990 the IG Metall had reached three agreements with Gesamtmetall that together reduce the workweek to thirty-five hours by 1995, thus ending a campaign begun over a decade before.[1] But the negotiations over working-time reduction introduced a relatively new feature into central bargaining, in that negotiations centered not only on the working-time issue, but also on the balance between central agreements and flexibility at the plant level. Until the late 1970s, under conditions of full employment and under the cyclical strain of inflationary pres-sures, collective bargaining revolved primarily around wages. Central contracts established universally binding "floors" on wages and working conditions. In the 1980s, central negotiations over working-time reduc-tion, however, produced no universally binding regulations, but instead defined the parameters for a second round of negotiations at the plant level. Opening clauses in the central agreements delegated important responsibilities to plant works councils, which are not to simply admin-ister the central agreements, but to actively shape their implementation in the plant.

Wolfgang Streeck's insightful analysis (1984c) provides a starting point for interpreting these pressures toward greater flexibility in central bargaining. He argues that the deterioration of labor's market power in the face of rising unemployment and the changing character of international competition have produced pressures for a decentrali-zation of bargaining. According to Streeck, neocorporatist bargaining under conditions of continuing high unemployment is increasingly characterized by employer efforts to relax the "rigidities" imposed by central bargaining and to exploit labor's market weakness to "restore flexibility to a bargained economy" through the reintroduction of market pressures into neocorporatist arrangements (1984c:298).

The deterioration of labor's market power now means that where central unions were once useful in maintaining wage stability, high unemployment now guarantees moderate wage settlements. In Streeck's words: "If trade unions...lack the clout to 'distort the market,' why should employers make any, even if only symbolic concessions to them for agreeing not to do so?" (1984c:293). At the same time, the growing

---

1. In fact, the demand for a thirty-five-hour workweek goes all the way back to 1977, when it was first discussed at the IG Metall's national congress. As discussed in Chapter 5, this became the union's demand for the steel industry the following year. The IG Metall first made a *general* reduction of weekly working hours its central demand in collective bargaining in 1984.

volatility of international markets has meant that employers now place a premium on their ability to respond flexibly to changes in demand. This flexibility is in their eyes incompatible with unified central bargaining, which produces "a body of (jointly agreed) central rules and regulations that, especially under critical economic conditions is experienced by the individual firm as rigid, inflexible, and severely constraining its adaptive responses to market contingencies" (1984c:294). This argument dovetails with the "plant egoism" argument discussed in the previous chapter, in that plant-level cooperation between labor and management, and the phenomenon of "workplace-based productivity alliances parallels and reinforces . . . the pressures from employers for a relaxation of corporatist controls over the work-place" (1984c:297; see also Hohn 1988: especially 168–69).

The new flexibility in central agreements on working time reduction in the German metalworking industries is surely related in part to a deterioration of labor's market power. Unemployment currently stands at 6.4 percent, after a post-reconstruction high of 9.3 percent in 1985 (*The Economist*, 23 February 1991:115; Adamy and Bosch 1989:272). As mentioned above, concession bargaining that exempts particular plants or firms from centrally negotiated regulations is difficult in the German context, since employers are reluctant to bargain with the union individually, and because works councils are legally bound to enforce and administer central bargains in the plant. But opening clauses in the central contracts on working-time reduction allowing for different working-time arrangements across plants inject new flexibility into central contracts by providing the basis for adapting the central bargain to the particular situation of individual firms. Such flexibility is what the union had to concede in exchange for progress on the working-time issue.

However, emphasizing labor's market weakness obscures the connection between this trend and the changing *content* of collective bargaining in the 1980s and 1990s. Understanding the trend toward "flexible" central bargains, as well as its implications for relations within the dual system, requires an examination as well of the changing political context of the struggle over working-time reduction. Furthermore, these developments demonstrate the tensions in Germany's dual system but also its continued resiliency. Pressures for a decentralization of bargaining have been resolved not in a wholesale retreat from central bargaining, nor even in the "hiving off" of particular plants or industries for exemption from central regulation, but rather by incorporating flexibility into central contracts themselves and assigning greater power to plant works councils.

Viewed in comparative perspective, it is clear that while plant egoism may be strong in Germany, the "superego" in the dual system (the central union) is also strong. The institutions of central bargaining still pose a powerful, countervailing, centripetal force, even in the face of new pressures for decentralization. In light of organized labor's relative market and political weakness in the 1980s (and compared to the effect neoliberalism has had on organized labor in Britain and the United States) what is in fact remarkable about the German case is that the "center" has held so well.

In Chapter 5 I argued that the trend in Germany since the mid-1970s has been toward the gradual abandonment of Keynesianism in favor of neoliberal, market-led solutions to adjustment. This shift constitutes a fundamental change in labor's political environment that has thrown into question the central union's traditional role in macroeconomic steering (Sabel 1986:47–51). The nature of the change and its implications for labor are summarized by Benjamin Coriat: "Labor, previously regarded as a constituent of demand and a stimulus to growth, [is increasingly] viewed as a cost, an obstacle to the accumulation of capital" (Coriat 1984:45). The reorientation in collective bargaining in the metalworking industry away from wage minimums and toward the terms of employment thus follows a macropolitical trend toward supply-side rather than demand-side macroeconomic steering: conflicts between labor and capital focus on labor as a factor of production and not of demand.

Employer strategies reflect the neoliberal agenda and respond to the changing character of competition in international markets to the extent that they now emphasize the need for labor flexibility—and not wage restraint—as the key to competitiveness. As noted above, employers increasingly stress their need to respond quickly not only to changes in the level of demand (through hiring and firing, the use of part-time or fixed-contract workers, and the use of overtime), but also in the content of demand (by reassigning workers within the plant, for example).

The IG Metall has responded as well to changes in the macropolitical and macroeconomic context, and of course to the agenda employers have set. Chapter 5 documented the union's increasing emphasis on "qualitative" issues such as employment and technological change. These "qualitative" demands speak directly to non-wage components of the labor process, and touch on questions of production organization that have become so contentious over the past decade (Katz and Sabel 1985; Sabel 1986). Where the union was once an unquestioning supporter of industrial modernization and restructuring, under conditions of high structural unemployment union strategies reflect a growing concern with such production questions. These issues are important in their own right; but the union also sees a return to full employment as a precondition for resuming the redistributive demands of the 1960s and 1970s. Or, put somewhat differently, the most pressing redistributive issue the union faced in the 1980s was a redistribution of employment, not wages.

Thus, along with a number of other authors, I subscribe to the thesis that the crisis of capital accumulation in the advanced capitalist countries that accompanied the macroeconomic changes of the late 1970s and 1980s poses particularly serious problems for national unions like the IG Metall (see for example, Streeck 1984c; Sabel 1986). But an examination of recent negotiations over working time reduction demonstrates not only the tensions in, but also the resiliency of, central bargaining in the dual system.

Specific macroeconomic and political shifts have provided the context for the current renegotiation of labor-capital relations in central collective bargaining in Germany. The IG Metall responded to the deterioration in the 1980s of its political and labor market power by adopting a strategy of reducing weekly working time in order to reduce unemployment. This initiative was pressed in three collective bargaining rounds—in 1984, 1987, and 1990—in which the union and employers clashed over both the working-time and the flexibility issues. These negotiations have been extremely important to relations between the central union leadership and the shop floor in terms both of stability and of change in the dual system.

LABOR MARKETS AND POLITICS UNDER THE CONSERVATIVE GOVERNMENT

The Social-Liberal government of the 1970s and early 1980s finally collapsed under the weight of growing conflicts within the coalition, primarily over economic policy. In 1982, the Free Democrats formed a coalition with the conservative Christian Democratic Union (CDU) and its Bavarian wing, the Christian Social Union (CSU). Werner Sengenberger sees this political shift as the culmination of a trend toward the gradual abandonment of what he calls "socially controlled welfare capitalism" for "unrestrained market capitalism" (1984:323, 326).

Despite growing criticism from the unions, the SPD–F.D.P. coalition never fundamentally abandoned the austerity course it charted in 1975. In fact, as one of its last acts in government, the coalition— primarily at the behest of the Free Democratic Party—pushed through further budget cuts on social and unemployment programs. The so-called Budget Operation 1982 consisted of two important measures. First a new, revised Budget Structure Law (Haushaltsstrukturgesetz) cut state unemployment benefits by tightening eligibility requirements through the redefinition of "acceptable work" and by excluding from the base figure for calculating benefits portions of workers' previous incomes such as "overtime payments, vacation allowances, and the (widespread) thirteenth month of wage and salary income" (Sengenberger

159

1984:334; also Bäcker 1984:250).[2] The second measure, the "Consolidation of the Work Promotion Law" (*Arbeitsförderungskonsolidierungsgesetz*) of the same year reduced government spending on active labor market policies by tightening eligibility requirements and allowances for state-sponsored training and retraining programs (Cichon 1986:33).

When the conservative government came to power in 1982, it increased government spending again on active labor market policies slightly, but continued the policy of fiscal austerity and further reduced benefits for various social programs. In 1984, for example, the CDU government cut unemployment benefits for persons with no children from sixty-eight percent to sixty-three percent of their previous net income (again, with supplemental payments left out of the base figure). The government also "reduced benefits for the handicapped, and altered maternity leave, state pensions and childrens' allowances" (Sengenberger 1984:335). With unemployment over two million and rising, critics of the government's social policy began to talk of the "new poor" in Germany and of the development of a "two-thirds society" in which the cleavage between the country's "haves" and "have nots" was growing (*Die Zeit*, 23 January 1987; Bäcker 1984:249–51).

The conservative shift in Germany was milder than in Britain and the United States. However, while the government's social policies left more of Germany's "social net" intact, the tone and thrust of economic policy under the conservatives took a decisive turn toward neoliberalism and an emphasis on market-led solutions to economic adjustment. As Sengenberger puts it: "It is no longer the fiscal problem that is the key argument for dismantling social policies. Now there is a more explicit advocacy of outright labor market competition on ideological grounds" (Sengenberger 1984:328).

Labor market policies reflected this shift. The government's answer to unemployment was to relax rigidities in the labor market that in its view impeded the free (and therefore most efficient) allocation and reallocation of resources. Through "deregulation" of the labor market the conservative government sought to "restore worker competition" (Sengenberger 1984:323).[3]

The centerpiece legislation in this market-oriented approach to unemployment was the Employment Promotion Act of 1985 (*Beschäftigungsförderungsgesetz*).[4] This law enhanced flexibility in the labor market in four ways (Bosch and Seifert 1984). First, the law allowed employers,

2. State employment compensation provided workers with 68 percent of previous net income. The exclusion of these allowances reduced benefits to between 57.6 and 63.6 percent of previous income (Sengenberger 1984:334).

3. This of course was not the whole of the Kohl government's campaign on unemployment. In 1984, for example, the government offered foreign ("guest") workers cash incentives to return to their homelands.

4. For a text of the law see *Bundesgesetzblatt* 21, 1985. For commentary on the law, see Kittner 1985.

without special justification, to hire new workers (or extend regular employment to graduating apprentices) on a fixed-term basis for up to eighteen months (Bosch 1986:276–80). In plants with fewer than twenty workers, the new law allowed for fixed contracts of up to two years (Kittner 1985:10). Second, the law relaxed limitations on firms' use of subcontracted ("loaned") workers (*Leiharbeiter*). It extended the maximum tenure of such workers from three to six months at a time (Bosch 1986:276–80; Kittner 1985:24).

Third, the 1985 law sought to encourage part-time work and job sharing by clarifying and regulating certain elements of their legal status. The use of such measures would allow employers to avoid the high wage-supplement costs of hiring full-time workers and to pursue "capacity-oriented," variable plant working time (Kittner 1985:13–18). And fourth, the new legislation impinged on codetermination by redefining some of the conditions under which employers must negotiate a "social plan" with their works councils over major layoffs not brought about in connection with changes in the plant (Kittner 1985:18–21). In short, the thrust of the law was to facilitate greater flexibility in plant personnel policy by making it easier to use workers whose status is less regulated through collective bargaining and codetermination.[5]

Thus, the core of the conservative government's employment policy was cutbacks in benefits for the unemployed on the one hand, and greater labor market flexibility on the other (Kreye 1986). The direction the CDU/CSU–F.D.P. coalition wanted to take German labor market policy (i.e. toward greater flexibility) was clear from the moment the government took office. And it was against the background of these political developments that the IG Metall introduced its demand for a general reduction of weekly working times to thirty-five hours as its alternative solution to Germany's unemployment problem.

THE BATTLE FOR WEEKLY WORKING-TIME REDUCTION

The union's campaign to reduce weekly working hours through collective bargaining was as much a sign of German labor's political weakness as it was of the IG Metall's industrial power and self-confidence. Between 1978 and 1983, unemployment in the Federal Republic had more than doubled, from just under one million to 2.3 million.[6] For the union, the idea behind weekly working-time reduction was to find a

5. See also Adamy, 1988, whose analysis of the law complements mine. Adamy stresses how the law promotes plant personnel policies based on external rather than internal flexibility (*unternehmensexterner Flexibilität*).

6. The unemployment rate shot from 4.3 percent to 9.1 percent between 1978 and 1983. See ILO *Yearbook of Labour Statistics* (Geneva: International Labour Office, 1986).

way to redistribute a shrinking volume of work across a larger number of workers in order to counteract a strong trend—reinforced by the government policies described above—toward divisions within the working class between the employed and the unemployed, between rationalization's winner and losers.

At its 1983 congress, union delegates voted to pursue the thirty-five-hour workweek not just for the steel industry (as in 1978), but for the metalworking industries as a whole, and indeed to make it the union's number one priority in collective bargaining.[7] With that, the stage was set for a showdown with the Association of West German Employers in the Metalworking Industries (Gesamtmetall); in demanding a thirty-five hour week the union went straight for an employer "taboo."

The 1984 Bargaining Round

For the IG Metall even more was at stake in the 1984 bargaining round than working time reduction. The previous three wage bargaining rounds had taken place in the context of recession, and the union had twice settled for real wage losses (in 1981 and 1982), a first since reconstruction. In 1983, the union's new president, Hans Mayr, declared: "We need again, finally, a success, after we have been able to show so little for the last three years" (quoted in Bahnmüller 1985:31). What was at stake for the union was its very ability to represent and defend workers' interests at a time when its political and market strength was low. Referring to the looming conflict over working-time reduction, the union's head of collective bargaining, Hans Janßen, stated: "We openly admit that... we are also defending our strength to defend workers' interests... [this] strength cannot be sealed up in a bottle and saved for better times" (quoted in Bahnmüller 1985:31).

From Gesamtmetall's perspective as well, the stakes in the 1984 conflict were very high. The national employers' association (BDA) categorically opposed any reduction of the regular workweek below forty hours. A settlement in the all-important metalworking industries would surely open the way for working-time reduction in all of German industry. It was up to Gesamtmetall to prevent this.

Thus, the stage was set for an historic conflict. Yet unlike the British miners' strike (which occurred at the same time), this conflict was not to be a fight to the death. The compromise solution in Germany was working-time reduction with flexibility in its implementation. Central bargaining only established the parameters for a second round of bargaining in the plant. Thus, when the dust from this historic central confrontation had settled, it was up to the plant works councils and

---

7. One of the compromises the IG Metall made in the 1978 bargaining round was to shelve its demand for reducing the workweek until at least 1983.

individual employers to determine the details of the implementation of the central agreement at the plant level.

The early (pre-negotiation) stages of the 1984 battle looked more like a national election campaign than the prelude to a collective bargaining round. The thirty-five-hour workweek became the focus of great public discussion and debate. Both employers and the union invested enormous resources into winning public support for their respective positions. Arguments and counterarguments supported by economic analyses and forecasts by both sides were daily fare in the national press.

The IG Metall launched a massive discussion and mobilization campaign in its plants in the months preceding the conflict. Indeed, surveys had shown that a large number of workers were not convinced by the union's posters, which proclaimed that thirty-five hours was "the right step" (Kurz-Scherf 1985:100–104; Bahnmüller 1985: chap. 3). After all, it was the presently employed who would have to endure the hardships of the strike (and almost certainly forego a higher wage settlement) on behalf of the unemployed. In the union's mobilization campaign, shop stewards and works councils argued that the thirty-five-hour workweek would not only reduce unemployment; it would also secure the jobs of the presently employed against labor-saving rationalization (Bahnmüller 1985:69–70).

The conservative government came out decisively against weekly working-time reduction. Chancellor Kohl publicly denounced the union's demand as "stupid and silly." Playing on tensions among the various DGB unions, the government introduced legislation to subsidize early retirement schemes in industries where unions signed contracts for lifetime employment reduction (early retirement) rather than weekly working-time reduction (*Frankfurter Allgemeine Zeitung*, 23 February 1984.[8] The timing of this maneuver was clearly designed to undermine support for the IG Metall's demand for *weekly* working-time reduction.[9] The union charged the government with taking sides in the conflict and encroaching on Germany's hallowed precept of "collective bargaining autonomy" (*Tarifautonomie*).

German workers may not be as class conscious as some of their European counterparts, but *union* consciousness runs deep in the metalworking industries. Despite the initial skepticism among the membership, the union won its strike votes handily. The mobilization campaign probably played a role, but so did the general feeling that a loss in the strike vote would irreparably cripple the union (Bahnmüller 1985:70). In May 1984, strike ballots were held in Baden-Württemberg and Hessen. In both districts, the union won with over 80 percent of the vote, a safe 5 percent margin over the 75 percent it needed by

8. Some of the unions—led by the IG Chemie—had expressed a preference for early retirement over weekly working-time reduction.
9. The law went into effect just two days before the first strike vote in Baden-Württemberg.

union statute to call what would become the longest strike in the history of the Federal Republic.

The story of the strike has been told elsewhere (see, for example, Bahnmüller 1985). Here, I will focus on the positions employers and the union took as the bargaining process unfolded, and on the outcome itself. Intransigence on both sides at the outset of the conflict gradually gave way to negotiations over parameters rather than absolute levels of working-time reduction, or in other words, over what working-time issues would be centrally regulated and what would be decided at the plant level. The core of the compromise, then, was the incorporation of "flexibility" into the central agreement.

The early stages of the conflict made clear that the struggle would be long. Four weeks into the strike the bargaining partners had made little progress toward a compromise. Gesamtmetall continued to pressure the union with massive lockouts and to oppose all proposals for a general reduction of weekly working hours.[10] The employers did offer shift workers a reduction to a thirty-nine-hour workweek starting in February 1985, which would later be reduced further to thirty-eight hours (*Spiegel*, 18 June 1984:19). Predictably, however, the IG Metall refused the offer, which the union calculated would affect a mere 15 percent of its constituency. The union's counteroffer was to reduce working time for all workers to thirty-eight hours in 1985, and to thirty-seven hours by 1987. In the union proposal, if by the end of 1987 over 500,000 workers were still unemployed, weekly working time would be reduced another two hours by 1989 (*Spiegel*, 18 June 1984:19). Gesamtmetall refused to budge from its position of maintaining the regular forty-hour workweek for the vast majority of workers. Thus, well into the strike, the forty-hour taboo still held "religious character" according to some observers (*Spiegel*, 18 June 1984:18), and neither side appeared willing to compromise (see also *Die Zeit*, 29 June 1984:24).

By the strike's fifth week, the union and employers were both under considerable public pressure to resolve the dispute. Facing a continued deadlock, the union called for impartial mediation, and employers accepted the offer. Negotiations then moved to a new phase, though still against the backdrop of strikes and lockouts. Georg Leber, former head of the (moderate) construction workers' union, chaired the mediation proceedings with the conservative law professor Bernd Rüthers at his side (*Die Zeit*, 29 June 1984:18).

After almost a week of negotiations, culminating in an all-night session on 25–26 June, Leber announced his compromise solution. His plan called for a 3.3 percent wage increase for 1984 and a 1.5 hour

10. All told, 60,000 workers went on strike, 150,000 were locked out, and another 310,000 workers were idled due to parts and supply shortages related to the strike (the so-called cold lockout) (Silvia 1988:165; see also Kurz-Scherf 1985:113).

reduction in the workweek beginning 1 April 1985. To maintain wages in a shorter workweek, Leber proposed a 3.9 percent raise beginning on 1 April 1985 and a 2 percent wage increase beginning on the same date for the duration of the contract (*International Herald Tribune*, 27 June 1984:1). Leber's compromise solution allowed for flexibility in applying the bargain within the individual plants. According to his proposal, works councils and managers would negotiate in a second round of bargaining over how to implement working-time reduction, e.g., whether to cumulate the hours into free days or distribute them over all or some days of the week. Both sides agreed to the Leber compromise, which allowed for working-time reduction *with* flexibility through a second round of plant negotiations with works councils.

The core of the compromise, then, was a trade-off in which the employers agreed to a regular 38.5 hour workweek in exchange for flexibility in implementing the central bargain at the plant level.[11] The contract gave employers new flexibility in two forms, which in Germany are referred to as "differentiation" and "flexibilization." First, the contract's *differentiation* clause allowed employers (in negotiations with plant works councils) to distribute working-time reduction unevenly across the work force. That is, some workers could continue with a regular forty-hour workweek, while others worked shorter regular hours, so long as a 38.5 hour average was maintained across all workers in the plant. Gesamtmetall was particularly eager to exempt skilled workers from working-time reduction, anticipating skill shortages and higher production costs associated with hiring additional qualified workers. The differentiation clause was so important because it injected new flexibility into the very definition of full-time work. Whereas before employers generally faced a choice between hiring full-time workers (at forty hours) or part-time workers, the 1984 contract recast the question of working time in terms of a plant average. Working times for individual workers would be set in plant negotiations, with the parameters (thirty-seven to forty hours) specified in the central contract.

Second, the contract's *flexibilization* clause gave employers room for working time flexibility *over time*. Daily or weekly working time reductions were only one possibility. Other combinations were allowable, so long as the 38.5 average was achieved within a two-month "balancing" period (*Ausgleichszeit*).[12]

Both these issues—differentiated working times for different workers and flexibility over time—would be decided in plant-level negotiations between works councils and management. While the union billed the outcome as a great victory (a "broken taboo"), employers heralded the

11. The terms of the contract are laid out in Kurz-Scherf 1985:76–81.

12. Working-time reduction could, for example, be cumulated into free days, which employers viewed as less disruptive to production than union proposals such as one hour off on Fridays and another half-hour off on Thursdays.

retreat from "rigid central agreements" as an important step forward. The political analyst Theo Sommer wrote in July 1984 that with the new agreement "we have all entered uncharted territory. Flexibilization ... and the shift of important decisions from the central union and employers' organizations down to the plants fit with the differentiated and increasingly more differentiated modern working world, in which central, all-encompassing deals no longer make sense, but rather sectoral, and even firm-specific rules are more appropriate" (*Die Zeit*, 13 July 1984:1). The fact that both sides could claim victory in 1984 had to do with the common ground they had found: the union got the working-time reduction it had sought (though not to thirty-five hours), and employers won new flexibility in the working-time question.

Denouement in the Plant

The flexibility in the central contract on working-time reduction meant that the 1984 bargaining round was not over when union representatives and employers shook hands in the various bargaining regions. As soon as they signed the contract, both sides began counseling their respective constituencies on how to proceed. The IG Metall advised works councils not to negotiate without first receiving instructions and feedback from the union (*Handelsblatt*, 16 July 1984:1). The union prepared and disseminated a full explanation of the agreement with instructions, including model plant agreements. Above all, union leaders hoped to thwart employer efforts to exploit the contract's differentiation clause. Under the motto "38.5 for *all* workers," they urged works councils to resist attempts by employers to split the work force by negotiating different working-time rules for different groups of workers (*Frankfurter Allgemeine Zeitung*, 27 August 1984; *Handelsblatt*, 21 August 1984).

The employers meanwhile launched their own offensive, encouraging individual companies to take full advantage of the working-time flexibility won in the 1984 round. In a brochure distributed to member firms entitled "Working-Time Flexibilization: The New Collective Bargain as Opportunity," the national employers' association detailed several models of working-time rules showing how firms could use the differentiation and flexibilization clauses to avoid skill shortages and maximize investment returns by introducing or expanding shift work (BDA 1984b).

Plant negotiations over the application of the agreement ran from July 1984 to April 1985. Very early on it became clear that despite the entreaties of the employers' association, very few plant agreements included provisions for differentiated working times for different categories of workers. The IG Metall's vice president Franz Steinkühler had correctly predicted that works councils were likely to fight "differentiation" agreements that deprived some workers of any working time reduction. Or more to the point, skilled workers would resist being singled out to continue working a regular forty-hour workweek, if for no other reason because longer base working times would deprive them of overtime supplements for the extra hours (*Handelsblatt*, 27 August 1984). Equally important, the differentiation formulas worked out in the BDA brochure were simply too complex and unwieldy to spark great interest, especially in small- and middle-sized firms lacking a personnel department to administer complicated working time models.

In the end, works councils in only 13 percent of all plants concluded agreements using the contract's differentiation clause (WSI 1986). And even where they did, the number of workers affected was generally very small. A WSI survey of over 3,300 plants in the metalworking industries found that only 5.7 percent of all workers in the metalworking industries ended up with regular working times different from (i.e., either above or below) 38.5 hours (WSI 1986).[13] Thus, the union was by and large able to achieve its goal of 38.5 hours for all workers, though lack of interest in differentiation among employers had played a larger role in this outcome than anyone originally expected.

Where considerable variation did emerge in the second round of plant negotiations on the 1984 contract was working-time flexibility *over time*. Here a variety of models emerged. According to the same WSI report, just under 50 percent (47.7) had concluded *weekly* working-time reductions.[14] Another 8.3 percent distributed working-time reduction over two or more weeks. Thirty percent of all plant agreements called for cumulation of working-time reduction into free days, often situated on "window" days in between holidays and weekends (WSI 1986).[15]

As employers introduced a new generation of expensive production technologies, machine utilization rates became especially important. Employers used the flexibilization clause to relax the link between machine times and working times in order to more fully exploit their capital investments. Thus, in many plants, managers linked negotiations over the application of the central contract to locally bargained issues such as the introduction of shift work or other changes in working-time arrangements (interviews, 1985).

The 1984 bargaining round was a turning point in many respects. The union put much on the line and did not lose. In light of the

13. The WSI (Wirtschafts- und Sozialwissenschaftliches Institut des Deutschen Gewerkschaftsbundes, Institute of Economics and Social Science of the German Labor Federation) is a union-affiliated research institute.

14. These agreements reduced weekly working times variously—through daily reductions of eighteen minutes, or other combinations such as one hour on Fridays, one-half hour on Thursdays, or an hour and a half off on Fridays.

15. Fourteen percent of all plants in the survey had adopted various "mixed models," involving a combination of forms.

difficult market and political situation in which the IG Metall found itself at the start of the conflict, this achievement in itself is significant. The price the union paid was flexibility in the central contract. The critical task of actively implementing the agreement in the plants fell to the works councils. In the second round, differentiation was not as significant a factor as many had thought. But employers did gain new flexibility by linking negotiations over working-time reduction with efforts to extend machine utilization rates by decoupling machine times from working times. Three years later, another agreement on further working-time reduction would hinge on a similar compromise.

The 1987 Bargaining Round

The 1984 contract had stipulated that the issue of further working-time reduction could not be reopened until 1987. Throughout 1985 and 1986, however, the union emphasized that it would again make the thirty-five-hour workweek its primary demand in negotiations with Gesamtmetall in 1987.

In some respects, the political situation had grown worse for the union. In 1986 the conservative government had passed a new law that made it very difficult—if not impossible—for the union to wage the kind of national strike it had in 1984.[16] The new legislation—a revision of paragraph 116 of the Work Promotion Act, or AFG 116—eliminated unemployment benefits for workers affected by the so-called cold lockout that had figured so prominently in the previous strike. Workers in a "cold" lockout are those who are laid off because of parts shortages due to strikes and lockouts in other (non-struck) bargaining districts.

Depriving these workers of state benefits would undermine the union's "mini-max" strike strategy, which had proved so successful in 1984. By targeting a few key supplier plants, the union had been able to paralyze the entire automobile industry (thus producing a maximum impact while calling a minimum of workers out). Since it paid strike support only to workers in the struck districts, the union depended on other affected workers (those locked out "cold") being able to collect unemployment checks. But under the revised AFG 116 these workers are no longer entitled to state benefits if the union's demand in their own bargaining region is the same as in the struck district. The only way around the new law would be for the union to introduce substantial variation in its demands across bargaining districts. Either way, the new AFG 116 was designed to disrupt the union's national strategy and make it too costly for the IG Metall to hold out in a long national strike.

Despite the advantage the new law gave them, employers opted not to push the union toward a strike in 1987. Indeed, after the bitter clash

16. See especially Silvia's (1988) excellent analysis of the conflict over this law.

of 1984, and further conflict in 1986 over AFG 116, the tenor in both camps was surprisingly calm leading up to the 1987 bargaining round. The IG Metall president Hans Mayr, who had led the union through the 1984 strike, had been an interim president. When he retired in 1986, the leadership of the union passed to Franz Steinkühler, Mayr's vice president and a man long considered the union's enfant terrible by employers in the metalworking industries. As head of the union's stronghold of Baden-Württemberg in the 1970s, Steinkühler had earned a reputation as an important figure in the "new generation" of union leaders, whose rhetoric at least was more radical than that of Mayr and the older generation.

The 1987 collective bargaining round was the union's first with Steinkühler at the helm, but if any evidence of the new president's fundamental pragmatism was needed, this round provided it. Steinkühler had scarcely been in office two weeks when he declared that the IG Metall was not opposed to flexibility per se, so long as it served workers' rather than only employers' interests. As Steinkühler put it, "Flexibilization is not a union demand, but if it gives workers more working time sovereignty... and choice, we cannot oppose it" (*Nürnberger Nachrichten*, 7 November 1986). The union had a very different idea of flexibility in mind from the employers, to be sure. However, Steinkühler's remark seemed to signal some room for negotiation, for it indicated that the conflict would center not so much on whether there would be flexibility but rather on whose notion of it would prevail. In a move designed to appropriate the concept and imbue it with the union's own meaning, the IG Metall drew up a position paper specifying how it defined acceptable working-time flexibility (IG Metall 1986).

The tenor within the employers' organization had also shifted significantly since 1984. Working-time reduction was no longer taboo. Although Gesamtmetall still opposed in principle a further reduction of the workweek, the employers made it clear well before the bargaining round that they were willing to discuss the issue, provided further flexibility could be made part of the package. The head of Gesamtmetall's Baden-Württemberg bargaining district, Hans-Peter Stihl, asserted, "We can only talk about working-time reduction as soon as we know whether and to what extent the IG Metall will accept further flexibilization. They cannot have one without the other" (*Handelsblatt*, 23 February 1987).

The 1987 round is remarkable in that, for the first time ever, Gesamtmetall went into bargaining *with its own set of demands* (*Manager Magazin*, January 1987:26). Two of those demands dominated the pre-negotiation debates. First, employers wanted to use negotiations over working-time reduction to establish Saturday as a regular workday. This aspect of the 1987 bargaining round is hard to square with a strict "decentralization of bargaining" thesis. Existing contracts only specified that the regular workweek should not exceed five days. *Which* five days was always an issue that was settled in plant negotiations between works councils and managers. Thus, the "work-free Saturday" the union found itself defending in 1987 was a matter of established plant practice rather than a binding contract (interviews, IG Metall and Gesamtmetall, 1987). What employers had in mind in 1987 was securing contractually the flexibility they in fact already had.

The other employer demand was greater flexibility in the distribution of work across time. As mentioned above, the 1984 contract required that plant working time arrangements maintain an average of 38.5 hours per week over a (maximum) two-month period. In 1987, employers wanted to relax this constraint and demanded an extension of the "balancing" period to twelve months (*Handelsblatt*, 23 February 1987). This extension would better enable managers to adapt working times to seasonal fluctuations in demand, while avoiding the expense of overtime.

The union opened negotiations simultaneously in several bargaining districts in February 1987. Little progress was made in the first several weeks of negotiations, as employers simply rejected demands for further working-time reductions. The IG Metall resisted the employers' demand for further flexibilization and called the issue of Saturday a "provocation" (*Stuttgarter Zeitung*, 20 February 1987).

In early March, employers surprised everyone by making an offer in Nordrhein-Westfalen in which they conceded a further one-half-hour working-time reduction in return for extending the "balancing" period to one year and including Saturday as a normal workday.[17] The new head of collective bargaining at the IG Metall, Klaus Zwickel, rejected the offer as "insufficient" (*Presse- und Funk Nachrichten*, 11 March 1987), and the IG Metall stepped up warning strike activity in several bargaining districts.

By early April 1987, negotiations in virtually all bargaining districts had broken down. But by this point, time was working to Gesamtmetall's advantage. With Easter vacation approaching, a strike would have to wait until late April. That would have given the union only seven weeks to reach an agreement before summer vacations began in early June, not ideal conditions for mobilizing for a strike or even threatening one. On 6 April, Steinkühler called Gesamtmetall president Werner Stumpfe and declared he was prepared to discuss a possible resolution to the conflict "any day from now on" (*Spiegel*, 13 April 1987:130). After several days, Stumpfe agreed to peak negotiations with the IG Metall leadership.

District negotiations were halted as delegations from the central

17. The proposal offered a 2.7 percent wage increase for 1987, and one-half-hour working-time reduction in 1988 (plus a further wage increase of 1.5%), in a contract that would run until mid-1991 (see *Presse- und Funk Nachrichten*, 11 March 1987).

union and Gesamtmetall met. At crucial junctures, Steinkühler and Stumpfe met alone ("unter vier Augen"). After thirteen hours of negotiations, the two reached a skeletal agreement that each would recommend to his regional representatives as the basis for settlements in the individual bargaining districts (*Spiegel*, 27 April 1987:43). Once again the compromise hinged on the trade-off between working-time reduction and plant flexibility in its application. The agreement also called for an (unprecedented) *three*-year working-time *and* wage contract.[18] Average weekly working time would be reduced in two steps to thirty-seven hours, with one hour off beginning in April 1988 and another half hour in April 1989. Nominal wage increases of 3.7 percent for 1987, 2.0 percent for 1988, and 2.5 percent for 1989 were concluded (Kurz-Scherf 1988a:88–89).

The agreement broadened the parameters for "flexibilization" (over time), but narrowed those for "differentiation" (among workers).[19] The central settlement extended the "balancing period" from two to six months, a partial victory for employers. However, the 1987 contract narrowed the parameters for differentiated working times from three hours (37 to 40 hours) to two and a half hours (36.5 to 39 hours).[20] The "bottom limit" (36.5 hours) was especially important to the union. It meant that for every worker with a regular work week of 39 hours, four other workers would have to be employed at 36.5 hours (to achieve a plant average of 37 hours). Placing this 36.5 hour floor on differentiation would prevent new workers' incomes from falling far behind that for workers with more hours (interview with Klaus Lang, collective bargaining department, IG Metall, 1987).[21]

Subsequent negotiations in the individual bargaining districts all adopted the central guidelines as the basis for regional contracts. On issues such as Saturdays and overtime, on which no central guidelines were established, a variety of regional settlements were reached (IG Metall 1987b). Most do not place further limits on overtime, to the disappointment of the union. But on balance, the union prevailed on the issue of Saturday. While most regional contracts simply reaffirmed

18. Contracts governing such issues as working times, payment systems, and other working conditions are regularly multi-year contracts; however, wage contracts only very rarely exceed twelve months.

19. This skeletal agreement provided no guidelines on the Saturday question. That issue, as well as limits on overtime, would be taken up in regional negotiations.

20. Throughout the negotiations, the IG Metall demonstrated more of a willingness to compromise on "flexibilization" than on "differentiation," despite the fact that many more workers were affected by the former than the latter. For a more complete discussion of the different effects of differentiation and flexibilization, and an analysis of the 1984 and 1987 bargaining rounds from this perspective, see Thelen 1989a.

21. The wage compensation the union negotiated for workers with fewer than thirty-seven hours applied only to those employed when the contract was signed. All new workers hired at fewer than thirty-seven hours would simply be paid at an hourly rate for fewer hours.

the status quo (i.e., Saturday work permissible with works council approval), some district contracts placed new restrictions on employers' ability to schedule regular work on Saturday.[22] It was an open secret in Germany that the employers' Saturday "offensive" had backfired.

The 1987 compromise was in many ways simply an extension of the 1984 settlement. In both rounds, the union subordinated wage demands to the working-time issue. And in 1987, the key trade-off was between further working-time reduction and the renegotiation of the parameters for its "flexible" implementation in the plant. In 1987 as in 1984, opening clauses left to a second round of negotiations how working times would be arranged at the plant level. Again it was up to individual plant works councils to implement the terms of the contract.

The 1990 Bargaining Round

In May 1990, the IG Metall and Gesamtmetall reached agreement on the further reduction of weekly working times to thirty-five hours, thus ending the conflict that had dominated labor politics in Germany for over a decade.[23] The contract calls for a two-step reduction, to thirty-six hours beginning in April 1993, and to thirty-five hours in October 1995. As in 1987, negotiations took place under the shadow of AFG 116. This time the union began mobilizing for a strike. But in the end the bargaining partners were again able to reach a settlement without industrial strife. As in both the previous two contracts on this issue, the key trade-off on which the 1990 compromise hinged was working-time reduction in exchange for flexibility in its application at the plant level.

Achieving closure on its long campaign for the thirty-five-hour workweek was a crucial breakthrough for the IG Metall. As the union's president Franz Steinkühler himself noted, the demand for weekly working-time reduction had absorbed the union's organizational energies and resources for over a decade, and its realization frees the union to turn its attention to other issues (*Handelsblatt*, 7 May 1990; *Der Gewerkschafter*, July 1990:6). Especially in the union's stronger districts, members were eager to put this campaign behind them and concentrate again on wages. Such sentiments only intensified after 1987 when the union had committed its members to modest (and nominal) wage increases for three years. As it turned out, real wages rose only slightly

22. In Hessen, for example, regular work can be scheduled only until noon on Saturdays; in Berlin, Saturday work requires the approval not just of the works council, but of the local union as well. In Baden-Württemberg, if employers cannot secure works council approval for Saturday work, they also cannot force it through recourse to arbitration (interview with Klaus Lang, 1987; see also IG Metall 1987b).

23. For the terms of the agreement see *Handelsblatt*, 10 May 1990, or IG Metall, 1990b. The latter also contains a summary of the negotiations and a breakdown of the results by bargaining district.

in 1987 and 1988, and they fell by 0.8% in 1989 (*Presse- und Funk Nachrichten* 14 May 1990:3).[24]

Since the agreement will give German workers, who already enjoy among the longest vacations in Europe, the shortest regular work week as well, union leaders were justified in claiming an "historic success" (*New York Times*, 9 October 1989:D8; *Der Gewerkschafter*, July 1990:6). However, the victory had not come without a cost, and the union had to make significant concessions of its own (see especially *Handelsblatt*, 8 May 1990). First, employers resisted union encroachments on a range of issues related to working times such as further contractual limits on overtime and weekend work, and various protections against work intensification. Second, employers succeeded in delaying when the new reductions in the workweek take effect until after 1992, the target date for European integration. The IG Metall also agreed to a clause that commits union representatives to engage in discussions with Gesamtmetall three months before each of the two one-hour reductions go into effect. The purpose of these discussions is to review the agreement in light of the general economic situation and developments in German unification and in the European Community (particularly with respect to working times in other EC countries). The clause holds out the possibility for the two sides to agree to postpone scheduled working-time reductions. However, employers could not get the union to agree to automatic postponements based on objectively defined conditions, and the contract gives Gesamtmetall no way to force such postponement (*Handelsblatt*, 8 May 1990 and 10 May 1990; IG Metall 1990a).

Third, as in the previous two bargaining rounds, the most important concession the IG Metall made was on the issue of working-time flexibility. While the union resisted employer demands to expand the "flexibilization" clause in the 1987 contract from six to twelve months, employers scored a crucial victory on the issue of "differentiation." According to the new agreement, up to 18 percent of all workers in a plant can—on a strictly voluntary basis—agree to continue with a regular forty-hour workweek.[25] Those who opt to do so are entitled either to be paid their regular wage for the extra hours, or to accumulate free time, which they can take in one or more blocks within a twenty-four-month time period.

This new differentiation clause differs in important ways from the

24. The 1990 contract again decoupled working time and wage negotiations. Wages were again covered by an agreement that extended for the usual twelve months (a 6 percent increase for 1990, plus one-time flat payments totalling approximately DM 430). Not just the union, but employers too had an interest in a wage agreement of shorter duration because of the uncertainties they confronted with German unification and developments in the European Community.

25. Thirteen percent in some districts, depending in part on whether certain white-collar employees are counted in the base figure.

previous ones in the 1984 and 1987 contracts that it replaces. As pointed out above, differentiation under the old agreements had required complicated personnel calculations and maneuvers that in fact made it too cumbersome to be useful as an instrument of personnel planning. The new provision in the 1990 contract simplifies matters in two respects. First, employers need no longer negotiate with the works council to secure longer working times for particular workers; rather, they can conclude individual agreements directly with the workers they want. Second, employers no longer need to shorten the hours of some workers in order to lengthen those of others; the only limit is that the number of workers who agree to longer hours cannot exceed 18 percent of the total work force (or 13 percent, see note 25). By simplifying its administration in these ways, it is likely that more employers will take advantage of the possibilities for differentiated working times for different workers that are offered by the new contract.

The reason this was such a significant and controversial concession by the union is that the 18 percent rule breaks a fundamental principle of union bargaining, namely to secure uniform regulations covering all workers. The differentiation clauses in the previous two contracts had gone a step in this direction, but under those agreements employers still had to negotiate with the works council. The new clause in the 1990 agreement takes a further step toward individually rather than collectively negotiated flexibility by allowing employers to bargain directly with selected workers on this issue. As the head of collective bargaining Klaus Zwickel put it, it was not "the IG Metall's wish that works councils are left out" in this way (Der Gewerkschafter, July 1990:6). Critics of the new agreement fear that individual workers will be pressured into longer working times despite the clause on voluntarism. They also argue that the new provision promotes fragmentation and could especially exacerbate divisions between workers with higher skills (especially white-collar and technical personnel who are more likely to be affected by the 18 percent clause) and those with lower skills (Der Gewerkschafter, July 1990:6).[26]

26. No one is indifferent to or unaware of the dangers of this new arrangement to union solidarity. At the same time, some unionists have tried to characterize the outcome in a more positive light, citing the new possibilities it offers to some white-collar workers who previously had been excluded from all working-time reduction (Tageszeitung, 11 May 1990). Some of this is of course spin control. However, part of the ambivalence with which this aspect of the new agreement was received in union circles reflects a deeper debate within the union over what overall position the union should take on flexibility. The IG Metall's policy on this matter is not without contradictions, and some of these come out in the slightly schizophrenic paper the union distributed to the works councils as an aid in implementing the new agreement (IG Metall 1990c). While the overall tone of the document is very defensive, it also contains scattered references to new possibilities for greater individual "working time autonomy" (1990c:15, also 7–8) and points to

Works councils' only formal function in terms of the new differentiation clause is to ensure that employers not exceed the 18 percent quota. The contract requires employers to present the works council with the names of all workers who agree to longer working hours (in some regions, before they conclude such arrangements with the workers, in others only afterwards) (IG Metall 1990c:23). Beyond this, the union has charged works councils with informing workers of the options available to them and, especially, making sure that all agreements are truly voluntary. Above all, the union wants them to persuade workers affected by the new clause to opt for free time rather than monetary compensation (*Der Gewerkschafter*, July 1990:36–37; IG Metall 1990c).[27]

Besides the 18 percent clause, however, the implications of the new agreement for relations between works councils and the union are in many ways the same. As with the previous two agreements, the regulation of many aspects of the contract is still up to the works council, which continues to negotiate collective rules for the majority of workers in the plant. Thus, for example, new plant-level agreements have to be concluded in 1993 and 1995 when the hourly reductions in working times take effect. In addition, works councils still negotiate over working-time flexibility within the six-month parameters carried over from the 1987 contract. And because they have codetermination rights on related issues such as daily working schedules and the distribution of working times across the days of the week, works councils are still on the front line on those issues on which the IG Metall and employers did not reach new agreements. These include weekend work, the maximum length of the working day, and the highly contentious issue of overtime (IG Metall 1990c: especially 5, 8–9).

In sum, the 1990 contract carries over many of the features of the previous two agreements on working-time reduction, and to this extent involves a similar delegation of responsibility to works councils. Again, the important exception to this is the new differentiation clause, which is of a very different quality, since it gives employers the opportunity to achieve greater flexibility in plant working times not through, but around, the works council. If this were to become a trend, it would amount to a new phase in the flexibility debate in Germany, one with serious political implications for the union.

---

particular groups of workers (for example, foreign workers) who might benefit especially from longer blocks of free time (1990c:15).

27. It is too early to tell how the new clause will actually be used, but early indications are that at least some works councils are advising workers not to agree to longer regular working times on the grounds that they will simply lose overtime payments for the extra hours (interviews, 1990). Encouraging workers to turn down differentiation in favor of overtime is of course not what the IG Metall leadership had in mind, but this kind of argumentation could affect the overall number of workers affected by the new differentiation clause.

"Flexibility" and the Resiliency of the Dual System

In order to assess these developments in collective bargaining in light of the theoretical issues sketched out at the beginning of this chapter, it is first important to be clear on what has and has not changed. In itself, bargaining at the plant level that results in some deviation from central collective contracts is not new. As discussed above, works councils in economically strong plants have long been able to supplement centrally defined wage minimums through informal "second rounds" of plant negotiations, often in exchange for concessions on overtime or other plant issues. Wage drift has for decades made rigid central bargains upwardly flexible at the plant level. Moreover, opening clauses in central contracts that institutionalize and formalize a second round of plant bargaining with works councils are also not new. What did change, however, was the character of bargaining in the second round: beginning with the 1984 agreement, plant negotiations moved not forward from the collective and universally binding minimum, but flexibly *within* centrally defined parameters.[28]

This examination of the IG Metall's campaign for a shorter work-week thus confirms Streeck's (1984c) general observation that national unions in the 1980s would find themselves increasingly confronted with pressures to decentralize bargaining. However, it also suggests a qualification to this general observation, as well as several further conclusions about how these pressures have been played out in the German context.

The qualification is that employer pressures for greater flexibility in central bargaining appear to be limited to those "qualitative" issues that affect the ability of employers to deploy labor as they please. Flexibility has not been an issue in bargaining rounds focusing on wages, as the 1986 bargaining round, for example, demonstrated. Employers continue to agree to "rigid" wage minimums (that are sometimes upwardly flexible at a plant level), but insist on central bargains with flexible parameters on issues governing the supply of labor and the conditions under which workers are employed.

In this sense, collective bargaining between the IG Metall and Gesamtmetall over working-time reduction offers a picture of the kinds of general tensions that have accompanied neoliberalism and the new market pressures since the 1980s. In this context, not union wage demands but the issue of flexibility in the terms and conditions of employment dominate, and negotiations are in part over the limits of that flexibility. These conflicts in central collective bargaining in Germany thus echo the themes of the dominant supply-side agenda: labor as a factor of production rather than as a factor of demand.

28. And the new differentiation clause allowing for individually rather than collectively negotiated flexibility is, as pointed out above, unprecedented.

Furthermore, while the literature on the crisis of neocorporatism emphasizes the strains on centralized bargaining since the 1980s, what is equally striking and significant is the resiliency of centralized bargaining in Germany despite these strains. The continued viability of central bargaining owes much to the tradition of what Katzenstein (1987) calls Germany's "centralized society." The outcome of negotiations over working-time reduction suggests that this tradition is still strong. Employers show no signs of seeking to engage the union in an all-out battle, nor of retreating from central bargaining, though the price— five hours working-time reduction—has not been low.[29] Although the conservative government had given them exactly the strike law they wanted in AFG 116, employers twice chose not to capitalize on the opportunity it gave them to push the IG Metall to strike and then to "hold out . . . until the union collapses," as seemed reasonable to predict at one time (Silvia 1988:169). Clearly, German employers still want centrally defined rules, only more flexible ones.

However, it takes more than just institutional inertia and tradition to sustain centralized bargaining. It is well known, for example, that small and medium-sized firms have felt particularly hurt by working-time reduction and argued strongly within the employers' organization against further concessions to the union on this issue (*Handelsblatt* 8 May 1990). The reason these pressures within Gesamtmetall have not resulted in a breakdown of centralized bargaining is that even for these firms the advantages of sticking together still outweigh the disadvantages of trying to go it alone. As Gesamtmetall president Werner Stumpfe puts it, "One common interest outweighs" the many differences within Germany's diverse business community, and that is "to confront the big and powerful IG Metall together. Our position would be worse if we were to try to reach individual agreements with the IG Metall" (*Kölner Stadt Anzeiger*, 12 June 1987).[30]

Continued unity on the employers' side is thus closely related to the continued strength and unity of the union. The conflict over working-time reduction demonstrated that the IG Metall is still capable of defining a national agenda for labor and mobilizing its membership in support of that agenda. The union demonstrated remarkable cohesion

---

29. In another gesture that reveals a degree of trust in the union that is remarkable in comparative perspective, Gesamtmetall president Stumpfe voiced his confidence that the union would consider postponements in working-time reduction in more than a perfunctory way when the time comes (*Handelsblatt* 8 May 1990). Historical precedent justifies his trust. In 1964, the IG Metall agreed to postpone the last step toward the forty-hour workweek by a year, from 1965 to 1966 (IG Metall 1990a:14).

30. The situation in Germany contrasts sharply with that in Sweden, where larger firms (such as Volvo) have been the ones behind pressures for decentralization. In Sweden, where unemployment is low, small firms have to compete with large ones for workers; they thus have a strong interest in centralized bargaining to keep wages out of competition to the extent possible.

in the 1984 strike and again in 1986 in the protests against the AFG 116. These mobilizations both reflected and reinforced the organization's unity and resolve, and contributed to its ability to secure substantial concessions from employers even under what have arguably been the most difficult market and political conditions it has faced in the postwar period.

The continued stability of centralized bargaining is also related to the resilience of the dual system and the particular compromise the unions and employers were able to find within that structure. The outcome of negotiations reflected—but also addressed—precisely those tensions that are most salient within each camp. Thus, the IG Metall made several strategic concessions on flexibility, including no further limits on overtime, that ease the burden of working-time reduction for smaller firms.[31] But conversely, by agreeing to the thirty-five-hour work week (and by decoupling its introduction from wages in the 1990 contract), Gesamtmetall helped the union appease its strongest districts, where unemployment is low and the membership is more interested in the union's turning its attention again to other issues, especially wages.

One of the reasons that the conflict over working-time reduction did not deteriorate into an all-or-nothing battle over centralized bargaining itself is because, contrary to most characterizations of the crisis of neocorporatism, the core conflict in Germany was not between central rigidity and plant-level flexibility. To be sure, the issue of flexibilization is the subject of intense debate in union circles today. However, what is striking about these debates is how they have evolved since 1984. In that year, the controversy the Leber compromise evoked was whether or not to allow flexibility into the central contract.[32] Today, the core controversy within the union has shifted: the question is no longer whether or not to accept flexibility, but what kind, how much, and under what conditions. Indeed, top union officials are now explicitly advocating an "à la carte" collective bargaining policy that would allow works councils to negotiate locally, choosing among a "menu" of options laid out in central contracts.[33]

So far, then, the dual system has successfully absorbed the pressures

31. Small and medium-sized firms were especially fearful that the IG Metall would insist on further limits to overtime, which is their main source of flexibility (*Handelsblatt*, 8 May 1990).

32. More precisely, the extent to which works councils could be trusted to act in the interest of the national organization in implementing the contract (interview with Hans Mayr, then president of the union, 1989).

33. The advocates of such a policy include both the union's president Franz Steinkühler and the executive board member in charge of collective bargaining policy Klaus Zwickel. See *Kölner Stadt Anzeiger*, 27 August 1988; Klaus Zwickel's speech in IG Metall 1988c:11–28 (especially 18); and Steinkühler's remarks at the IG Metall's conference on technology (IG Metall 1988d:126–28). See also IG Metall, 1989a: especially 50; and *Der Gewerkschafter* 9a, September 1988:112–13.

for flexibility in ways that have averted disintegration on the labor side (cf. Weber 1986). Pressures for decentralization were resolved not through the breakdown of central bargaining, but rather through the flexibilization of central contracts and a shift in the balance within the dual system toward the growing importance of works councils. Indeed, strategic maneuvering by labor and capital and compromise *within* the dual system may in fact have helped avert an attack on it.[34]

However, the issue is not just working-time reduction. The next chapter deals with the responsibilities works councils have inherited over the past decade in the union's technology policy. It documents how the shift toward the growing importance of plant works councils is also part of a more aggressive strategy by the IG Metall. Whereas the union was *driven* to concede more powers to works councils on the working-time issue, on the technology question it is *drawn* to the plant and the prospect of using the legal rights of works councils to influence the pace and form of technological change.

34. This argument fits well with Katzenstein's characterization of change in Germany through "experimentation" and "flexibility" within stable institutions (1989).

CHAPTER EIGHT

Contemporary Trends in Union Technology Policy

Technological change is of course not a new problem for the IG Metall. For as long as unions have existed, they have been concerned about the effects of technology. However, the advent of microelectronics has made the problem for unions even more pressing, and the technology issue has risen to the top of union agendas throughout the advanced industrial world.

Three factors contribute to the urgency of the problem of technological change. First, while the base technology for programmable automation has been available for decades, prices have fallen steadily to a point that allows more and more employers to introduce such technologies on a broad scale. Second, unlike other technologies whose impact was profound but narrower, affecting a relatively small number of workers (such as the linotype), the development of microelectronics has had broad implications for work in a range of sectors virtually economy-wide. Third, technology is a growing concern because the economic context since the 1970s is different from the full employment context of the 1950s and 1960s. For all of these reasons, unions across the advanced industrial world now view technology as an area of growing importance. For these reasons as well, references to the current "revolution in production" may be somewhat overdrawn, but they are not completely inappropriate.

German unions in general, and the IG Metall in particular, are still fundamentally receptive to technological change. However, the employment, skill, and income effects of new technologies have become points of ever-greater contention since the economic upheavals in the mid-1970s. This chapter traces the development of union technology policy in response to these changes.[1] As in the case of collective bargaining, works councils have come to occupy an increasingly important position in union technology policy in the 1980s.

Partly, works councils have simply been drawn into the union's strategy by the advance of technology itself. Works councils negotiate on a range of issues related to the introduction of new technologies: job reclassifications and transfers, for example. In addition, works councils play an important role in adapting regionally negotiated "framework" agreements on wage determination methods to specific plant conditions. These framework agreements were negotiated decades ago, and technological change has raised issues that they did not anticipate. As Klaus Lang, head of the IG Metall's collective bargaining department puts it: "The job of adapting our old wage framework agreements to the new problems has necessarily fallen to the works councils" (interview, 1987).

Beyond this, however, works councils figure prominently in the union's current strategy of going beyond securing compensation for workers adversely affected by new technologies to actively influencing the organization of production itself. The union sees work organization (*Gestaltung*) as central to the defense of workers' skills and incomes. Lose the battle over the organization of production and you can do little more than soften the blow (*abfedern*) for workers adversely affected by technological change.

Thus, beyond the obvious and growing importance of the technology issue to the union, an examination of the evolution of the union's response to technological change offers another window on the changing relations between the central union and works councils. Indeed, technology in many ways epitomizes the broader challenges currently confronting the IG Metall that have contributed to the shift in the locus of conflict within the dual system to the plant.

The rapid advance of technological change "blurs" the line between quantitative (wage) and "qualitative" issues (skills, employment). In Germany, this blurring of issues has also blurred the traditional division of labor between the central union and works councils. As mentioned above, labor law in Germany specifies fairly neatly and explicitly that unions shall conduct negotiations over wages and broad working conditions, while works councils shall deal with a range of plant-level issues such as plant working times, changes in the organization and flow of production, and plant payment methods. The "blurring" of issues means that central bargaining gains—be they "quantitative" or "qualitative"

---

1. For another, more comprehensive and detailed analysis of the IG Metall's technology policy, see Kaßebaum, 1990.

—can be lost again at a plant level. Just as the employment effects of centrally bargained working-time reduction hinge crucially on how works councils apply it in the plant, centrally bargained wage increases may be significantly diluted, unless works councils can successfully defend workers against job downgrading. The extent to which the union can influence such outcomes will hinge therefore on its ability to work through works councils.

Moreover, some of the union's technology goals are difficult to achieve directly through central bargaining. Certain forms of protection against job and income loss for workers adversely affected by technological change can be negotiated in encompassing agreements. But other union goals contain distinctly *nonquantifiable* components that make them difficult to achieve centrally (see also Sandberg 1986). Union goals relating to the organization of production such as job enrichment, job rotation, and group work are examples of demands for which central bargains can provide a framework, but not directly regulate in individual plants. Thus, the union's move toward a more active interest in the politics of production organization (*Gestaltungspolitik*), with its nonquantifiable, plant-specific characteristics, has also contributed to a shift toward works councils in the dual system. Contemporary technology policy targets the plant and aims to use works councils' rights as a lever for achieving the union's technology goals in these areas.

Thus, the trend in union technology policy—as in the case of the union's struggle in central bargaining for a thirty-five-hour workweek—is toward the growing importance of works councils in Germany's negotiated adjustment. But if the trend is the same, the impetus is slightly different, for in this case the move toward the plant is at least in part driven by changes in *union* goals and strategies. Debates on decentralization and flexibilization tend to be cast in terms of union givebacks. But recent developments in union technology policy provide an example of a search on the union side for a more plant-oriented (one might also say more flexible) approach to the problems raised by technological change.

THE EVOLUTION OF UNION TECHNOLOGY POLICY
WITHIN THE DUAL SYSTEM

The IG Metall's goals and strategies in the area of technology have evolved in response to changes in the macroeconomic and political context. The rapid advance of technology and the more zero-sum economic context since the oil crises of the 1970s have of course driven broad changes in the union's views and objectives on technology. Beyond this, however, the union's strategy has flowed in channels that reflect the specific constellation of opportunities and constraints the IG Metall has faced since the 1970s. Strategic maneuvering by the union in response to new openings and new challenges helps account for the shifting balance within the dual system.

Prior to the 1970s, union technology policy was embedded in what might be called a more or less stable "coalition for industrial modernization" between the IG Metall and employers. As discussed above, labor was politically weak until the Social Democratic party came to power in 1969, but the union enjoyed considerable market strength in the period of the economic miracle. The "coalition for industrial modernization" involved a (largely implicit) trade-off: in exchange for its acceptance of and even active support for rationalization and technological change to support Germany's export-dependent industries, the union demanded that workers be allowed to share in the resulting productivity gains through increased benefits, shorter working times, and better working conditions. Bargaining was centralized in this period, and technology policy was an implicit ingredient of wage bargaining.

The 1970s were especially important as a formative decade in union technology policy. This period began with the establishment of the Social-Liberal coalition in 1969, which ushered in the "reform euphoria" of the early 1970s (see Markovits 1986:117). The revised Works Constitution Act was one of the most important fruits of this period. The new rights won by the works councils were an important precondition for the union's subsequent plant-based strategy. But "reform euphoria" had more direct implications for union technology policy as well, for it opened up new political avenues to extend the terms of the previous "coalition for industrial modernization." The union's technology stance maintained most of the basic features of the previous period, but it also went further, demanding that labor's payoff include other non-wage benefits. The most important project in this area was the "humanization of working life" program sponsored by the Social Democrats.

The excitement that accompanied the "humanization" initiatives at the beginning of the 1970s gradually faded. As economic growth slowed and unemployment grew under Chancellor Helmut Schmidt, the Social Democrats' commitment to "humanization" projects waned, and the union's orientation toward technology became more guarded and critical. As political avenues for achieving union technology goals began to yield more modest and even ambiguous results, the union returned to a reliance on industrial action and collective bargaining as the primary arena for pursuing its technology policy. However, employer resistance in general, and specifically resistance to concessions to the union on "qualitative" issues, grew stronger and more determined in the late 1970s.

The IG Metall's current technology policy was shaped in important ways by this constellation of new opportunities and new constraints coming out of the 1970s. On the one hand, the emphasis on plant-level bargaining capitalizes on new opportunities created during the period of "reform euphoria," most importantly, the new rights won in the revised Works Constitution Act. Although the law gives works councils only limited rights on the introduction of technology itself, their stronger rights on the range of personnel issues that are affected by technological change give them a lever on the technology issue. The union's new Gestaltungs strategy is virtually unthinkable apart from the new rights plant-level labor representatives won in 1972.

On the other hand, the new emphasis on plant-level bargaining also responds to the narrowing political opportunities and deteriorating market situation that followed the "reform euphoria" period. The paralysis that accompanied this confluence of market weakness and political exclusion forced the union to reevaluate its position and its strategy. While the union will continue to make gains through central-ized collective bargaining where it can, the current period is character-ized by a partial retreat from both its former reliance on the state's reform policies and its own previously more centralized approach. The result has been a strategic shift toward the plant and union locals, in order to tap plant-level resources and enlist plant and local labor representatives as active proponents of union technology policy.

The dual system has helped to shore up negotiated adjustment by providing the unions with a stable second avenue for addressing technology even as the room for concessions—particularly on qualita-tive issues—narrowed in central collective bargaining. Beyond this, the dual system has provided the union with the flexibility it needed to pursue its more aggressive strategy on work organization.

The rest of this chapter traces the process through which strategic adjustments by the union to changing macroeconomic conditions and political developments have contributed to a shift within the dual system toward the increasing importance of works councils in union technology policy. My discussion focuses primarily on the 1970s and 1980s. However, it is useful to begin with a brief description of union technology policy before the crisis.

The Coalition for Industrial Modernization, 1955–1969

The period up to about 1969 can be characterized in terms of what might be called a "coalition for modernization" between German labor and capital. During the German economic "miracle" the economy grew steadily and at a rather spectacular rate. The country's first postwar recession in 1966–67 was brief and in retrospect very mild. At that time, the IG Metall's technology department was called the Department for Technology and Atomic Power, and what union publications are now more careful to call "technological change" they once referred to more optimistically as "technological progress." The union's position on technological change was sanguine, even generally enthusiastic, throughout the 1960s.

As in many other countries, the advent of the computer era provoked a more critical discussion of technological change and its potentially negative effects on workers, but sustained economic growth throughout this period made converts of even the most skeptical and quickly defused the "automation scare" of the early 1960s. In a union-sponsored conference "Automation: Risk or Opportunity" in 1965, it was the opportunities that new technologies presented which predominated (see, for example, IG Metall 1965). The union's resolution on automation and technology at the national congress in the same year summed up the core of the IG Metall's position. It described technological progress as a necessary precondition for economic growth. Technological change made possible "better and fuller lives through a growing social product, higher wages and salaries, an increase in welfare, shorter working times, longer vacations, and relief from physically demanding work" (quoted in Müller 1968:114).

The IG Metall was keenly aware of German industry's dependence on exports and saw technology as playing a key role in its continued success: "If companies do not adapt in time to the technological standards in their sectors they will lose their competitiveness and be out of business" (IG Metall *Geschäftsbericht 1960–61*:61). Thus, the union accepted the necessity of technological change, and the condition for their participation in the "coalition for industrial modernization" in the 1960s was that workers reap their fair share of productivity gains, especially through higher wages and working-time reduction.

This overall positive position on technological change also survived the Federal Republic's first recession in 1966–67. True, the recession had given a glimpse of the dangers of rationalization in a more zero-sum context, and in 1968 the union and employers concluded a national-level "Rationalization Protection Agreement" to shield especially vulnerable workers (in particular, older workers) from the negative employment and income consequences of technological change (*Der Gewerkschafter*, February 1968). However, in that same year, IG Metall president Otto Brenner reemphasized the union's basically positive position on technology:

> In contrast to some western industrial countries, it is to the credit of the German unions that historically they have never tried to hinder or impede progress. They have simply insisted on preempting its negative social consequences. Moreover, it has been the unions themselves who have spoken out in favor of an accelerated introduction of modern

technologies, often very much to the dismay [*zum Kummer*] of certain enterprises (e.g., nuclear energy, computers, numerical machines, general automation). [IG Metall 1971, 2:1121]

Thus, despite the economic downturn in the late 1960s, the IG Metall had not lost its faith in the positive effects of technology, and indeed saw innovation and technological change as the antidote to the recession: "The unions have an interest in technically advanced, productive and efficient industry. Industrial productivity is a precondition for rising incomes, better working conditions and full employment. Higher wages and salaries depend among other things on modern and efficient plant.... The standard of living will only rise if the economy is further rationalized and modernized" (IG Metall 1971, 2:1123).

In terms of both goals and strategies, the union's technology policy until the late 1960s reflected auspicious economic conditions. Union leaders today stress how the IG Metall's current emphasis on plant-level initiatives contrasts sharply with the more "top-heavy," centralized approach of the 1960s (interview with Andreas Drinkuth, head of the IG Metall technology department, 1985). But a decentralized strategy was neither possible nor necessary in this period. It was not until the Works Constitution Act was revised in 1972 that works councils were granted stronger information and consultation rights on the introduction of new technologies and stronger codetermination rights on a range of issues related to the effects of technology on workers. Prior to that time, works councils were not viable vehicles for union technology policy. But more importantly, because technology policy was implicitly embedded in the union's collective bargaining policy over wages and working time, the role for works councils was minimal.

"Reformeuphorie" and Disappointment in the 1970s

The early 1970s (until the oil shock of November 1973) were heady years for the unions. German industry was prospering and hence able to hold up its end of the productivity deal that had developed over the previous decade. The atmosphere of "reform euphoria" (*Reformeuphorie*) that the Social Democrats brought with them also affected the union's technology demands.[2]

In 1972 the IG Metall hosted a major international conference on automation and technological change with the title "Task for the Future: Quality of Life" (IG Metall 1972). This theme reflected the union's continued optimism concerning technological change, but it also went a step further. Not only should workers be protected from the possible adverse effects of technological change and allowed to

2. For a more general account of the "reform euphoria" period see Markovits 1986: especially 114–26.

share in its benefits, but technology should positively serve the interests of workers in more humane jobs and work environments (*Der Gewerkschafter*, April 1972:123). The IG Metall's (then) vice president Eugen Loderer captured the mood of the time in his summary of the results of the conference: "In contrast to earlier conferences, the IG Metall went a significant step further at this one. The question was no longer economic and sociopolitical adjustment to the more advanced technologies, but rather the application of technology in the interest of improving the quality of life" (IG Metall 1972, 10:7).

The union took up the banner of the "humanization of working life" and pursued it both in collective bargaining and through its demands for political reform. In the area of collective bargaining, the IG Metall struck in 1973 in the union stronghold of Nord-Württemberg/Nord-Baden for a new wage framework agreement, the heralded *Lohn-rahmentarifvertrag II* (hereafter LRTV II). LRTV II included a range of goals relating to working conditions. The most important measures the union achieved were additional five-minute (paid) work breaks for assembly-line and piece-rate workers, minimum work-cycle times of one and a half minutes, and income guarantees for workers over age fifty-five (Laube 1981:235–42).

The union's humanization accomplishments in Nord-Württemberg/Nord-Baden were substantial. Indeed, the union hoped through LRTV II to create the preconditions for labor influence on the organization of production itself. So for example, increasing minimum work-cycle times to ninety seconds would not just reduce the pressure of the assembly line; the union saw it as well as a precondition for more thoroughgoing changes—the introduction of job rotation or group work, for example. As such, the central agreement created a frame-work within which ultimately other, more far-reaching goals could then be achieved (Brumlop and Rosenbaum 1979). The only dark spot in this otherwise important victory was the union's inability to generalize the contract to other bargaining districts and thus make it the industry pattern.[3]

The political flank of the union's strategy aimed at working with and through the new Social Democratic government. With "its" party in power, the union resurrected the agenda for political reform it had shelved in the 1960s when the conservatives controlled the government. As discussed above (Chapter 4), the revised Works Constitution Act passed in 1972 extended works councils' rights in a number of areas. The new law enhanced their rights to receive information on the

3. Recall that collective bargaining in the metalworking industries is formally carried out by the union's regional bargaining units. In almost all cases of wage negotiations, the union engages in "pattern" bargaining, in which their signing any agreement reached in a given district is made contingent on the results being carried over to the industry as a whole.

introduction of new technologies or other significant alterations in plant or equipment and to be consulted on questions relating to certain aspects of the structure and organization of work, working conditions, and job design (Works Constitution Act, paragraphs 90, 91). The law especially strengthened their rights on issues affected by technology, for example, in the areas of plant wage systems and plant personnel policy generally.

The unions' political lobbying also bore fruit in the form of a new government-sponsored "Humanization of Working Life" program (*Humanisierung des Arbeitslebens*, hereafter HdA). In May 1974 the Federal Ministry of Research and Technology (Bundesministerium für Forschung und Technologie, BMFT) and the Ministry of Labor (Bundesministerium für Arbeit, BMA) jointly initiated the program. HdA combined the goals of both its sponsors: the BMFT's goal of supporting the technical-organizational modernization of industry and the labor ministry's goal of worker protection and the improvement of working conditions (Peter 1979:39). The Minister of Research and Technology, Hans Matthöfer saw the goals of modernization and humanization not only as compatible, but complementary: "A more humane (*menschengerechtere*) organization of work...need not at all be at odds with economic necessities and goals. On the contrary: whoever thinks they can ensure their long-term competitiveness in international markets by striving for cost advantage at the expense of humane working conditions cannot reap lasting success" (Matthöfer 1976:162; see also Matthöfer 1980: especially 39–42).[4]

Straddling as it did the dual goals of industrial modernization and humanization, the HdA program in many ways epitomizes the positive-sum way the unions themselves viewed technological modernization and the interests of workers. Concretely, the program's goals were four:

(1) to develop worker protection measures, and establish minimum standards for machines, systems and plants;
(2) to develop "humane" production technologies;
(3) to devise and test new modes of work organization and job structures for subsequent diffusion; and
(4) to disseminate and apply "humanization" findings and plant experiences. [Pöhler 1979:9]

Still a champion of plant-based initiative, Matthöfer secured works council participation in individual plant-based HdA projects in 1975 when he pushed through a provision that made government funding for such projects contingent on the works councils' approval. At the same time, the minister pulled union representatives into the national

---

4. Chancellor Helmut Schmidt appointed Matthöfer to head the BMFT in 1974.

HdA administration as members of the boards that decide which projects would receive federal "humanization" funding (Peter 1982:213).

In this period, the union strove—often in the context of HdA plant projects—to create a set of model plants for the humane application of new technologies. Early efforts in this regard, and the most publicized cases, were at Volkswagen, Bosch, and Ruhrkohle AG. At VW, for example, the union sought to achieve a model plant solution to production organization by working with the works council in a HdA project to reorganize motor assembly. The result was the abandonment of traditional assembly line techniques and the establishment of a production system that gave individual workers maximum autonomy in performing their jobs, which could be accomplished either individually or in work groups (interview, 1985).

On balance, the years of reform euphoria did not so much constitute a departure from the "coalition for industrial modernization" of the 1960s as they did its extension to include a series of non-wage reforms in addition to labor's longstanding demands for wage and work-time compensation for increases in productivity. The union pursued these qualitative goals through its traditional strength in collective bargaining, but also through a renewed reliance on union-government cooperation.

In general, works councils played only a secondary and subordinate role in union technology policy. However, a partial exception to this is the agreement (LRTV II) achieved in Nord-Württemberg/Nord-Baden. Here, works councils were assigned a crucial role not only in implementing the agreement, but also in adapting it to their particular plant situation (Brumlop and Rosenbaum 1979:288–90). The central union saw its role as creating the framework (*Rahmen*) within which plant actors could then attempt to shape the organization of production further. For example, by establishing minimum cycle times, the agreement facilitated (but did not directly implement) union goals such as job enrichment through group work. In this sense the union saw central union agreements like LRTV II as a precondition for plant and local action. Since the union was not able to turn the agreement in this district into an industry standard, opening up such possibilities in other plants in other districts had to be postponed.

The idea behind the model plants created under HdA auspices was similar. In most instances the central union worked closely and directly with a select number of plants. In the creation of these models the central union largely leapfrogged and preempted intermediate (local and district) actors. What was missing in both cases—and what began to emerge in the 1980s—was a broader mobilization and an increasing reliance on intermediate union bodies and especially on works councils as a primary vehicle for union technology policy.

The "reform euphoria" that characterized the early years of the Social Democratic government began to buckle under the weight of the new pressures of structural unemployment and uneven growth in the late 1970s. Tensions between the union and the Schmidt government surfaced in the union's growing criticism of government technology policy and in particular the HdA program. "The [HdA] program was created under conditions of economic growth and full employment as well as political reform plans.... This situation ... influenced the point of departure and focus of the program, which was meant to develop 'humane' technologies and models for work organization through which demands for the 'quality of life' could also be realized at work" (Trautwein-Kalms and Gerlach 1980:207). What none of the participants could see in 1974 when the HdA program was created became increasingly clear in the subsequent years: the Humanization of Working Life program would be squeezed in the conflict over which goal—humanization or rationalization—would predominate in the leaner years following the oil crisis of November 1973 (Naschold 1980: Pöhler 1980).

As Frieder Naschold points out, the coalition for HdA was unstable to begin with. The program juxtaposed the "partly overlapping and partly contradictory interests ... of enterprises and unions, Social Democratic party and state apparatus," which produced "an unstable sociopolitical balance of compromise" (1980:223). Under changed economic and political conditions in the late 1970s, this unstable coalition slowly came apart. The balance struck in the period of prosperity between industrial modernization in the interests of international competitiveness on the one hand and humanization on the other hand seemed to the IG Metall to be tilting increasingly toward the former.

Personnel changes in the HdA program administration contributed to the union's growing skepticism. In 1978 Schmidt appointed the less union-oriented Volker Hauff to replace the outgoing Matthöfer as head of the Ministry for Research and Technology.[5] As a consequence, the HdA program itself became a contentious issue between the government and the union.

In March 1979, Karl-Heinz Janzen, the IG Metall executive board member responsible for the Automation and Technology Department, criticized the Ministry's technology policy for its massive support of "job-destroying rationalization measures" (Janzen 1979:5). While the union was still committed to the original idea and goals of the Humanization Program, Janzen concluded that the results of HdA had so far been "sobering.... The express goal of the humanization of working conditions has in practice stayed on paper. Nothing or only very little has come out [of the program] for the affected workers." (1979:7).

The union's objections to HdA were both procedural and substantive. The procedural component had to do with a perceived discrepan-

5. Gerd Peter describes the significance of this ministerial shift, as well as the departure (apparently a resignation the government encouraged) of the pro-union Willy Pöhler as head of the HdA program two years later (Peter 1982:218).

cy between the goals of the program as a whole and the implementation of individual projects. As mentioned above, HdA was unique among the projects sponsored by the BMFT in that funding was granted for plant projects only after they had received the approval of plant labor representatives. Still, only employers could apply for funding for such projects; works councils could not initiate them. This seemed to the unions to clash with the program's rationale (or at least one of them)—the improvement of working conditions in the interests of workers. Presumably, workers' representatives are best able to assess the needs of the workers (Pöhler 1980:233).

The union's substantive objections were based on its evaluation of the results of already-completed and ongoing HdA projects. These—or a majority of them—seemed to have little to do with developing creative and durable solutions to the problem of more "humane" work. The IG Metall increasingly charged employers with using HdA funding as a ruse and vehicle for state-subsidized rationalization projects.

Their growing skepticism of the results of HdA research left the unions in a quandary:

> The unions, as the Humanization of Work Program's necessary sponsors, increasingly saw themselves caught in the trap of having cooperated in a government humanization policy that had resulted in mostly negative social consequences for workers and hence bearing part of the responsibility. Thus they criticized ever more sharply employers' strategies of circumventing the goals of the humanization program while receiving program money, and also—especially—the insufficient support and supervision capacity and cooperation on the part of the state bureaucracy. [Naschold 1980:223]

The fact that union representatives sit (in equal numbers with employers) on the boards that approve specific HdA projects made the union's dilemma more uncomfortable yet. Karl-Heinz Janzen, member of the IG Metall executive board, claimed that the problem was in part one of a manpower shortage. The labor representatives on HdA boards frequently did not have time to follow up the specific projects in the implementation phase (Janzen 1979:5).

Although the critique of HdA continued, the union could never bring itself to abandon support for the program entirely. Nonetheless, the IG Metall's experiences in the late 1970s disabused the union of the idea that strong and unequivocal measures by the government to alleviate the negative effects on workers of new technologies were forthcoming. This realization gave birth to a shift in strategy on the part of the union away from the political arena and toward collective bargaining to achieve the goals it saw neglected and even distorted in the HdA program.[6]

6. See also the discussion of the IG Metall's strategy of "self-reliance" in Chapter 5 above.

The first concrete expression of this shift came in 1978 when the union waged a bitter strike, again in Nord-Württemberg/Nord-Baden, for protection for workers adversely affected by technological change. The centerpiece of the agreement the IG Metall reached was protection against downgrading through an eighteen-month income guarantee for workers transferred to lower-paying jobs as a result of rationalization. Yet on other, more far-reaching demands the union was not so successful. For example, employers resisted the union initiative to "freeze" existing wage structures, which would have provided a "collective guarantee" against the longer-term downgrading of whole work forces (Streeck 1981; see also Chapter 5). More importantly perhaps than this, the union was again unable to make to the agreement reached in Nord-Württemberg/Nord-Baden into an industry pattern.

The limitations the union encountered in its strategic shift to collective bargaining were discussed in Chapter 5. Union technology demands were in some ways bound to encounter especially strong resistance in central bargaining, since they centered on those "qualitative" aspects of the labor process over which employers were least willing to negotiate. In light of the increasingly volatile international markets in the late 1970s, employers were particularly opposed to centrally negotiated blanket regulations that would impinge on their ability to rearrange production and introduce technologies as they pleased. The union's experience in the 1978 bargaining round confirmed this.

In terms of technology policy, the 1970s had been something of a roller coaster for the IG Metall. The decade began with full employment and the promise of strong government support for the union's "humanization" agenda. But labor's initial "reform euphoria" soon faded, and by the end of the 1970s, there was a clear change in the union's attitude toward technology and the first signs of a shift in strategy. Massive rationalization in the context of rising unemployment had caused a growing number of unionists to call into question the organization's longstanding view that modernization and automation were not only compatible with, but prerequisites for, improving workers' standards of living (Steinkühler 1984). And even if the union did not abandon its fundamental acceptance of technological change, it was seriously rethinking the terms of its participation in the "coalition for industrial modernization" that had held for most of the postwar period.

But at the same time—and for many of the same reasons—the union was running up against the limits to the pursuit of its technology goals through collective bargaining. Growing levels of industrial conflict were a sign of increasingly acrimonious relations between labor and capital.[7] While the union did not emerge from the 1978 conflict in Nord-Württemberg/Nord-Baden empty-handed, the outcome fell far short of

7. The year 1978 was the most strike-ridden for the IG Metall to that point in the postwar period.

the union's original goals, and it had taken a six-week strike that had cost the union dearly. Moreover, the IG Metall's inability to generalize the agreement to the entire metalworking industry was a clear signal of employers' resolve and their increasingly effective resistance. The other flank of the union's efforts—reform through state policy—was yielding similarly modest and ambiguous results even before the SPD left office. Going into the 1980s, the IG Metall was casting about for new answers to the problem of technology, which had become more pressing than ever before in the postwar period.

Plant Bargaining and Union Technology Policy since the 1980s

Continuing high unemployment and the conservative *"Wende"* since 1982 mean that union technology policy is now formulated in an economic and political context that is very remote from that which prevailed in the 1960s and early 1970s. The mood in the IG Metall on technological change has become more critical:

> The economic boom in the Federal Republic in the first twenty-five years of its existence was founded on a fundamental consensus between the unions, employers, and the government. The unions did not fundamentally challenge rationalization and new technology; through their collective bargaining and worker protection policy they were able to reap for their members the fruits of productivity gains in the form of wage increases, working time reduction, and job and health protection. Developments in recent years make this social consensus more and more fragile [*brüchiger*].... Rationalization in recent years has been at the expense of workers, in the growth of mass unemployment and worsening working conditions. [IG Metall, *Geschäftsbericht, 1980–82*:413]

These developments prompted a new discussion within the IG Metall, to "reconsider...the union's previously positive position on technological change" (Janzen, quoted in Fricke, Krahn, and Peter 1985:33). The union has not suddenly begun actively resisting technological change, but its position has shifted from what has been described as a "yes, but..." to a "no, unless..." stance (Fricke, Krahn, and Peter 1985:33).

Stalled at the political level and preoccupied with the question of unemployment and the thirty-five-hour workweek at the industrial level, the IG Metall has been moving toward an increased reliance on plant works councils and intermediate-level union actors as vehicles for the union's technology policy. Beyond the limited room for initiatives at other levels, however, two further factors have driven this trend toward a more plant-based technology strategy. First, a more important role has simply fallen to works councils as technological change revealed the deficits and weaknesses of "framework" regulations the union had negotiated previously, but under very different political, economic, and technological conditions. Second, works councils are key actors in the union's more aggressive strategy to influence work organization (*Arbeitsgestaltung*).

The problem of "disjunctures" between region-wide "framework" regulations (negotiated previously) and new developments in technology has been especially pronounced in the area of wages. As mentioned above (Chapter 6) the widespread "analytic" system of wage determination in Germany compensates workers rather generously for physical exertion and environmental strains (for example, noise or dust) on the job. Automation very often decreases physical strain and/or alleviates negative environmental factors (sometimes by eliminating dangerous or hazardous jobs altogether). In Germany this means that job reclassification or transfer in the course of technological change can have an immediate and dramatic effect on a worker's income.

In addition, wage determination methods for a large share of production work in Germany are based on calculations of a worker's output (a combination of hourly and piece-rate pay). Despite the dictum "Akkord ist Mord" (piecework is murder), various forms of performance pay systems are more prevalent in Germany than in the United States. The reason has to do with the structure of labor representation. Works councils have full codetermination rights on the setting of piece and premium rates and similar performance-related remuneration (WCA, paragraph 87). They can exercise greater control over the relationship between performance and pay under such systems than with hourly wages and often prefer them for that reason (interviews, 1985).

The problem now is that the introduction of new technologies changes the relationship between output and payment, and often breaks the link between the two altogether, for example as workers' jobs increasingly consist of overseeing automated production processes. Such developments create a hiatus between the current wage determination system and shop-floor reality. In the words of Klaus Lang, the head of the IG Metall collective bargaining division:

> Our current wage framework agreements date back to the 1960s. They represent an adaptation to the technological and organizational stage of development embodied in mass production. We are now in a period of upheaval [*Umbruchsphase*], when technological and organizational production standards have changed. The old contracts fit the previous standards, but now [with rapid technological change] they leave a lot of questions unanswered and problems unregulated. [Interview, 1987]

In both areas, personnel maneuvers and the adaptation of wage determination methods, works councils have filled the gaps created by the "upheavals" Lang cites. Works councils negotiate over job transfers and reclassifications, but also over plant wage issues in ways that "patch" these disjunctures and attempt to shield workers from the negative income and employment consequences of new technologies.[8]

Beyond these ad hoc, defensive maneuvers, however, union technology policy now explicitly assigns to works councils an increasingly important role in its attempts to influence technology and work organization in a more positive way as well. In this respect, the shift toward the plant is closely related to the union's goals on work organization, or Gestaltung. This more aggressive aspect of the trend toward a certain decentralization in union technology policy can be traced in three separate but related developments: the adoption in 1984 of a new plant-based "Action Program" for technology, recent initiatives in central bargaining to bolster the influence of works councils in the area of skills and training, and the evolution of union policy concerning quality circles.

The clearest signal of the union's move toward strengthening works councils and assigning them a more prominent role in union technology policy is the IG Metall's current "Action Program" (IG Metall 1984a).[9] Preliminary work on the new technology program began in 1980, when delegates to the IG Metall National Congress commissioned the union's executive board to draw up a new strategy on the technology question (IG Metall, *Geschäftsbericht 1980–82*:419–20). As a first step the union undertook a survey of 1,100 plants in 1982–83 to assess the current state of rationalization in the metalworking industries (IG Metall 1983). The results of that survey summarize what the union considers to be the "danger areas" posed by new technologies (employment, wages, skills, and health), and thus the focus of attention for regulation.

On the basis of the survey, the union's technology department drew up the "Action Program" (entitled "Work and Technology"), which the union's top executive board ratified and adopted in November 1984. The program describes a new strategy of greater reliance on works councils and union locals in union technology policy as part of an integrated strategy to coordinate centrally the decentralized implementation of the union's technology goals.

The union's 1982 annual report describes the reasons behind the union's shift toward increased reliance on plant labor representatives in implementing the union's technology demands: "[The growing number of plants and workers adversely affected by technological change] confirms the need to move away from more targeted assistance... toward stronger, more systematic support of the whole organization. The goal... is to create a broad impact within the context of a comprehensive union concept and to provide [plant labor representatives] with 'help to help themselves'" (IG Metall, *Geschäftsbericht 1980–82*:418). The 1984 Action Program describes how the central union will organize this campaign.

8. As one union official put it: "You can't do everything at once in collective bargaining" (interview, 1985).

9. See also the English translation, "Action Program Work and Technology: People Must Stay!" (IG Metall 1984a).

The program "seeks in the first instance to improve... prospects for successful union shop-floor politics concerning the organization of work and technology" (IG Metall 1984a:32). It "concentrates on the plant level—where rationalization is taking place, and where new technologies are being introduced.... Concrete alternatives to employers' rationalization plans... must be developed and 'carried' politically by works councils, shop steward committees, and the affected workers" (IG Metall 1984a:9). So, for example, the program recommends that special technology committees be formed within works councils. It calls for the inclusion of shop stewards in work groups to help develop alternative production organizations to bring into negotiations with management.

The head of the union's technology department describes the difference between the union's technology policy of the past and that described in the new Action Program: "The difference is that technology is no longer just a question for top union officials. The goal is to make it an issue for the membership more generally and on a broader scale in the plants. We are aware that we will not be successful everywhere, but some of us think it is better to have a 50 percent success rate in a thousand plants than an 80 percent success rate in a hundred" (interview, 1985).

Union technology advisers work with selected plants to develop and implement solutions to particular technology problems. But these model plants are not an end in themselves. Rather, the union uses them as instructional devices, to show works councils what they can achieve for themselves. So for example, on the basis of plant experiences, the union technology department has developed a series of handbooks (*Aktionsmappen*) that other works councils can use as aids in their negotiations with management. The central union acts as a clearing house for generating and disseminating these materials. In that sense, the union's model plant initiatives are very much a part of the more general strategy to equip works councils with a set of tools which will then allow them to "help themselves."[10]

The goal of the union technology advisers is to educate works councils and ultimately to make them more self-sufficient in dealing with the problems technology raises at the plant level. For this the Action Program assigns a pivotal role to intermediate union bodies, and especially to union locals, which have close and multiple links to

10. A union-affiliated "Humanization of Working Life" (HdA) advisory group, consisting of ten full-time technology advisers (originally funded in 1980 by the then–Social Democratic government) has been working closely with the IG Metall's own Technology Department to develop these plant models. An obvious response to the union's criticism in the 1970s of the government's humanization program, this group's focus has been to bring union influence into federally funded HdA projects and to strengthen the links between union headquarters and the various plants receiving HdA support. Government funding has also allowed the union to set up two regional technology centers, also staffed by union appointees and charged with advising plant works councils, shop stewards, and union locals in technology questions.

the plants. The role of the locals in the union's technology policy before the Action Program was much less central, according to the head of the technology department. "Mostly it was a case in which the central union worked with plant representatives directly. The idea [of the Action Program] is that locals have to assume the burden. We noticed in the 1970s that in some plants good things were being done, but they disappeared again because locals and plant representatives were not prepared and able to sustain them" (interview, 1985).

The central union has charged each of its over 170 local offices with drawing up its own action program, tailored to the particular needs of the plants in that region. Locals should also create their own set of pilot cases "to demonstrate the viability of alternative [production organizations] and thereby... provide an impetus for activities in other plants" (IG Metall 1984a:37). Union locals are charged with developing their own advisory capacity to assist plants with technology problems. The central union thus sees the strengthening of intermediate union bodies as a crucial part of its mobilization effort and vital to the success of the Action Program.

In sum, the IG Metall's 1984 Technology Program describes a strategy of plant and local mobilization that the union will coordinate centrally, but which ultimately places the weight of responsibility for implementing union technology policy on works councils, working together with plant shop stewards and the union locals. In contrast even to the LRTV II, the union is now saying that local representatives cannot wait for the central union to solve their technology problems: "The... political goal that underlies this program... must be fought for and achieved in the plants themselves. Only the workers themselves who are affected by rationalization and their shop-floor representatives... can do it" (IG Metall 1984a:33).

The issue of skills has also become particularly salient with the accelerated introduction of new technologies. A recently concluded "Wage and Salary Framework Agreement" in Nord-Württemberg/Nord-Baden (LGRTV-I) shows how in this area, too, the IG Metall has come increasingly to rely on works councils to translate union goals and centrally bargained agreements into plant outcomes (IG Metall 1988a; see also Kurz-Scherf 1988b). This agreement addresses the link between the skills workers command and the wages they receive. It reflects the union's dual goal of promoting a continual upgrading of skills and of linking a worker's pay to the skills he or she possesses rather than the particular job he or she performs (i.e., precisely the kind of pay-for-knowledge system that U.S. unions often reject).

The agreement mandates yearly consultation between works councils and management to assess the plant's upcoming skill requirements and to plan and implement retraining programs to meet them. Employers bear the cost of any training measures undertaken, which take place during (paid) working time. The new agreement does not establish a full-fledged "pay-for-knowledge" system, but it does ensure that a worker who receives training but is not bumped up to the higher skill (and thus higher wage) job on a permanent basis is nonetheless entitled to receive the higher wage for a specified "bridge" period. Thus, workers who have not been placed in higher-skill jobs four months after they have completed training are entitled to additional wages amounting to three percent of their monthly wages for at least ten months (Kurz-Scherf 1988b:517). The idea behind the agreement is that the best way to protect workers against deskilling and income loss in the long run is to push for an ongoing upgrading of worker skills.[11]

The agreement strengthens and institutionalizes the role of works councils in promoting ongoing retraining and encouraging a closer wage-skill fit. The agreement does not give works councils full codetermination rights on the assessment of the plant's skill requirements. However, as Kurz-Scherf points out, combined with the rights works councils already possess in the area of training (e.g., paragraph 98 of the Works Constitution Act), the new agreement gives them potentially quite powerful tools with which to affect plant-level skills and training (Kurz-Scherf 1988b:517–18). In this sense the agreement empowers and challenges works councils to adopt a more aggressive stand on these issues (Kurz-Scherf 1988b:517).

While the general goals behind this agreement are the same as those of its predecessor of a decade earlier (the 1978 "Wage Framework" Agreement described in Chapter 5), the approach is quite different. The solution to the problem of deskilling embodied in the 1978 contract was more passive—income guarantees in the event of downward classification. The new 1988 agreement, in contrast, turns the wage-skill problem around by putting the skill issue first and empowers works councils to adopt a more aggressive stance in plant training initiatives. In addition, in 1978, both the union's demand for a "collective" income guarantee, and the more watered-down individual guarantees it actually got, represented uniform "blanket" regulations negotiated above the plant level and simply administered by the works council. In the 1988 agreement, in contrast, works councils play a central role, adapting general guidelines set down in the contract to their individual plant conditions. Indeed, this kind of flexibility may account for why employers found this new agreement more palatable than the first. In 1988, unlike in 1978, employers and the union reached a compromise without industrial strife.

Finally, signs of a strategic shift toward a greater reliance on works councils to achieve the central union's technology demands are also apparent in the current discussion of quality circles. Until recently, the IG Metall's official position on quality circles was to advise works

---

11. The union's collective bargaining department is also discussing a more thorough revamping of existing wage framework agreements, which would establish closer links between wages, work organization, and skills (see IG Metall 1989b).

councils to withhold all cooperation (IG Metall 1984c). Union leaders are now rethinking this policy. While the issue remains controversial, the debate has shifted toward contemplating a more differentiated approach to various kinds of employer-initiated programs for worker participation.

This discussion revolves around the question of whether it would be possible to use union cooperation in some such programs as a lever for achieving union demands on skills and technology (Herzer et al. 1988; IG Metall 1988b). Where worker participation programs are linked to changes in work organization, plant-level labor representatives might cooperate strategically, agreeing to participate so long as the working groups could develop projects serving labor's and not just management's goals. The idea would be then to use them as a forum for discussing the union's Gestaltung goals, and as a vehicle for gaining greater labor influence on questions of job design and work organization.

This discussion of union responses to employer-initiated programs for worker participation is in fact part of a broader debate within the union (but especially in the technology department). The question is whether works councils themselves need to restructure their work so that the workers who are affected by work reorganization and other changes in the plant are more involved in the process of formulating demands and pushing for their implementation. Ironically, some aspects of this debate are reminiscent of the discussion of "on the job codetermination" in the early 1970s (see Chapter 4). The concrete proposals that were so controversial then (legally based work groups and/or group leaders) are no longer on the table. However, it is perhaps not surprising that the kind of direct worker involvement that is being called for, for example in the union Action Program on technology, has helped rekindle a discussion of what Mitbestimmung am Arbeitsplatz might mean today.[12]

This reorientation in the IG Metall's strategy on quality circles is another example of the union's attempts to formulate a more differentiated policy that responds to the particular situation labor representatives confront in their own plants. Like the union's new technology program and the 1988 agreement on skills described above, the idea is for works councils to play a more prominent role in formulating and implementing plant-level solutions to the specific problems they face.

UNION TECHNOLOGY POLICY IN THE DUAL SYSTEM

The shift in union technology policy toward the increasing importance of works councils and plant-level bargaining grew out of the new opportunities and constraints the IG Metall encountered, especially

12. See, for example, Lecher 1991, as well as the DGB's new initiative for Mitbestimmung am Arbeitsplatz (DGB 1985b).

since the 1970s. The expansion of works councils' rights in areas directly and indirectly affected by technology strengthened (if not laid) the basis for a more decentralized strategy, although the union still of course considers the rights of work councils (particularly on the introduction of technology itself) insufficient. But if the reforms of the early 1970s made such a strategy increasingly viable, the disappointments later in the decade—in the "humanization" politics of the government and in collective bargaining—made the strategy increasingly attractive. In this sense, the shift to the plant level is a response to blocked opportunities in other arenas.

But that is not the whole story, for the shift toward a more plant-based approach has also been driven by the nature of the union's own goals on technology. As I have argued, demands such as job enrichment through group work and job rotation are by their very nature difficult to secure directly in broad and encompassing contracts. The union's own Action Program also stresses how the plant-specific character of union demands for Gestaltung necessarily enhances the importance of plant-level bargaining in union technology policy (IG Metall 1984a: passim). Of course, just because the union is behind this kind of plant-oriented strategy does not mean that employers oppose it. On the contrary, if the contrast between the 1978 and 1988 agreements in Baden-Württemberg just described is any indication, the very flexibility such decentralized solutions offer may make it easier for the union and employers to find common ground for compromise in central framework agreements.

The evolution of the IG Metall's technology policy since the 1970s thus also points toward another critical source of resiliency in the dual system. In this case, and unlike in the case of centralized bargaining over working-time reduction, the IG Metall is at least as much drawn as it is driven to integrate works councils more closely into central union strategies. As the 1988 agreement on skills shows, this plant-based strategy does not preclude centralized bargaining and is certainly not conceived as a substitute for it. However, labor's relatively strong plant-level rights on issues directly or indirectly related to technological change have given the unions a crucial second avenue to negotiate the effects of technology at the plant level even when, as in the late 1970s, such qualitative issues were the source of great tensions at the national level. In addition, these rights have given the union a point of departure to address the particular problems technology raises in different sectoral and plant contexts. As in the case of the union's campaign to reduce weekly working times, works councils are becoming an increasingly important locus of conflict and cooperation between labor and capital in Germany's negotiated adjustment.

CHAPTER NINE

The Politics of Work Reorganization: A Comparative Perspective

Chapters 7 and 8 document intensified maneuvering between German employers and the IG Metall within the dual system. They show how the union has been both pushed and pulled to incorporate works councils more closely into central union policy, but how in both cases the dual system has provided a source of resiliency and stability in West Germany's negotiated adjustment. This chapter returns to a comparative perspective, highlighting what is distinctive about West Germany by comparing the politics of work reorganization there with Sweden and the United States.

Employers throughout the advanced capitalist world are experimenting with new work designs in an effort to enhance the flexibility of their production processes and their work forces. Group work and job rotation are examples of the kinds of innovations they are introducing to reduce shop-floor rigidities, improve product quality, and raise productivity. Such changes are associated with the heralded crisis in Fordism and the search for new ways to organize work in the increasingly volatile markets since the 1980s (Piore and Sabel 1984).

The politics of work reorganization epitomize the more general pressures for labor flexibility and for decentralization that now figure more prominently in labor politics throughout the advanced industrial world. One of the prime motives for reorganizing work is to enhance the flexibility of labor, among other things, by adapting job assignments and manning levels to evolving production requirements and by training workers in a variety of skills. Furthermore, because so many of these changes deal with plant-specific production issues, work reorganization necessarily involves plant-level negotiations and thus raises questions about the balance between centralized and decentralized bargaining.

From labor's perspective work reorganization implies both new opportunities and new risks (Coriat and Zarifan 1986). The relaxation of Fordist work organization can enrich jobs, enhance skills, reduce monotony, and dismantle oppressive plant hierarchies (Sabel 1986:51–54). But work reorganization can also lead to layoffs and disguise old-fashioned speed-ups (Parker and Slaughter 1988: especially chap. 3). The balance struck between the opportunities and the risks varies cross-nationally in ways that reveal much about labor's role in the restructuring.

Work reorganization provides a good window on national differences in contemporary labor politics because, while the trend toward restructuring is pervasive, labor strategies and the politics of the process vary dramatically from one country to another. In Britain and the United States unions often oppose the introduction of "flexible" forms of work organization such as teamwork (Parker 1985; Parker and Slaughter 1988).[1] In countries like Sweden and West Germany, in contrast, work reorganization along similar lines has been accomplished more consensually and with greater input and participation from organized labor. Indeed, unions in these countries have welcomed innovations such as group work and job rotation, which they see as compatible with goals they themselves have been promoting for decades (Sandberg 1984; Auer 1985; and Thelen 1987b; see also Chapter 8).

Differences in labor goals and participation derive in large part from differences in the institutional context, especially union organization and the institutions for negotiation and conflict resolution between unions and employers. Union goals are shaped by the organization of labor interests: for example, the goals of craft unions are different from those of industrial and multi-industrial unions like the IG Metall. In addition, however, the institutions of labor relations structure conflicts over work reorganization in ways that affect both the goals of unions and the outcomes of their interactions with management. The structure of labor relations matters because, as Zysman puts it: "What is attempted and achieved is affected by how it must be done" (1983:79).

West Germany and Sweden share certain characteristics, most notably a relatively unified labor movement, that distinguish them sharply from the American case. However, the mechanisms for negotiation and conflict resolution in Germany are more decentralized and legalistic than in Sweden, and on this dimension German labor relations resemble those in the United States in some respects. Comparisons of the politics of work reorganization in West Germany with those in Sweden and the United States illustrate the impact of these two variables— union organization and the institutions of labor relations—on the

---

1. Although union responses to such initiatives vary across sectors and plants (see, e.g., Kochan, Katz, and Mauer 1984).

politics of production reorganization and highlight the distinctive features of West Germany's dual system.

Swedish and German unions pursue similar goals in work reorganization, but they do so through very different channels. The similarity in goals derives from the structure of the labor movements, in particular the organizational unity and pervasive presence of unions in both countries. However, Swedish unions rely more on political avenues (national corporatist bargaining and a more politicized version of plant-level codetermination) to achieve their goals. Lacking similar national political power, German unions are forced to pursue their goals through different channels—collective bargaining and especially Germany's more legalistic version of codetermination at the plant and company levels. The comparison of the politics of work reorganization in Sweden and West Germany thus echoes and reinforces the conclusions in Chapter 2: West Germany's negotiated adjustment is not simply a weaker version of Swedish corporatism, but differs systematically from the classic corporatist model. It is more privatized, more decentralized, and more legalistic.

The comparison of West Germany and the United States bounds the analysis of the German case from the other side and illustrates the difference between the two kinds of legalism (premised on broad framing principles versus detailed rules) identified in Chapter 2. American and German unions pursue very different goals with respect to work reorganization, but in both cases plant-level bargaining is key, and the primary channels for negotiation and conflict resolution there are legalistic. The different structures of the two labor movements help account for their very different goals. However, shop-floor labor relations in Germany—like those in the unionized sector in the United States—are subject to extensive procedural regulations governing the adjudication of grievances and conflicts. This legalistic basis for labor politics not only distinguishes Germany from "classic" corporatist countries like Sweden, but distinguishes both the United States and Germany from other countries like France and Great Britain, where labor relations are less codified, more highly politicized, and generally more volatile.[2]

However, a comparison of the politics of work reorganization in the United States and West Germany also shows that different types of legalism lead to very different outcomes. I distinguish between the *contractually based* rights of American unions and the *constitutionally anchored* rights of their German counterparts, and show how the latter facilitate restructuring with positive union participation, whereas the former impede restructuring and foment conflict over work reorganization, which is eventually accomplished anyway, but with much lower levels of union participation.

2. On France, see especially Daley 1988; on Britain, see Kahn 1987.

Swedish Corporatism versus German Legalism

At first glance one is struck more by the similarities than the differences between the Swedish and West German cases. While differences between them exist, the relative political and market strength of the unions in both countries, as well as labor's considerable powers at the plant level, contribute to a higher overall degree of labor influence on work reorganization than in many other advanced capitalist countries. Moreover, Swedish and German unions wield their power toward similar ends: instead of opposing or impeding restructuring, they participate in and shape work reorganization to achieve union goals.

Multi-industrial unionism contributes to the positive orientation of both labor movements toward work reorganization. Craft unions or even narrowly based industrial unions often oppose change because the decline of the skills and sectors they organize threatens the unions themselves with extinction (Slichter 1941; Olson 1982). But multi-industrial unions in Sweden and Germany have less interest in protecting particular jobs in particular factories or trades. In both countries the idea is much more to ease the movement of workers into jobs with a future rather than attempt to guarantee their tenure in jobs without one. The active labor market policies and subsidies for retraining that have emerged as national policy out of tripartite bargaining between employers, unions, and the government in Sweden are precisely designed to shift workers out of declining professions and industries and into growing ones.

In Germany, too, organized labor's goal is to facilitate workers' adjustment to restructuring rather than oppose it, as a 1984 agreement between the IG Metall and Gesamtmetall attests. This agreement reorganized skills and apprenticeship training for the metalworking and electronics industries, collapsing fifty-four previously separate trades into ten new, more broadly defined ones (*Der Gewerkschafter*, January 1985:15–34).[3] The idea behind the reorganization was to promote a closer fit between the vocational training that workers receive and contemporary changes in industrial organization and technology that demand more diversified skills. The reorganization eliminated narrowly based, traditional trades by merging them with others to produce a smaller number of trades embodying a broader range of skills. However, the union welcomed the restructuring because the broader base of skills it provides allows workers to keep pace with technological change and enhances their opportunities in the labor market.[4]

3. In the metalworking industries, forty-two previously distinct trades were reduced to six new ones, with sixteen different specializations possible; in electronics, four new trades (with eight possible specializations) replace the previous twelve separate trades.

4. Many academics tend to romanticize a very traditional notion of the skilled craftsman and often cite Germany as the country that has best nurtured and preserved

Not only are German and Swedish unions generally amenable to adjustment and restructuring; both union movements in the past have advocated specific measures that are strikingly similar to the kinds of changes that managers are now promoting. For example, unions in both countries have long championed innovations such as group work and job rotation that employers are now embracing in the interests of plant flexibility.[5] Although their motives are different from those of employers (job and income security, skill enhancement, and "humanization of work" for the unions; efficiency, productivity, and flexibility for employers), unions in both countries (but especially in Germany) view employers' recent initiatives in work reorganization as an opportunity to revive demands that have long been on their agenda but whose realization was delayed by the economic crisis in the 1970s.[6] The head of the IG Metall technology department described this goal colorfully, saying that his union's strategy was premised on the "jujitsu principle" (interview, April 1989). The union wants to use the weight and momentum of its stronger employer-opponents (who are themselves now questioning traditional forms of production organization) but redirect it toward realizing longstanding union goals in the area of work organization.

Political and institutional differences at both the national and shop-floor levels reveal why German and Swedish unions pursue their similar goals through different channels. The same factors that distinguish West Germany's negotiated adjustment from that of the corporatist

this endangered species. However, discussions with German unionists show that their conceptions of skilled work are generally much more dynamic and are premised more firmly on a fundamental acceptance of the need to adapt skills to ongoing organizational and technological change (statements by members of the IG Metall technology department and the DGB Technology Advisory Center at a union workshop on technology, April 1989).

5. The Swedish case is a little more complicated. There, some of the first experiments with teamwork in the early 1970s (e.g., at Volvo in Kalmar) were initiated by employers who were seeking to lower absenteeism and turnover by increasing job satisfaction. At the time, unions feared that teamwork systems might be used to undermine codetermination (Pontusson 1990:315–16). Since then, however, Swedish unions (like German ones) have been active proponents of models of group work and job rotation that broaden skills, enrich jobs, and upgrade assembly work. Both the Swedish and the German metalworkers unions have developed criteria for how they would like to see group work implemented; in fact, the IG Metall's criteria were explicitly based on those of the Swedish Metalworkers' Union, though adapted to the particular conditions in German factories (interviews with members of the technology department at IG Metall, 1989; for the criteria themselves, see Muster 1988a). On the Swedish case, see Swedish Metalworkers' Union 1985b: especially 35–36; Sandberg 1984; Auer 1985; and Auer and Riegler 1988. On Germany, see Muster and Wannöffel 1989; Muster 1988a, 1988b; Roth and Kohl 1988; and Thelen 1987b.

6. Again, the Swedish case is slightly different because of the different role employers played in the "humanization of work" debates in the early 1970s (see note 5). But even there, employers often lost interest in the experiments they had initiated as the economic crisis deepened (see, for example, Pontusson 1990:314–15).

democracies also account for different patterns of union involvement in work reorganization at the plant level. What Swedish unions can accomplish through political avenues because of their close relationship with a hegemonic Social Democratic party, German unions must seek through collective bargaining and greater reliance on labor's legal rights under codetermination.

National Politics and Work Reorganization

Swedish labor's political strength at the national level affects both general macroeconomic conditions and specific public policies in ways that support labor's agenda for work reorganization. Labor influence in macroeconomic decision making has helped sustain near-full employment, and tight labor markets have in turn spurred innovation in work design by individual employers. In addition, specific policies and legislation have provided direct support for union influence exercised through codetermination bargaining at the plant level and ensured labor participation in the restructuring of production.

Swedish managers cite tight labor markets as an indirect source of pressure to experiment with new forms of work organization that not only are compatible with the requirements of economic efficiency but also benefit workers. Consistently low unemployment in Sweden (between 1 and 3 percent throughout the 1970s and 1980s) sustains active competition among firms for workers. At the same time, the LO's solidaristic wage bargaining has compressed wage differentials across industries and plants, limiting the ability of employers to compete for workers on the basis of wages. In this context, firms have turned to other inducements, including desirable working conditions, to attract and hold qualified employees. This is precisely how managers explain the adoption of measures such as group work and job rotation. For example at Luxor, a major producer of consumer (and other) electronics, high labor turnover and absenteeism motivated the company to reorganize work along these lines in the hope that more diversified jobs would improve worker satisfaction (interview with production manager, April 1989). This strategy of enhancing work content in order to attract and retain workers plays an even greater role in industries that employ more skilled workers than the electronics industry does (see also Pontusson 1990).[7]

7. The Swedish Metalworkers' Union (Metall) wants to capitalize on employers' growing interest in work reorganization and skills by launching a new initiative for what the union calls a "solidaristic work policy." Just as the LO's longstanding solidaristic wage policy was designed to decrease wage differentials among workers in different plants and sectors, the goal of solidaristic work policy is to narrow skill differentials among workers through aggressive training and retraining initiatives (interviews with Christer Markin and Ingemar Göransson of the research department at Metall headquarters, April 1989).

Low unemployment not only affects the incentives employers face in the market; it also influences what workers themselves demand of their jobs. It is often hard to mobilize workers around abstract and seemingly exotic demands to "humanize" work by improving the work environment or job design. Certainly such goals enjoy far lower priority than more basic and tangible demands such as wages and job security. But as a representative of the Swedish Metalworkers Union pointed out, the relative job and income security that Swedish workers already enjoy allows them to think beyond such concerns (interview, April 1989). While American unions grapple with these basic survival issues, Swedish unions are freer to devote greater attention to others, including working conditions and work organization.[8]

Swedish employers do not feel the effects of labor's political power only through the indirect influence of near-full employment. Corporatist bargaining has also produced policies at the national level whose effects reverberate at the plant level and directly support union influence in work reorganization. The codetermination legislation of the 1970s (discussed below) is one example. Another is the "renewal fund" law of 1984.[9] In that year, the Social Democratic government passed a bill requiring all companies earning over SKr 500,000 (approximately $80,000) in profits in 1985 to deposit ten percent of them into a non–interest-bearing account administered by the Swedish National Bank. These so-called renewal funds would be held in the company's name, tax-free, for five years and could be used for particular kinds of investments including worker training, research and development of new products, or innovations to improve plant safety and/or working conditions. A withdrawal from the fund required the approval of the plant union (*Verkstadsklubb*), which insured labor's input into the projects from the start. Those funds not used in the five-year period would be subject to taxation as profits.

The renewal fund legislation was linked to wage negotiations between Swedish employers and unions in 1984.[10] As such, it provides a good example of how national-level corporatist negotiations can produce public policy that enhances the bargaining position of plant-level

8. It could also be argued that because of low unemployment Swedish workers know they can easily find a job elsewhere and thus have less incentive to work to improve their present working conditions. This alternative hypothesis was generally not borne out in my own observations in the electronics industry, but further research would be needed to determine the conditions under which either effect might obtain.

9. This account of the renewal fund legislation is based primarily on interviews at Metall headquarters, Stockholm, April 1989; and a Metall memorandum, 4 February 1985. See also Milner 1989:137.

10. As a Metall memorandum puts it: "The [Renewal Fund] Act should be seen as a measure taken to ease wage negotiations. In light of the high profits some employers were reaping, the low wage increases that would have been necessary to fight inflation would otherwise not have been tenable" (Swedish Metalworkers Union 1985a:1).

representatives and supports their participation in production reorganization. This law not only gave employers a financial incentive to invest in worker training and other work reorganization projects; the stipulation that they could access the funds only with the consent of the Verkstadsklubb ensured that management negotiate with the union over planned projects. Indeed, it gave the local union veto power in the bargaining process, since employers could not get at their money without reaching an agreement with labor over the use to which it would be put.

Although the renewal fund legislation did not enjoy uniformly high success,[11] in many cases it provided an incentive for both managers and local unions to develop ideas and to negotiate over worker training programs and work reorganization. Group work and job rotation at Ericsson (a producer of telecommunications equipment), for example, grew out of experiments in production reorganization that were financed out of the renewal funds. The primary goal of these measures—which were in fact initiated by the union locals at Ericsson—was to reduce injury and sickness rates among workers through work redesign (interview with union adviser to the project, 1989). The heralded Volvo project at Uddevalla for job enrichment and skill enhancement through group work was also partly financed out of these funds (interview with members of Metall research department, 1989).[12] More generally, representatives of the Swedish Metalworkers' Union emphasize how the legislation sparked a broad discussion within and among local unions of alternative concepts for worker training and work organization.

At this macropolitical level, the contrast to Germany is stark. There, continuing high unemployment weakens labor's bargaining position and removes an incentive for employers to cater to the interests of workers when they redesign production. Moreover, public policy in West Germany over the last decade, particularly under the conservative government, has not supported increased union participation in work reorganization. National legislation has promoted investment in new technologies, but without an equivalent to the Swedish renewal fund legislation that ensures labor influence over how these technologies are introduced. Union appeals for stronger codetermination rights for works councils on technology issues have likewise brought no results. Indeed, other labor legislation such as the Employment Promotion Act of 1985 has if anything undermined or circumscribed the rights of works councils in aspects of decision making at the plant level that bear on work organization issues (see Chapter 7).

11. For example, some companies deliberately drove down 1985 profits in order to avoid or minimize their commitments under the law (interviews at Metall headquarters, Stockholm, April 1989).

12. Although Volvo had begun experimenting with work redesign at other plants well before the 1984 law. For a description of work organization at Uddevalla, see Auer and Riegler 1988:39–41; and Pontusson 1989.

In light of these developments, German unions have turned to other avenues such as collective bargaining to influence work reorganization. The IG Metall has achieved results similar to those of the Swedish renewal fund legislation, but through negotiations with Gesamtmetall rather than through public policy. The "Wage and Salary Framework Agreement" for Baden-Württemburg (described in the previous chapter) encourages labor input into worker training by mandating yearly discussions of this issue between works councils and plant managers. Like the Swedish renewal funds, this agreement in effect extends the consultation rights of works councils in the area of worker training and—at least potentially—also in related questions of work organization.[13]

Thus, despite the similar goals espoused by Swedish and German unions, the channels through which they pursue them depend on their power to influence legislation and their market strength. Lacking the same institutionalized voice in national policymaking as their Swedish counterparts, German unions have been forced to pursue their objectives with less public policy support and more "on their own strength." One avenue for German unions to influence work reorganization has been collective bargaining. The other, perhaps more important one, is the exercise of labor's legal rights at a decentralized level under codetermination.

Plant Bargaining and Work Reorganization

Both Sweden and Germany have well-developed systems of codetermination that give unions a presence on company boards and a voice in plant-level decision making on a broad scale. Company- and plant-level codetermination facilitates union participation in work reorganization in both countries, and this distinguishes them from many of their European neighbors. But there remain important differences between the two that affect the politics of production reorganization and support the general argument that Germany's negotiated adjustment is on balance more decentralized and legalistic than Sweden's.[14] Swedish labor's plant-level rights derive rather directly from the unions' political power at the national level. German unions, in contrast, arrived at

13. Indeed, this aspect of the new agreement in Germany is what makes it so significant, especially since labor's efforts to extend the codetermination rights of works councils through political pressure for new national legislation have been unsuccessful.

14. This section will focus on labor's rights at the plant level. However, company-level codetermination in the two countries also differs. Indeed, Swedish unions explicitly rejected the German model of company-level codetermination (Martin 1977:52; Auer 1985:4). West German unions have always sought full parity representation on company supervisory boards, the goal being to participate equally in decision making at that level. Wary of the possible conflict of interest posed for labor representatives codirecting capitalist firms, Swedish unions have been content to settle for a more modest union presence on company boards in order to keep themselves informed concerning management's plans.

comparable plant-level powers less directly, and the legal rights of works councils there if anything now compensate for the weaker political position of the central unions. Related to this, Swedish codetermination is an extension of the collective bargaining relationship between union and employers, while German codetermination is more codified and statute-driven.

Earlier chapters document the evolution of the rights of works councils in West Germany and make the case that these have helped to buttress the strength of central unions and thus to sustain negotiated adjustment in the absence of classic corporatist bargaining. Plant-level codetermination in Sweden, in contrast, is much more an extension of national-level corporatism and an expression of the continued national political and economic power of Swedish unions. As in West Germany, plant militancy in the late 1960s provided an impetus for legislative reforms to enhance labor's powers at the plant level.[15] But in West Germany subsequent attempts (after 1972) to extend union rights enjoyed at best mixed results. In Sweden, in contrast, the initial legislation was only the first in a series of reforms sought and achieved by the unions as an explicit response to the growing importance of production issues and shop-floor bargaining (see, for example, Martin 1977:66; Auer 1985:3–4).

Between 1972 and 1976 several new laws significantly extended labor's plant-level rights in Sweden.[16] Legislation in the early 1970s established union representation on company boards of directors, strengthened the rights of union health and safety stewards (and empowered them to halt work considered dangerous), and placed new restrictions on employers' ability to lay off workers (Heclo and Madsen 1987:123). These measures were followed in 1976 by the landmark Codetermination at Work Act, passed by a broad parliamentary coalition (including both the Social Democrats and bourgeois parties).[17] This law laid down general guidelines for expanding the powers of shop stewards and called for negotiations between the national trade union and employers' confederations to establish new parameters for plant-level labor relations.

Although these negotiations were delayed for several years, in 1982 the LO reached an agreement with the Swedish Employers' Confedera-

---

15. Indeed, Andrew Martin's (1977) explanation of the LO's demands for greater plant rights is similar to my explanation of the German case above, in which a part of the impetus lay in the desire to neutralize the challenge to the central union leadership from shop-floor militants.

16. On the whole range of legislative reforms that have enhanced Swedish unions' plant powers since the 1970s, see Edlund and Nyström 1988; Auer 1985; Martin 1977, 1984; Gustavsen 1985; and Broström 1982.

17. For a description of the law, see Milner 1989:138–44; and Heclo and Madsen 1987: chap. 3.

tion (SAF) that enhanced the powers of shop stewards substantially.[18] Among other things, their "Development Agreement"[19] allows local unions to initiate discussions and negotiations with management over work organization (paragraph 3.1), encourages the introduction of group work, job rotation, and job enrichment (paragraph 3.4), ensures union participation in technical changes that involve major adjustments for workers (paragraph 4.3), and entitles union members to five hours of paid working time to participate in union meetings on matters connected with union activities in their company (paragraph 10).[20] In sum, codetermination legislation in Sweden has flowed out of national-level corporatist bargaining, and Swedish labor's stronger political position has allowed the unions to respond to the growing importance of plant-level bargaining by negotiating stronger codetermination rights at that level.

West German labor, in contrast, arrived at similarly strong plant-level rights, but through the somewhat more circuitous route described in Chapters 3 and 4. German unions achieved a breakthrough on codetermination in 1972, but unlike in Sweden they have basically been stalemated ever since.[21] Equally important, however, West German unions entered the crisis of the mid-1970s with relatively strong plant-level powers already in place, which despite even the conservative "Wende" in 1983 virtually no one is seriously trying to dismantle. Much more than in Sweden, labor's shop-floor rights are less the explicit product of ongoing corporatist bargaining than they are a source of stability in Germany's negotiated adjustment *despite* labor's weakened national political and market power.

These differences in the evolution of labor's shop-floor rights affect bargaining at the plant level and reflect its relationship to the broader structure of labor politics. In Sweden, plant-level codetermination is integrated into the larger structure of unionism; indeed, it basically extends collective bargaining to the shop floor. This is what Martin calls "codetermination through collective bargaining" (Martin 1977:52–53). The "dualism" of the German system prohibits this kind of formal integration, and plant-level bargaining is more legalistic and codified.

The German Works Constitution Act enumerates in great detail the rules governing works councils' interactions with management. The rights of works councils to participate in decision making are broken

18. Conflict over the wage-earner funds was primarily responsible for the delay.
19. This employers' association calls it the "Agreement on Efficiency and Participation."
20. For a text of the agreement, see Swedish Employers' Confederation 1982.
21. In the same year that the Swedish parliament passed the Codetermination at Work Act by an overwhelming majority, the German Bundestag was engaged in a highly partisan battle over extending the Montan model of company-level codetermination to other industries, a battle which resulted in a compromise that disappointed the unions and heightened tensions between them and employers.

down into three "layers" representing different degrees of strength: on some issues (e.g., the introduction of new technologies) managers must simply inform the work council of their plans; on others (e.g., changes in plant layout), employers must consult with the works council; and on still others (e.g., overtime, major layoff plans) they must negotiate and reach agreement with the works council before implementing the proposed changes. When the two sides cannot reach agreement on an issue in which the works council has full codetermination rights, either party can call for conciliation chaired by a neutral outsider who casts the deciding vote (*Einigungsstelle*). While the works council has the right to seek the advice of outside consultants (such as representatives from union headquarters), the process of conflict resolution involves neither the central union nor the employers' organization formally.

The rights of Swedish shop stewards, in contrast, are not enumerated in the same way.[22] Unlike in the German case, Swedish managers are under no obligation to consult with labor representatives on particular, specified issues. But also unlike the German case, the local union can simply demand consultation and negotiations over a much wider range of issues (see, for example, Martin 1984:263).[23] The range of issues on which union representatives are included in plant decision making is thus more expansive than in West Germany, where enumerated rules bind management, but also set boundaries on management's strict obligations under the law.[24]

Conflict resolution in Sweden is also more often negotiated than adjudicated. Only cases of alleged violations of the law (e.g., where employers withhold information or refuse even to consult with the local union) are subject to adjudication through the labor courts. A simple failure by plant management and the Verkstadsklubb to reach agreement on an issue does not make the conflict subject to arbitration or conciliation.[25] Rather, the case is referred upward for discussion and

22. Except the rights of safety stewards, which are explicitly enumerated in law.

23. On important issues they do not need to demand it. Because of labor's rather pervasive powers, Swedish managers consult with the union on most important decisions as a matter of course (plant interviews, 1989).

24. Even basic issues such as the number of plant labor representatives and how they organize their work are open for negotiation in Sweden. The German Works Constitution Act specifies precisely how many full-time labor representatives a work force of a particular size is entitled to. The work of a Swedish Verkstadsklubb is much more fluidly defined. Elected members can take the time they need to fulfill their duties. Moreover, other workers (not elected to the Verkstadsklubb) can also be relieved of work responsibilities to do union work during working hours. Managers who are concerned about personnel planning sometimes pressure the union to negotiate a "time budget" for union work, which specifies the number of hours they expect to devote to union activities in a given year (plant interviews, 1989).

25. By the same token, the local union's right to be consulted on various issues does not include an obligation that management also reach agreement with the union. And in this respect, the rights of German works councils—at least on a narrow range of questions that are subject to full codetermination and conciliation—are perhaps stronger.

negotiation at higher levels within the union and the employers' association.

These micro-level differences between Sweden and West Germany also affect the politics of work reorganization. The more expansive (though less well defined) rights of Swedish shop stewards allow them to directly initiate negotiations over work reorganization. An example is ABB-Automation in Västeras, where the impetus for introducing job rotation came from union suggestions to lower injury rates in the plant. In Germany, in contrast, the Works Constitution Act gives works councils only relatively weak rights in the specific areas of work organization and technological change. However, German works councils can force negotiations over work reorganization by linking it to other bargaining issues where they have stronger codetermination rights. For example, the works council at Volkswagen in Braunschweig linked its approval of changes in working times, manning levels, and wage grades (issues on which the works council has strong rights) to demands for broader jobs and group work (*ganzheitliche Arbeit in Gruppen*), to maintain and indeed expand the skills of the affected workers (presentation by works councillor at IG Metall conference, Oberhausen, 1989). The strategy on technology and work reorganization sketched out in the IG Metall's technology program is premised on just such linkages at the plant level, using the rights of works councils on personnel matters as a lever for influencing work organization.

Hence, while it is possible for plant-level labor representatives to get work organization on the agenda in both countries, this requires somewhat more strategy and creativity in West Germany. The legal rights of German works councils provide an important lever in negotiations, but they still give the works council only indirect means for forcing the issue on management. Sweden's less "statute-driven" version of codetermination constrains employers less in strictly procedural and legal terms, but it also allows unions more room for maneuver and opens up the possibility for labor influence over a wider range of issues.

Despite the way the particular rules of the Works Constitution Act can circumscribe union influence over work reorganization, German codetermination does provide a more general and indirect incentive for employers to experiment with forms of work organization such as job rotation and group work that the union can endorse. As argued above, the strong rights of works councils in personnel policy turn labor, in Streeck's words, into more of a "fixed cost" for employers (Streeck 1983:30). Where it is costly for them to engage in a policy of hiring and firing, flexibility in personnel policy depends on flexible *internal* labor markets (multiskilled workers, flexibility in job assignments). In the end, the rigidities imposed on employers by labor's strong plant-level rights in West Germany have effects similar to that of low unemployment in Sweden discussed above: whereas Swedish employers have an incentive to reorganize work in order to hold on to scarce workers, West German employers are pushed to do so because they cannot easily let workers go. In this way, too, German labor's legally based rights at the plant level compensate for their weaker market and political position at the national level.

In sum, the differences between the politics of work reorganization in Sweden and West Germany support the general conclusion that West Germany's negotiated adjustment is different from Swedish corporatism not only in degree but in kind. The two systems of labor relations in many ways produce similar outcomes, but through different means.

WEST GERMANY AND THE UNITED STATES: VARIETIES OF LEGALISM

A comparison of West Germany's dual system with another model of labor relations, that in the United States, will illuminate the distinctive features of the German model from another perspective.[26] U.S. industrial relations, like Germany's and unlike Sweden's, are relatively "privatized" and legalistic. As in Germany, the government in the United States is generally averse to intervening directly in labor-capital relations, and prefers the role of referee.[27] Unlike Sweden, but also in contrast to more politicized and decentralized systems such as those in Italy, France, and Great Britain, both the United States and West Germany are renowned for the highly legalistic character of labor relations, especially at the plant level.[28]

Despite these similarities, striking differences characterize labor-capital relations and affect the politics of work reorganization in the two countries. American unions have adopted a more defensive stance on work reorganization and have been less successful in influencing the process. Innovations such as teamwork and job rotation have been far more controversial in labor circles in the United States than in West Germany, and U.S. locals are more apt to oppose employers initiatives to introduce such changes. Moreover, even where they have participated in production reorganization, U.S. unions have been less successful in incorporating labor interests into the resulting work design.

Again, these differences can be traced back to the two factors cited

26. Parts of this argument are also laid out in Thelen 1989b and Thelen 1991, both of which, however, focus primarily on the U.S. case, including plant case studies.

27. There are of course exceptions to this in both cases: from President Cleveland's interventions in the great railroad strike of 1894 to Reagan's firing of striking PATCO workers in the United States, and the Concerted Action discussions of the late 1960s in Germany. However, neither government is involved to the same extent as the Swedish in actively mediating and negotiating trade-offs between labor and capital on an ongoing, long-term basis.

28. On the legalism of U.S. labor relations, see Bok 1971; and Rogers 1984.

above: the organization of labor interests (which shapes the goals of unions) and the broader institutional context of labor relations (which defines the channels available to them to participate in work reorganization). Greater fragmentation in the U.S. labor movement both makes many individual unions less amenable to work reorganization and makes unions as a group more vulnerable to employer strategies that use competition among plants and regions as a lever to achieve their goals.

In addition, differences between the German and American variants of "legalism" highlight differences in the channels of bargaining that also help to explain outcomes in the two cases. The basic difference is closely related to the distinction described in Chapter 2 between broad framework regulations (Rahmenbedingungen) and detailed, highly specific rules (see also Katz and Sabel 1985; and Piore and Sabel 1984: chaps. 5 and 6). The contractually based rights of American unions are closely tied to the structure of production under Fordism; hence the retreat from Fordist work organization itself undermines their traditional sources of shop-floor power (Piore 1982). In contrast, the more broadly defined rights of German works councils (anchored in the Works Constitution Act of 1972) are not linked to any particular form of work organization, and thus provide a more stable basis or framework (Rahmen) for union participation in restructuring. In short, the legal channels available to unions in the United States mediate against their positive participation in work reorganization, whereas those in Germany encourage, support, and sustain such participation.

National Politics and Work Reorganization

Two institutional features of the national political economy in the United States circumscribe unions' options and shape their strategies for dealing with management initiatives on work reorganization: the size of the unionized sector in the national economy and the structure of the organized labor movement itself.

First, while union membership in West Germany has been quite stable since the 1960s, the unionized sector in the United States is small and shrinking. The national unionization rate peaked in the mid-1950s at around 35 percent, and since then membership has steadily declined to its current level of approximately 17 percent (Kochan, Katz, and McKersie 1986:48). Unionization rates also vary tremendously on a regional basis: they are higher in northern industrial states such as Michigan and Ohio where unions are more entrenched, especially in heavy industry and manufacturing, and much lower in the southern "right-to-work" states, which place greater restrictions on union organizing (Freeman and Medoff 1984:31).

The uneven market presence and national political weakness of

American unions undermine their position in bargaining over work reorganization. Plant restructuring often involves changes in work rules and job classifications that must be negotiated with the local union. Should these negotiations become difficult or cumbersome, employers can threaten to opt for the simpler route of avoiding unions altogether.[29] Honda (Marysville, Ohio), Nissan (Smyrna, Tennessee), and IBM (everywhere) are pursing precisely this strategy. And at the GM-Toyota joint venture in Fremont, California, the condition for reopening the plant and recalling UAW workers was the union's acceptance of the plant's teamwork system (interview with UAW local president, 1985).[30] The availability of a nonunion option in the United States creates enormous temptations for employers to undertake restructuring without union participation, or to use the threat of moving production to nonunion sites as a lever to extract greater concessions from labor on work organization (see also Katz 1985:186ff; Kochan and Cutcher-Gershenfeld 1988; Turner 1988:5; and Parker and Slaughter 1988).

The relative ease with which employers can avoid and threaten unions in the United States contrasts sharply with the situation in Germany. This kind of confrontational union-avoidance strategy plays a less important role in Germany where membership levels have been more stable and union coverage is more encompassing, both through collective bargaining and the Works Constitution Act.[31] German unions are in a better position to influence work reorganization in large part because their presence throughout the economy forces German employers to negotiate with, rather than try to avoid, organized labor.

Second, the relative fragmentation of the American labor movement helps explain why some U.S. unions oppose work reorganization and accounts as well for the difficulty American unions have in formulating a cohesive and unified response to employer initiatives.[32] While many industries (e.g., automobiles and steel) are organized along industrial lines, others such as construction are still craft-based.[33] Work reorganization involving changes that blur the lines among traditionally separate crafts can make labor unity difficult and even actively incite conflict among unions. Combining and broadening skills to enhance plant

29. This threat can be explicit or implicit, and it can assume a number of forms. In poorly or only partially unionized sectors, it can be a direct threat to transfer production to nonunion regions or plants. But even in well-organized sectors such as automobile assembly, employers have pressed their local unions for work rule concessions against the threat of contracting out production (often to nonunion suppliers).

30. Indeed, GM first experimented with production reorganization in its nonunionized southern plants, although the UAW subsequently reached an agreement with the automaker to extend union coverage to these work forces (Katz 1985:90).

31. Although German employers, too, often try to provoke competition among works councils as a bargaining strategy.

32. See Kochan and Katz, 1988:120–36, for a summary of the variety of types of bargaining units in the United States and its implications for union bargaining.

33. And the industrial unions in the United States are also narrower than multi-industrial unions in Europe such as the IG Metall.

flexibility can threaten some craft unions with extinction, which accounts for why such measures have been especially controversial among unions organizing particular skilled trades. Conversely, it is not surprising that the most successful examples of positive union participation in work reorganization in the United States have come out of industries (such as automobiles and steel) that are dominated by national unions organized along industrial lines.[34]

Moreover, like the nonunion option, labor fragmentation and rivalries among unions can be used as a wedge by employers. For example, at a major electronics plant organized into two separate bargaining units, one represented by the International Union of Electrical Workers (IUE), and the other by the International Brotherhood of Electrical Workers (IBEW), management was able to encourage concessions on work rules and job classifications from the IUE local by first striking a deal with the less militant IBEW local (interviews, 1989) (see also Kochan and Katz 1988:132–33). Another form of such "whipsawing" is possible where a company with many production sites can foster competition among locals within a more broadly defined, but decentralized, union structure. For example, GM and other carmakers have been accused of using such tactics to elicit concessions on job classifications.[35] And finally, jurisdictional disputes among different unions for the right to organize particular plants create tensions that employers can also exploit for leverage in bargaining.

In sum, the U.S. labor movement's weaker and more uneven presence in the economy, as well as its relative fragmentation into a variety of different and sometimes competing unions, undermine attempts at a coherent, coordinated effort to participate positively in work reorganization. Because they are more pervasive, German unions are harder for employers to avoid or ignore. And because they are more centralized, they are less vulnerable to employer-instigated competition. In contrast to the United States, these national-level factors—the organization of labor interests and the broad presence and strength of the unions—support labor participation in industrial restructuring in Germany; they promote greater unity in the labor movement and encourage negotiation and compromise rather than conflict between labor and capital on work reorganization.

Plant Bargaining and Work Reorganization

The scope and character of labor's rights at the plant level influence union goals and the politics of work reorganization even more directly

34. I am indebted to Kirsten Wever for this point.
35. See, for example, Turner's account of how GM based its decision on which of two plants to concentrate production of Camaros and Pontiac Firebirds (and which to close) on the relative willingness of the two UAW locals to cooperate in the implementation of a team system (1988:12).

than the national-level political factors discussed above. The institutions of labor relations in both Germany and the United States are highly legalistic, but the rules of American labor relations impede, while those of German labor relations enhance, labor's ability to participate in work reorganization. First, codetermination gives West German unions the opportunity to participate proactively in work reorganization, while American unions are generally limited to more defensive participation. Second, in contrast to German codetermination, labor's institutionalized rights under American "job control" unionism are themselves closely linked to Fordist work organization (Piore 1982). American labor's defense of certain "rigid" shop-floor practices stems from this linkage, since making work more flexible by dismantling Fordist work organization can have the side effect of undermining labor's traditional sources of shop-floor control (see also Katz and Sabel 1985).

In demanding codetermination, West German unions historically have sought to ensure labor input into the management of capitalist enterprises. "Business unionism" in the United States, in contrast, largely cedes the issue of managerial prerogative; indeed unions actively eschew sharing responsibilities normally assumed by management.[36] Although different unions have different ideological leanings, the overall philosophy that has prevailed in the United States assigns unions more of a "watchdog" function to protect workers from the effects of managerial decisions and to win as large a "slice of the pie" as possible.

American labor law follows this tradition and institutionalizes a system of plant-level rights that is essentially reactive and defensive.[37] In the United States the norm is "management acts, and workers and their unions grieve" (Kochan, Katz, and McKersie 1986:27). Conflict resolution procedures are premised on the interpretation of labor contracts, and union powers are based substantially on their right to redress employer transgressions of the contract. Unlike German works councils, which can block certain employer actions at least temporarily (pending negotiations and/or agreement with plant labor representatives), U.S. unions can only rarely prevent management from acting, though they can contest actions once taken and redress injuries to workers that result from them through various legal and quasi-judicial channels. Kochan, Katz, and McKersie aptly describe this aspect of the

36. Of course, "business unionism" was not simply a matter of union choice, and alternative ideologies played an important role in American labor history. However, in the United States, all attempts that were made to secure labor's right to (even limited) incursions into the realm of managerial prerogatives were roundly defeated. One of the most famous of these struggles was the UAW strike of 1945–46, which sought to force General Motors Corporation to open its books to the union (see, e.g., Gartman 1986:267–68).

37. This is not to say that the rights of American unions are insignificant. As many authors have pointed out, they place substantial constraints on employers, for example, on transfers and layoffs (see, for example, Slichter, Healy, and Livernash 1960; Chamberlain 1948). The point, rather, is when and how they affect managerial decision making.

U.S. system as "a particular form of industrial jurisprudence" (1986:29) in which managers initiate and unions litigate.[38]

This issue of reactive rather than proactive (or coactive) rights is especially significant in the current context of work reorganization. American managers are not under the same legal obligations as German ones to provide unions with advance information on their plans and to consult with them over the terms of their implementation. As a consequence, U.S. unions are more often cast in the role of protesting against management initiatives on the basis of procedural violations of the terms of the contract, rather than participating in shaping plant outcomes directly.[39] While West German works councils do not have full codetermination rights in the areas of technology and work organization, they do have much stronger information rights than American shop stewards. In addition, and as pointed out above, works councils can use their stronger codetermination and consultation rights in related areas for leverage on work organization issues.

More generally, and perhaps more importantly, German managers are simply more accustomed to ongoing consultation and negotiation with labor because of the long tradition of codetermination and works council participation in plant-level decision making. This tradition itself makes union involvement in new issues like work reorganization less contentious, more natural, and thus more likely in Germany. The case of Volkswagen in Braunschweig is again illustrative. In a major restructuring project at the plant in the mid-1980s, the works council was in on the plans from the start, even taking part in the company's discussions with the manufactures of alternative technologies (presentation at union technology conference, Oberhausen, 1989). This is a somewhat extreme case, but other evidence points in the same direction. For instance, a video advertisement for a German firm that supplies software for machine tools features the IG Metall's expert on numerically controlled machine tools endorsing the firm's product as being compatible with the union's goals for shop-floor programming (video advertisement for Keller). The implication is that the acceptability of certain technologies to unions and works councils can be a source of competitive advantage in the German market. Examples of compa-

38. Another source of shop-floor power is, of course, the right of union locals to strike over certain issues. This right, explicitly denied to German works councils under the Works Constitution Act, has been enormously important in the history of U.S. labor relations. However, the leverage it gives unions depends on the broader context; the current political and market weakness of U.S. unions has drastically curtailed the ability of unions to exploit this source of power.

39. Piore and Sabel (1984: chap. 5) refer to this difference as one of "substantive" versus "procedural" rights. See also Katz and Sabel 1985, who make a complementary argument, emphasizing the difference between two broad models of industrial relations, one premised on narrowly defined jobs (United States), the other premised on broadly defined jobs (Germany), and each associated with a different role for the union.

rable influence by American unions on management decision making are hard to find.

The second feature of labor relations that distinguishes the U.S. from the German case is the closeness of the link between Fordist work organization and U.S. labor's formal rights. The building blocks in the American system of "job-control unionism" are detailed job classifications, work rules, and seniority.[40] Not only is a worker's income pegged to the job he or she performs,[41] work rules attached to the various job classifications specify who can do what jobs in the plant. Taken together, job classifications define a sort of plant hierarchy in which gradations are based on income and working conditions. Competition among workers in the allocation of work within this hierarchy is often governed at least partially by seniority rules.[42]

Work rules, job classifications, and seniority have been the key elements in the traditional structure of organized labor's rights in the United States. Once rules surrounding them have been established contractually, employer transgressions are subject to grievance by the union. The labor contract and the regulations it sets down thus provide the union with the leverage to defend worker interests. For example, work rules that specify the rights and obligations of workers in particular jobs (including the type and amount of work expected of them) can be used to prevent foremen from assigning additional tasks to workers who have worked fast enough to get ahead of the assembly line and thus earn themselves a break. By extension, such work rules can help maintain stable employment by preventing managers from doubling up job assignments for some and laying off others in a period of slack demand.

American managers now regularly criticize unions for defending "rigid" work rules and the "outmoded, traditional" job classifications on which they are based. But employers and not unions are responsible for having introduced job classifications in the first place.[43] Indeed, the

40. The best analyses of the structure and functioning of job control unionism can be found in Kochan, Katz, and McKersie 1986; Kochan and Katz 1988; and Katz 1985: especially 38–47. My account draws on these works, in addition to my own plant-level research in selected plants in the automobile, steel, and electronics industries. While my analysis is compatible with that of Katz in particular, some of the analytic categories I use differ from his in order to highlight comparisons with the German case.

41. In this respect, job classifications are not so different from German wage determination methods, and particularly the "Analytik" method, which also bases workers' pay on the characteristics of the jobs they perform.

42. Seniority provisions take many forms and are usually not the only criterion in work allocation. However, in most unionized plants, workers with greater seniority have bidding rights over plant vacancies and enjoy preference in competition for easier and/or better paying jobs in the plant.

43. This brief historical section draws on Lichtenstein 1982, 1988; Gartman 1986; McPherson 1940; Katz 1985; Piore and Sabel 1984; Slichter, Healy, and Livernash 1960; Jacoby 1985; and Chamberlain 1948.

use of job classifications predates widespread unionization (see Gartman 1986; chap. 11; McPherson 1940: especially 80). In the 1920s, "Ford and other modern manufacturing firms ... set up elaborate job classification systems" with hundreds of distinct occupations to determine pay rates (Lichtenstein 1988:66). Choice jobs in the plant hierarchy were doled out unilaterally by management and on an arbitrary basis, a procedure that naturally enhanced divisions and heightened competition among workers (see also Gartman 1986:234–41; Jacoby 1985:251).

As they grew in the 1920s and 1930s, U.S. unions sometimes challenged the bureaucratic job structure that employers had created (Gartman 1986: chap. 12). But mostly they sought to purge the system of managerial caprice and favoritism, and to impose more egalitarian and universalistic criteria for determining who should advance in the plant hierarchy and who should be entitled to which jobs (and thus to what pay rate) (see, e.g., McPherson 1940:82; Jacoby 1985: chap. 8 passim). Work rules that clarified a worker's contractual obligations to employers reduced the room for arbitrary managerial actions. And seniority rights were a crucial union victory since they replaced foremen's whims in determining who could "bid" for vacancies within the plant to move up the skill, job, and income ladders.[44] In short, seniority became the principle on which conflicts among workers for better jobs and better pay in the plant would be routinized and removed from the realm of managerial discretion. And work rules, in spelling out the individual worker's rights and obligations, would alleviate competition among workers in the context of ongoing production.

Thus, American unions originally had no interest in job classifications per se, only in minimizing their use by employers to incite competition among workers and to pick the winners and losers arbitrarily. But once union rights had been defined in connection with job classifications, organized labor developed a certain stake in the job structure they formed (see also Piore 1982). Developments during and after the war solidified these patterns (see especially Lichtenstein 1982) and gave unions an interest not only in the maintenance of job classifications, but in their proliferation.

Wartime controls in the 1940s reinforced unions' dependence on differentiated plant hierarchies based on job classifications.[45] A wage freeze prevented the unions from raising wages through collective bargaining, but wage increases due to movement to a higher job classification did not have to be cleared by the War Labor Board. Shifting workers within the plant hierarchy became the primary means for raising the incomes of workers during the war. Employers collaborated in this process to retain workers in a period of intense labor shortages.

44. In addition, and most importantly, perhaps, seniority became a basis for determining who would be affected first in the event of layoffs.
45. This paragraph is based on Jacoby's account (1985: especially 262–69).

In this way, as Jacoby argues, "The war did much to forge a distinctively American pattern of internal career ladders composed of rigidly defined jobs" (Jacoby 1985:265).[46]

In addition, in 1947 several arbitration rulings "confirmed that workers could rely on their seniority if they sought a permanent transfer or promotion to an entirely new job classification, but that the foreman's authority governed transfers to a new job assignment within a classification" (Lichtenstein 1988:72). Hence, a larger number of job classifications meant that movement across a greater proportion of jobs in the plant would be governed by seniority rules (and thus subject to union intervention) rather than decided unilaterally by employers and supervisors.

This historical legacy puts an entirely different spin on work reorganization and explains why American unions are often less receptive than German unions to employer initiatives to relax the "rigidities" of Fordist production methods. Changes that German unions embrace in the interests of enriching jobs, upgrading skills, and "humanizing" work are much more controversial in union circles in the United States. Introducing group work and job rotation, for example, often means reducing job classifications and relaxing work rules. But such changes affect the very basis on which organized labor has traditionally been able to prevent speedups and fight layoffs. Likewise, reducing the number of job classifications can weaken the seniority principle. The right of older workers to priority consideration for easier or better-paying jobs is diluted to the extent that fewer job classifications translates into a flatter plant hierarchy and a smaller number of more homogeneous (equally demanding and remunerated) jobs.[47]

Different U.S. unions—and, within unions, often different locals—have taken varying positions on work reorganization (see, for example, Turner 1991). But even where labor has cooperated in new production concepts (e.g., teamwork systems) the decision to do so has frequently sparked controversy. Opponents of such systems of course have nothing against job enrichment through job rotation or group work that enables workers to learn a variety of skills. Rather, what makes these issues contentious is that they involve changes that undermine the traditional rights and role of unions at the plant level. Critics fear that relinquishing or relaxing traditional controls will open the door for a return to the earlier days of managerial caprice and favoritism (see, e.g., Parker and Slaughter 1988). They argue that without the right to combat violations of work rules and classifications, managers would be free to assign

---

46. On how World War II shaped U.S. labor relations, see also Lichtenstein 1982b.

47. This helps explain why workers with long seniority are often most adamantly opposed to innovation in work organization. However, some aspects of seniority rights would be unaffected by fewer job classifications. For example, it would be possible for the union and employers to agree to continue to use seniority criteria on layoffs.

and reassign workers and combine jobs without union "interference."[48]

Clearly, German works councils must also guard against work reorganization that causes speedups and layoffs. However, the basis of their rights to fight these side effects (the Works Constitution Act) is untouched by the work organization changes themselves. Thus, the key difference is that in Germany, works councils negotiate over work organization *on the basis of* a set of stable shop-floor rights, whereas in the United States, negotiations over work reorganization are perforce and by definition inextricably linked to negotiations *over* labor's core rights in the plant. This difference helps explain why American unions often find themselves internally divided over this issue and, more generally, why employer initiatives to reorganize production have provoked a deeper crisis—of strategy, but also of identity—among American unions (Piore 1982). This situation contrasts sharply with that in Germany, where labor has been able to capitalize on the new interest employers have shown in work reorganization to strive, jujitsu-style, for old union demands.[49]

The core difference between the legalism of West German labor relations and that of American labor relations can be characterized as the difference between contractually based rights in the United States and constitutionally anchored ones in Germany.[50] Plant labor relations in the United States revolve around the adjudication of disputes by interpreting and applying specific provisions in detailed contracts. All union grievances and all management counterarguments are premised on the language of the contract. Although certain arbitration awards may be accorded some precedent-setting value, the particular language of individual contracts is decisive and may vary considerably from plant to plant.[51] In the U.S. system, then, contracts typically evolve by

48. New forms of union involvement and new guarantees against such abuses of course can be negotiated and included in new contracts in return for reducing job classifications. Indeed, such agreements have formed the basis for the most successful cases of labor-management cooperation in work reorganization (e.g., GM's Saturn project). In other cases, however, (for all the reasons cited above), unions have been pushed to make concessions on work rules and job classifications on less favorable terms.

49. The policies of the two union movements on worker involvement programs (such as "quality circles") is another example of the same point of contrast. The IG Metall is considering ways of using quality circles as a lever in its work organization strategy, i.e., aggressively using them as a forum to initiate union-oriented changes in work design. The typical pattern in the United States, in contrast, is for unions to attempt to decouple worker involvement programs from changes in work organization. Thus, where they agree to participate in quality circles, U.S. unions often make their participation contingent on management's agreeing not to use these as a forum for addressing contractual issues and by extension questions of work organization.

50. See also Harry Katz and Charles Sabel's (1985) argument stressing the differences between the narrowly based rights of U.S. unions and the more broadly defined rights of German works councils, which captures a part of the difference I am emphasizing here.

51. Awards under one contract may be influential in subsequent cases, though strictly speaking they have no precedent weight under another contract.

growing increasingly complex as further detailed instructions are added on how to deal with new problems. What is now happening, however, is that a growing number of employers are pushing for a more thorough-going renegotiation of contracts to replace detailed job classifications and work rules with teamwork systems and new forms of worker involvement. Already on the defensive, union locals often fear such a wholesale renegotiation of labor's role in the plant and resist giving up "solid" work rules in favor of what to them appear to be vague promises of greater union participation in management decisions. Many prefer to attempt to defend these older rules negotiated in periods of relative labor market strength.

In contrast, the German Works Constitution Act spells out general rights and obligations of management and of works councils for plants throughout the country. More detailed shop-floor agreements may "fill out" or augment the Works Constitution Act or regulate plant-specific issues. However, the basic principles and rules that govern labor's and capital's interactions on the shop floor are both uniform across plants and stable in the sense that they are not subject to renegotiation at the local level. Not designed to cover every contingency, the Works Constitution Act has proved adaptable and capable of accommodating changes in the political, economic, legal, and technological environments. The character of labor's shop-floor rights thus reflects Germany's general pattern of regulation through broad and flexible Rahmenbedingungen (Allen 1990) and contrasts with the American pattern of shop-floor relations premised on detailed contracts, which are themselves in turn embedded in a broader system of state regulation resting on a "tangled web of statute and precedent" (Bok 1971:1394).

Thus, political and institutional differences at the national level, as well as variation in the basis of legalism at the plant level, go a long way toward explaining differences in the politics of work reorganization in Germany and the United States. The overarching system of industrial unionism in Germany gives unions there a more positive orientation toward industrial change; their presence throughout the economy ensures their participation in these changes. These national-level factors are buttressed by the structure of labor's rights at the plant level, which give works councils a more stable basis for negotiating the terms of shop-floor flexibility through work reorganization than is available to union locals in the United States.

WORK REORGANIZATION IN COMPARATIVE PERSPECTIVE

Cross-national variation in the structure of unionism and the institutions of labor relations account for different patterns of conflict and cooperation between labor and capital over work reorganization. Differences at the national-political and shop-floor levels have affected plant bargaining over flexible work organization, influencing both the goals of unions and the channels through which they pursue them in ways that shape labor's role in the restructuring.

In Sweden and Germany, where the labor movement is unified and relatively centralized, labor's overall goals are quite similar, attempting to capitalize on employers' new initiatives in work reorganization to achieve old union demands such as the humanization of work, the upgrading of skills, and a narrowing of plant income differentials. But unions in the two countries pursue their goals through different avenues. Where Swedish unions emphasize political channels and reform through state policy and corporatist bargaining, German unions are more dependent on collective bargaining with employers and on legal avenues under codetermination.

German unions are in some ways more constrained than Swedish unions by the legalism of the dual system. But at the same time, the legal anchoring of labor's rights has been more important in shoring up the strength of German unions, which lack the same strong political position enjoyed by their Swedish counterparts. Swedish unions were able to respond to the growing importance of plant-level bargaining and bolster the powers of shop stewards over the last fifteen years, both through legislative action and subsequent negotiations with employers. German unions, in contrast, have not been as successful in gaining new rights since 1972, but they met the economic crisis already armed with relatively strong plant-level rights. And in both cases strong shop-floor powers are a crucial complement to central union strength in the face of the new challenges since the 1980s.

The U.S.–West German comparison highlights another aspect of the relationship between the institutions of labor relations and labor's goals and strategies. In this case, differences in the structure of unionism and the way labor's rights have been institutionalized explain the different goals of the two labor movements, although both rely on legalistic avenues to achieve them. The way German unions are organized, and also, especially, the way their rights are institutionalized at the plant level, allow them not only to endorse flexible work organization but to participate positively in the restructuring from a position of relative strength. The more tenuous position of American unions within the national political economy, in contrast, excludes or marginalizes them in the process of work reorganization, which only reinforces their more defensive role in the process. This pattern is strengthened further by job-control unionism at the plant level, which poses another barrier to union participation in work reorganization.[52]

52. The difficulties and controversy—also within the labor movement—of rethinking and renegotiating labor's traditional rights became especially clear in the recent discussion within the AFL–CIO over the idea of introducing some kind of statutory "Worker Representation Committees." The proposal was buried when it encountered stiff opposition from within the federation itself (*Los Angeles Times*, 28 February 1989, part 4:1).

This analysis yields a more fine-grained picture of the German case, and again shows that Germany is not simply a "weaker" case of corporatism, but differs qualitatively from the democratic corporatist countries. Comparisons with the Swedish and American systems reveal the "hybrid" characteristics of the German model, which combines labor unity and pervasive union influence at the national level with strong shop-floor rights and a type of legalism that complements and supports negotiated adjustment at the plant level. One of the distinctive features of Germany's dual system of labor relations is how it juxtaposes elements of centralization and decentralization in this way.

CHAPTER TEN

Labor Politics and Industrial Adjustment

By now it is clear that the stability of German labor relations is not the "fair weather" phenomenon some observers claimed it was two decades ago. Labor participation in industrial adjustment and cooperative labor relations held up remarkably well through the economic and political strains of the 1970s and 1980s. One important source of stability has been the resiliency inherent in Germany's dual system of labor relations.

What Germany shares with the "classic" corporatist democracies such as Sweden and Austria is an institutional framework that supports negotiated adjustment. As in these other countries, industrial adjustment in Germany can be characterized in terms of bargained trade-offs between the interests of labor and capital (see also Katzenstein 1985; Wilensky 1983). But the specific institutions that sustain such bargaining distinguish Germany from the more corporatist countries.

The centralization of business interests and the pivotal leadership role played by the IG Metall help compensate for the rather lower overall organization level of the German working class. The strong tradition of what Katzenstein (1987) calls West Germany's "centralized society"—in this case, the centralization of business interests, industrial unionism, and centralized collective bargaining—is a crucial feature of the German model. In the face of centrifugal strains since the 1970s, this tradition has been a powerful centripetal force in labor relations.

But where the West German model of negotiated adjustment is most different from the corporatist democracies is in the role of the state. Organized labor in Germany is still a powerful political lobby compared to unions in many other countries. However, other institutional and political features of the German political economy have inhibited the kind of stable national-level bargaining among business, labor, and the state that is characteristic of Sweden, Austria, and other examples of corporatism. In particular, the autonomy of the German Central Bank (Bundesbank) and the pivotal position of the Free Democrats in German party politics have complicated the national-level negotiation of trade-offs across related policy areas (monetary, fiscal, incomes, active labor market, and social policies) that sustains tripartite cooperation among the major economic actors in the corporatist democracies.

As a result, the government's role in Germany's negotiated adjustment has been less direct and less active in manipulating economic policy to mediate labor's and capital's conflicting interests. But where the state has been important in Germany is in establishing the legal framework (Rahmenbedingungen) that structures labor and capital's interactions in the market. The legalism of German industrial relations and, in particular, the institutions of codetermination are a crucial "second leg" in the German model. Codetermination at the plant and company levels has shored up Germany's negotiated adjustment as tensions between labor and capital at the national level have grown since the mid-1970s. Moreover, the presence of the unions within the statutory framework of codetermination has also helped stabilize central union power as labor's marketplace strength has waned. As Katzenstein puts it: "West Germany's labor laws may have constrained union militancy in times of prosperity, but they secure the unions' position in harder times" (1987:356).

While similar institutions for labor participation (especially at the plant level) are also in place in some of the corporatist countries, they differ from German codetermination in their origins and in their significance. German unions do not organize (proportionally) the same number of workers as in these other countries, but they are pervasive. Since works councillors even in little-organized plants in Germany are overwhelmingly union members, the works council system only in part *expresses* central union strength; it also *magnifies* the presence of Germany's unions in the economy.

This outcome is somewhat paradoxical in light of the history of the works councils. Two turning points were particularly important in shaping relations between the IG Metall and works councils in the postwar period. The first, in 1952, was a political defeat for the unions. Codetermination has been one of German labor's key demands since at least the turn of the century. However, the creation of the works council system in the Federal Republic—under conservative auspices—institutionalized a system of labor representation that the unions at the time could not endorse and indeed against which they fought. Rather than meeting their demands for stronger unions rights on the shop floor, the conservative government created a parallel structure for labor representation at the plant level, emphasizing its formal separation from Germany's multi-industrial unions. In the ensuing years, however, the IG Metall was able to accomplish a de facto incorporation of works councils into the union apparatus through its dominance in plant elections.

By the time of the second turning point—the shop-floor unrest of the late 1960s—the union had internalized the works councils system. Indeed, the IG Metall's response to rank-and-file militancy in this period in some ways reinforced the dualism of the dual system, even as it drove forward its development through the revised Works Constitution Act of 1972. The IG Metall was able to capitalize on auspicious economic conditions and the reform euphoria of the first years of the Social-Liberal coalition to defuse plant militancy through a twofold strategy. Rapid economic growth allowed the central union to recapture the initiative in collective bargaining with a series of substantial wage increases. At the same time, the SPD victory in 1969 created the political space within which the union could pursue legislative reforms that enhanced the powers of the works councils. In effect, the IG Metall redefined and transformed the conflict over centralized versus decentralized authority within the union into separate battles. It defended central authority in the all-important area of collective bargaining, but extended the power of labor representatives (vis-à-vis employers) on the shop floor as well.

The way the IG Metall now confronts the challenges of the 1990s must be understood in terms of the way these previous battles were resolved. The union had resisted decentralization in the crucial area of wages, but it also won new rights for labor at the plant level. This combination of strong labor participation at both levels of the dual system has lent the German model of negotiated adjustment considerable resiliency. The significance of labor's plant-level rights may not have been fully apparent in 1972, but they have become a crucial factor sustaining labor strength since then, as economic growth slowed and labor's market power waned. Macroeconomic and political changes in the late 1970s and 1980s were resolved in part through a shift in the locus of conflict and cooperation. As relations between the IG Metall, employers, and the Social Democratic government deteriorated in the late 1970s, subnational bargaining under codetermination sustained collaborative, negotiated adjustment.

The shift in the dual system is related as well to the changing character of the challenges facing labor. The crisis of Keynesianism in the 1970s and the German government's turn toward neoliberalism in the 1980s have refocused the political agenda away from demand management and toward supply-side efforts to restart growth. Employers' increasing emphasis on flexibility in the deployment of labor (as opposed to wages) as the key to competitiveness in the current period reflects this new agenda and responds as well to the changing character of international competition. The IG Metall's own agenda also responds to shifts in the national economic and political context and focuses increasingly on qualitative demands such as employment and technology. In short, the character and content of the interactions of labor and capital are in transition; more and more, the emphasis is on labor as a factor of production rather than demand.

This reorientation has contributed to the growing importance of works councils to the central union's strategy for the 1980s and 1990s. The IG Metall is both pushed and pulled to the plant. In the case of bargaining over weekly working-time reduction, the IG Metall was pushed to incorporate works councils into central bargaining through opening clauses in contracts that delegate to plant representatives new responsibilities in actively implementing the terms of the agreements. This compromise within the dual system was one that accommodated both the union's demand for working-time reduction and employers' demand for flexibility in the deployment of labor.

In the case of the IG Metall's technology policy, the union is drawn to the plant level by the prospect of using the legal rights of works councils as an alternative avenue for achieving the union's goals on technology and skills in a period of relative market weakness. The union also sees labor's plant-level rights as an important lever in its more proactive Gestaltungspolitik, to ensure labor participation in the reorganization of production. The IG Metall's strategy is to use at the subnational level its de facto shop-floor influence and the de jure rights and powers of works councils to attain the political goals it has set itself at the national level.

These episodes in the evolution of the dual system illustrate a pattern of what I have called strategic maneuvering within dynamic constraints. The formal institutional arrangements of labor relations in Germany shape labor and capital's interactions in the market in important ways. But institutions only constrain and do not determine outcomes. Strategic maneuvering within these institutional constraints by both the union and employers in response to openings and challenges created by changes in the broader economic and political context have influenced in subtle ways the parameters of the dual system, as well as the balance within it. And in the end, not institutional rigidity, but resiliency and flexibility, is what accounts for the continued stability of negotiated adjustment in Germany through the economic and political strains of the last decades.

UNION "SUCCESS" IN THE 1990S: THE ADVANTAGES OF DUALISM

Along with a number of other authors, I subscribe to the thesis that this is a period of crisis for organized labor in the advanced industrial countries (Piore and Sabel 1984; Sabel 1986; Coriat 1984; Gourevitch et al. 1984; Streeck 1984c; and Katz 1985). Over the past decades the character of competition in international markets has shifted. Changes in the international division of labor, the accelerated introduction of microelectronics-based production automation, and greater volatility in traditional mass markets have all contributed to a situation in the advanced countries in which the agenda has shifted from a primary focus on wage restraint at a national level to the growing importance of productive restructuring at the industry and firm levels.

These macroeconomic changes, or what has been called the current "crisis of capital accumulation" (e.g., Coriat 1984; Golden and Pontusson, forthcoming) have in many countries not only upset the basis of the postwar Keynesian economic policies and the compromise between labor and capital; they have also called into question the traditional role of national unions in macroeconomic steering (Sabel 1986). These political and economic trends are what lie behind the growing literature on the "crisis" of centralized, neocorporatist bargaining.

Volker Schneiders draws an important distinction between two different interpretations of this crisis, one attributing it to a "neoliberal offensive" by employers, the other to broader, structural changes associated with the crisis of mass production (Schneiders 1987:50–60).[1] A brief characterization of the differences between these two perspectives on the nature of the crisis will help frame my own argument on the general issue of union "success" in the 1980s and 1990s and provide the basis for an assessment of the developments I have described within the IG Metall.

In the "neoliberal offensive" interpretation, what is behind the crisis of neocorporatism is pressure by employers—often reinforced by state policy—to relax the "rigidities" imposed by corporatist bargaining and to strengthen market forces as a way of disciplining labor (Schneiders 1987:52–53, 55).[2] Pressures to decentralize bargaining are often combined with efforts by employers to coopt labor at the plant level, with offers of job security or new forms of participation for example. High unemployment strengthens the effectiveness of employers' strategies at both levels, for it weakens labor's national-level defenses even as it fuels tendencies toward "plant egoism."

---

1. Schneiders bases this distinction on a very insightful juxtaposition of the work of Wolfgang Streeck and Charles Sabel. My analysis draws on the core distinction Schneiders identifies, though I use it to slightly different ends. What Schneiders does not draw out fully, and what I emphasize here, are the different implications of the two perspectives for the question of centralization or decentralization, and how this relates to the more general issue of union success in the 1990s.

2. Schneiders bases his characterization of the "neoliberal offensive" interpretation on Streeck's (1984c) analysis. However, the basic argument is explicitly or implicitly embraced by many other authors as well. See, for example, Sengenberger 1984; Hohn 1988; Lange, Ross, and Vannicelli 1982; and Gourevitch et al. 1984, among others.

The second theoretical perspective, associated especially with the work of Sabel and Piore, links the crisis of neocorporatism to a deeper crisis of mass production and the whole system of regulation (including Keynesianism and centralized bargaining) with which it was associated in the 1950s and 1960s (Schneiders 1987:53–55). At that time, national unions played a key role in maintaining a balance between demand and production capacity, but this system of regulation no longer "fits" with an emerging, alternative paradigm premised on "permanent innovation" (or what Piore and Sabel call "flexible specialization"). Indeed, in this view, for unions to attempt to defend their old role in macroeconomic steering would only undermine their own goal of creating the productive basis that is necessary to achieve their redistributive goals (Schneiders 1987:58).

For Schneiders, what is key is how these two perspectives converge in ways that underscore the strategic dilemmas unions now face. One such dilemma is that unions' defense of previous (centralized) organizational forms that are now under attack from neoliberals may in fact hinder rather than facilitate economic expansion under flexible specialization and would thus undermine the basis for labor's own redistributive agenda (Schneiders 1987:58). The other dilemma, related to this, is how the more decentralized and flexible structures that the neoliberals want, but that are also in fact better adapted to the new requirements of capital accumulation, can be reconciled with labor solidarity, on which union strength ultimately rests (Schneiders 1987:57).

For my purposes here what is important is how the two views of the crisis give different meanings to the decentralization of bargaining, and here it is useful to begin by taking Schneiders's distinction a step further. The "plant egoism" thesis cited above generally rests more or less explicitly on the "neoliberal offensive" interpretation: national unions face a two-front attack on centralized bargaining as both employers and labor representatives at the plant level come to favor a relaxation of neocorporatist controls. This perspective emphasizes the negative effects on labor solidarity of decentralization. In this view, the continued viability of central unions hinges at least in part on their "resistance . . . to a 'downward' transfer of bargaining issues to the work-place" (Streeck 1984c:297).

The second interpretation leads to somewhat different conclusions. Sabel alludes to a decentralization of bargaining and warns of the danger of enterprise unionism (Sabel 1986:56). However, for Sabel such decentralization seems not to imply only dangers but also opportunities for labor. Flexible specialization reintroduces the importance of skills and thus rejuvenates a source of union power that mass production had eliminated (Sabel 1986:54). This emphasis on skills points to new sources of power for labor at the shop-floor level that for him appear partly to compensate for the declining power of national unions in neocorporatist bargaining.[3]

The different implications of decentralization and of union responses to it follow from the differences in emphasis between the two perspectives. The "neoliberal offensive" interpretation stresses the changed *context* of bargaining, especially labor's current market weakness. To the extent that the challenge unions confront is defined in terms of a fragmentation of working class interests, then labor's fate appears to hinge on the ability of unions to resist flexibilization and to control plant egoism. The "flexible specialization" interpretation, in contrast, stresses the changing *content* of bargaining. From this perspective, unions must redefine their role by launching their own offensive on production issues, not so much to resist flexibilization but to define on whose terms flexibility will be achieved. The former stresses the pitfalls of decentralization (fragmentation and the growth of "enterprise unionism"), while the latter points to the opportunities (e.g., worker influence over production organization).

However, what both lines of argument tend to obscure is the *interaction* of central union strategies and shop-floor politics. As in the literature on the crisis of neocorporatism generally, the tendency is to reduce this interaction to a question of centralization or decentralization.[4] But posing the question in this way misses the truly important point: Where in the 1970s the viability of central unions hinged on the passive support of the shop-floor, since the 1980s it has increasingly depended on its active support. This is true not only because central unions must defend against employers' "fragmentation" strategies, but also because of the kinds of challenges labor now faces.

The changing character of the challenges labor currently confronts forces us to reexamine the formula for union "success." The framework of industrial relations that proved so successful at regulating wages, dampening inflation, and maintaining employment in the 1970s (peak-level, tripartite bargaining) may be less appropriate for the battles over *production* issues since the 1980s. How organized labor weathers the

3. Sabel's analysis is vague on the character and organization of labor interests under flexible specialization. He argues that unions should forge links among workers in plants connected by flexible specialization (e.g., workers in core plants and in their suppliers), as well as across regions (1986:57–58). However, the overarching organization of labor interests seems to be something of a dependent variable that depends on how flexible specialization itself develops.

4. In fact, Streeck and Sabel and Piore are themselves less prone to such dichotomous characterizations than others who have followed and expanded on their basic insights. However, in the case of Piore and Sabel, there is still some ambiguity in the role of central unions under flexible specialization. Sabel's argument about linkages among workers in plants connected by flexible specialization (see previous note) provides only part of an answer. It is not at all clear, for example, that such linkages can simply be "summed" into an overarching program for the labor movement as a whole.

crisis depends crucially on the political and organizational resources unions command to meet these new challenges. It depends, to use Pizzorno's phrase, on organized labor's "capacity for strategy" (Pizzorno 1978:287; see also Golden and Pontusson, forthcoming). But as the problems labor faces shift, so too does the formula for "strategic capacity."

Central strength will still be crucial to union success, but central strength alone may not be sufficient. National unions can ill afford to lose their ability to define labor's agenda, or agendas, but this ability to coordinate and define must not be confused with centralized bargaining per se. A central union may choose or be forced to pursue centrally defined goals decentrally. Moreover, the case of the IG Metall demonstrates that what national unions can accomplish in centralized bargaining is limited not just by their market weakness but also by the character of the challenges they now face.

To the extent that these challenges increasingly present themselves at various subnational levels, it is there that central unions must meet them. What workers are going to earn, how many will have jobs, and at what skill levels they will be employed are issues that are only in part being decided in national-level bargaining. They are also profoundly influenced by developments at the firm and plant levels in the course of productive restructuring currently underway. If unions are unable to influence these developments at that level, then no amount of macroeconomic steering can help them later on. What is increasingly important is organized labor's ability to work with and through its intermediate and local representatives to address these concrete sectoral and plant challenges. The issue is not really centralization or decentralization because central unions do not have a choice between the two.

Where unions are decentralized and fragmented, as in the United States, the threat faced by organized labor in the current crisis is nothing short of extinction. In such countries, unions are looking abroad for models of successful adaptation, and they are rediscovering the virtues of centralization. The AFL–CIO's recent initiatives in this direction are indicative of this (even if the organization's leadership faces dim prospects for successfully acting on them), as is the growing number of union mergers currently underway in the United States and Britain.

But at the same time, and in other countries, highly centralized labor movements are discovering the limits to central action, and the advantages if not of decentralization in a strict sense, then at least of strengthening labor's rights and representation at various subnational levels. The Swedish LO's initiatives in the 1970s to enhance plant- and company-level codetermination illustrate this trend.

In Germany, the challenges labor now faces require some organizational rethinking on the part of central unions, but not dramatic restructuring.

The dual system is something of a hybrid that combines the strengths of both centralization and decentralization. This system emerged, I have argued, as the consequence of a series of legal and political struggles in the 1950s, 1960s, and early 1970s that has resulted in the organizational juxtaposition and a politically fought integration of labor representation at the national and plant levels. However, the mix of centralization and decentralization that characterizes the dual system of labor relations in Germany is a formula that now lends the labor movement substantial flexibility in the face of the new challenges since the 1980s.

The overarching system of centralized bargaining and industrial unionism in Germany provides a crucial countervailing force to the centrifugal strains stressed by the "neoliberal offensive" view. But equally important, the outcome of previous battles in Germany has left the union firmly entrenched at the plant level and armed with a set of relatively strong rights. This combination of centralized and decentralized strength leaves the IG Metall organizationally well positioned to address the new challenges, not so much to block flexibility as to participate in it and to influence (to return to Sabel) on whose terms flexibility will be achieved. Indeed, what Sabel sees as organized labor's need to "seize the initiative" in the emerging production paradigm (1986:42) may in fact mean that unions themselves need to develop the capacity to respond "flexibly" to challenges as they present themselves not just at the national level but at various subnational levels as well. And seen from this perspective, German labor's strong rights at the plant and firm levels are not so much part of the central union's problem (as in the "plant egoism" theory) as they are part of the solution.

The fact that Germany's dual system combines powerful central unionism with well-established decentralized channels for labor influence at the plant and company levels may in fact turn out to be its greatest strength. Relations between the IG Metall and its works councils are not always smooth, to be sure, but union presence through works councils in even little-organized plants gives the union a crucial organizational foothold that enables it to meet employers' "flexibilization" strategies in the plant. I have argued that changes in the economic and political context have shifted the balance within the dual system, but conflicts between labor and capital are still mediated through a relatively stable structure, and importantly, a structure flexible enough to accommodate the changing strategies of both employers and the union. Labor relations thus conform (and contribute) to what Katzenstein has described as a general pattern of adjustment in Germany in which flexibility and stability converge (1989a:308).

In sum, the nature of the economic and structural transformations of the current period may require a more nuanced picture of the organizational formula for union "success" in the 1990s. Where others warn of the liabilities and pitfalls of an inadvertent slide into decentralization, I have argued that local- and intermediate-level strength may turn out to be central unions' best (or only) defense against employers' fragmentation and flexibilization strategies. Strength at the subnational level opens up the possibility for national unions to fight plant battles and to shape plant outcomes. My analysis thus suggests that national unions will have to do a lot more than just defend central bargaining. Not just their central strength, but their organizational depth as well, will determine how labor weathers the current crisis.

Unions need to find new organizational forms that combine centralization and organizational depth, and new strategies that combine central coordination with flexibility at subnational levels. Decentralization without coordination leaves them vulnerable to flexibility on employers' terms—"fragmentation." But centralization without strong subnational enforcement and implementation may produce the same result. The challenge central unions like the IG Metall now confront is not just that they are weakened centrally, but also that weak defenses at the plant level could render their central successes irrelevant.

Bibliography

Aaron, Benjamin, and K. W. Wedderburn, eds. 1972. *Industrial Conflict: A Comparative Legal Survey*. London: Longmans.

Adamy, Wilhelm. 1988. "Deregulierung des Arbeitsmarktes: Zwischenbilanz des Beschäftigungsförderungsgesetz." *WSI Mitteilungen* 8.

Adamy, Wilhelm, and Gerhard Bosch. 1989. "Arbeitsmarkt." In Michael Kittner, ed., *Gewerkschaftsjahrbuch 1989*. Cologne: Bund Verlag.

Alexis, Marion. 1983. "Neo-Corporatism and Industrial Relations: The Case of German Trade Unions." *West European Politics* 6 (January).

Allen, Christopher S. 1989a. "Corporatism and Regional Economic Policies in the Federal Republic of Germany: The 'Meso' Politics of Industrial Adjustment." *Publius: The Journal of Federalism* 19 (Fall).

Allen, Christopher S. 1989b. "Ideas, Institutions, and Capital Investment in the United States and West Germany: Laissez Faire vs. Organized Capitalism." Paper presented at the meetings of the American Political Science Assocation, Atlanta, Georgia, 31 August–3 September.

Allen, Christopher S. 1989c. "Political Consequences of Change: The Chemical Industry." In Peter J. Katzenstein, ed., *Industry and Politics in West Germany*.

Allen, Christopher S. 1989d. "The Underdevelopment of Keynesianism in the Federal Republic of Germany." In Peter A. Hall, ed., *The Political Power of Economic Ideas: Keynesianism across Nations*. Princeton: Princeton University Press.

Allen, Christopher S. 1990. "Democratic Politics and Private Investment: Banks and Stock Markets in West Germany and the United States." Johns Hopkins University, American Institute for Contemporary German Studies Research Report # 3 (March).

Allen, Christopher S., and Jeremiah M. Riemer. 1985. "The Reindustrialization Debate in West Germany." Paper presented at the meetings of the American Political Science Association, New Orleans, La., 28 August–1 September.

Armingeon, Klaus. 1983. "Co-operative Unionism in Austria and the Federal Republic of Germany: A Review of Recent Literature." *European Journal of Political Research* 11.

Atkinson, Michael M., and William D. Coleman. 1985. "Corporatism and Industrial Policy." In Alan Cawson, ed., *Organized Interests and the State*.

Auer, Peter. 1985. "Industrial Relations, Work Organization, and New Technology: The Volvo Case." *Swedish Center for Working Life Discussion Paper.* Stockholm: Arbetslivscentrum.

Auer, Peter, and Claudius Riegler. 1988. "Gruppenarbeit bei Volvo: Aktuelle Tendenzen und Hintergründe." *Discussion Paper FS I 88-5.* Berlin: Wissenschaftzentrum Berlin für Sozialforschung.

BAA (Bundesanstalt für Arbeit). 1985. *Amtliche Nachrichten: Arbeitsstatistik 1984— Jahreszahlen.* Nuremberg: Bundesanstalt für Arbeit, July 18.

Bäcker, Gerd. 1984. "Sozialpolitik." In Michael Kittner, ed., *Gewerkschaftsjahrbuch 1984.* Cologne: Bund Verlag.

Bäcker, Gerd. 1985. "Sozialpolitik." In Michael Kittner, ed., *Gewerkschaftsjahrbuch 1985.* Cologne: Bund Verlag.

Bahnmüller, Reinhard. 1985. *Der Streik: Tarifkonflikt um Arbeitszeitverkürzung in der Metallindustrie, 1984.* Hamburg: VSA Verlag.

Balduin, Siegfried. 1981. "Vom Rationalisierungsschutz zu einer umfassenden Sicherungsstrategie." *IIVG Discussion Paper* dp81–207. Berlin: IIVG, January.

BAS (Bundesministerium für Arbeit- und Sozialordnung). 1980. *Codetermination in the Federal Republic of Germany.* Bonn: Bundesministerium für Arbeit- und Sozialordnung.

BAS (Bundesministerium für Arbeit- und Sozialordnung). 1986. *Statistisches Taschenbuch: Arbeits- und Sozialstatistik.* Bonn: Bundesministerium für Arbeit- und Sozialordnung.

BAS (Bundesministerium für Arbeit- und Sozialordnung). 1988. *Statistisches Taschenbuch: Arbeits- und Sozialstatistik.* Bonn: Bundesministerium für Arbeit- und Sozialordnung.

BDA (Bundesvereinigung der Deutschen Arbeitgeberverbände). 1984a. *Arbeitgeber: Jahresbericht der BDA.* Bonn–Bad Godesberg: BDA, December 6.

BDA (Bundesvereinigung der Deutschen Arbeitgeberverbände). 1984b. *Flexibilisierung der Arbeitszeit: Neue Tarifregelungen als Chance.* Cologne: BDA.

Becker, Hans. 1979. "Montanmitbestimmung in der betrieblichen Praxis." In Rudolf Judith, ed., *Montanmitbestimmung: Geschichte, Idee, Wirklichkeit.* Cologne: Bund Verlag.

Bergmann, Joachim, Otto Jacobi, and Walther Müller-Jentsch. 1979. *Gewerkschaften in der Bundesrepublik.* 3d ed. Frankfurt: Campus Verlag.

Bergmann, Joachim, and Walther Müller-Jentsch. 1983. "The Federal Republic of Germany: Cooperative Unionism and Dual Bargaining System Challenged." In Solomon Barkin, ed., *Worker Militancy and Its Consequences.* 2d ed. New York: Praeger.

Berthelot, Marcel. 1924. *Works Councils in Germany.* Geneva: International Labour Office.

Biedenkopf Commission. 1970. "Mitbestimmung im Unternehmen: Bericht der Sachverständigenkommission zur Auswertung der bisherigen Erfahrungen bei der Mitbestimmung." Full text appears in Bonn: Deutscher Bundestag, 6. Wahlperiode (Drucksache VI/334).

Blackaby, Frank, ed. 1978. *De-industrialisation.* London: Heinemann Educational.

Blank, Michael, and Hermann Unterhinninghofen. 1983. "Betriebsstillegungen und Gegenwehr." *WSI Mitteilungen* 1.

Bok, Derek C. 1971. "Reflections on the Distinctive Character of American Labor Laws." *Harvard Law Review* 84 (April).

Borsdorf, Ulrich, Hans O. Hemmer, and Martin Martiny, eds., 1977. *Grundlagen der Einheitsgewerkschaft: Historische Dokumente und Materialien.* Cologne: Europäische Verlagsanstalt.

Bosch, Gerhard. 1981. "Das Arbeitsmarktpolitische Sonderprogramm der Bundesregierung von 1979." *Soziale Sicherheit* 3.

Bosch, Gerhard. 1986. "Arbeitsmarkt." In Michael Kittner, ed., *Gewerkschaftsjahrbuch 1986.* Cologne: Bund Verlag.

Bosch, Gerhard, and Hartmut Seifert. 1984. "Das Geplante Beschäftigungsförderungsgesetz: Ein Arbeitsmarktpolitisches Notstandsgesetz." *WSI Mitteilungen* 10.

Bosch, Gerhard, and Werner Sengenberger. 1984. "Employment Policy, the State, and the Unions in the Federal Republic of Germany." Report prepared for the Sixth Annual Conference of the International Working Party on Labour Market Segmentation, Budapest, Hungary, 24–28 July.

Boyer, Robert. 1984. "Wage Labor, Capital Accumulation, and the Crisis, 1968–82." In Mark Kesselman, ed., *The French Workers' Movement: Economic Crisis and Political Change.* London: George Allen and Unwin.

Brandt, Gerhard. 1984. "Industrial Relations in the Federal Republic of Germany under Conditions of Economic Crisis." In Tokunaga Shigeyoshi and Joachim Bergmann, eds., *Industrial Relations in Transition.*

Braunthal, Gerhard. 1978. *Socialist Labor and Politics in Weimar Germany.* Hamden, Conn.: Archon Books.

Brenner, Otto. 1972. "Wie leben wir morgen?" *Der Gewerkschafter* 4 (April).

Brigl-Matthiaβ, Kurt. 1926. "Das Betriebsräteproblem in der Weimarer Republik." In R. Crusius, G. Schiefelbein, and M. Wilke, eds., *Die Betriebsräte in der Weimarer Republik.* Vol. 2.

Britscho, Winfried. 1978. "Opel Rüsselsheim: Konflikte um Sonderschichten." In O. Jacobi, W. Müller-Jentsch, and E. Schmidt, eds., *Gewerkschaftspolitik in der Krise: Kritisches Gewerkschaftsjahrbuch 1977/78.* Berlin: Rotbuch Verlag.

Brock, Adolf. 1978. "Die Arbeiter- und Soldatenräte von der revolutionären Aktion zur Integration." Introduction to R. Crusius, G. Schiefelbein, and M. Wilke, eds., *Die Betriebsräte in der Weimarer Republik.* Vol. 1.

Broström, Anders. 1982. "Industrial and Economic Democracy in Sweden: Approach and Problems." Paper presented at the Bologna Conference on Industrial and Economic Democracy, May. Swedish Center for Working Life Discussion Paper. Stockholm: Arbetslivscentrum.

Brumlop, Eva, and Ulrich Jürgens. 1983. "Rationalisation and Industrial Relations in the West German Automobile Industry: A Case Study of Volkswagen." IIVG Discussion Paper dp83-216. Berlin: IIVG, September.

Brumlop, Eva, and Wolf Rosenbaum. 1979. "'Humanisierung der Arbeitsbedingungen' durch gewerkschaftliche Tarifpolitik." In Joachim Bergmann, ed., *Beiträge zur Soziologie der Gewerkschaften.* Frankfurt: Suhrkamp.

Bührig, Erich. 1952. "Das Betriebsverfassungsrecht." *Gewerkschaftliche Monatshefte* 3 (March).

Bureau of Labor Statistics, U.S. Department of Labor. 1919. "Agreement between Trade Unions and Employers' Associations in Germany." *Monthly Labor Review* 8.

Bureau of Labor Statistics, U.S. Department of Labor. 1920. "German Works Council Law." *Monthly Labor Review* 10.

Burgi, Noelle. 1985. "Neo-corporatist Strategies in the British Energy Sector." In Alan Cawson, ed., *Organized Interests and the State.*

Cameron, David. 1984. "Social Democracy, Corporatism, Labour Quiescence, and the Representation of Economic Interest in Advanced Capitalist Society." In John H. Goldthorpe, ed., *Order and Conflict in Contemporary Capitalism.*

Cawson, Alan. 1985a. "Introduction: Varieties of Corporatism: The Importance of the Meso-Level of Interest Intermediation." In Alan Cawson, ed., *Organized Interests and the State.*

Cawson, Alan, ed. 1985b. *Organized Interests and the State: Studies in Meso-Corporatism.* Beverly Hills, Calif.: Sage.

Chamberlain, Neil W. 1948. *The Union Challenge to Management Control.* New York: Harper and Brothers.

Cichon, Deborah. 1986. "The Labor Market Policies of West Germany." In Howard Rosen, ed., *Comparative Labor Market Policies of Japan, West Germany, United Kingdom, France, Australia*. Conference Proceedings of the National Council on Employment Policy, 25 April 1985. Washington, D.C.: National Council on Employment Policy.

Clegg, Hugh A. 1960. *A New Approach to Industrial Democracy*. Oxford: Blackwell.

Cohen, Stephen S., and John Zysman. 1987. *Manufacturing Matters: The Myth of the Post-Industrial Economy*. New York: Basic Books.

Coriat, Benjamin. 1984. "Labor and Capital in the Crisis: France, 1966–82." In Mark Kesselman, ed., *The French Workers' Movement: Economic Crisis and Political Change*. London: George Allen and Unwin.

Coriat, Benjamin, and Philippe Zarifan. 1986. "Tendenzen der Automatisierung und Neuzusammensetzung der industriellen Lohnarbeit." *Prokla* 62 (March).

Craig, Gordon. 1980. *Germany: 1866–1945*. New York: Oxford University Press.

Crouch, Colin. 1978. "The Changing Role of the State in Industrial Relations in Western Europe." In Colin Crouch and Alessandro Pizzorno, eds., *The Resurgence of Class Conflict in Western Europe Since 1968*. Vol. 2.

Crouch, Colin, and Alessandro Pizzorno, ed., 1978. *The Resurgence of Class Conflict in Western Europe Since 1968*. Vol. 1 and 2. New York: Holmes and Meier.

Crusius, R., G. Schiefelbein, and M. Wilke, eds., 1978. *Die Betriebsräte in der Weimarer Republik*. Vol. 1 and 2. Berlin: Verlag Olle & Wolter.

Daley, Tony. 1988. "Labor and Industrial Change: The Politics of Steel in France." Ph.D. diss., University of California, Berkeley.

Degen, Barbara, Gerd Siebert, and Wolfgang Stöhr. 1979. *Handbuch für den Arbeitskampf*. Frankfurt: Nachrichten-Verlag Gesellschaft.

Deppe, F. 1977. "Der Deutsche Gewerkschaftsbund 1949–1965." In F. Deppe, G. Fülberth, and J. Harrer, eds., *Geschichte der deutschen Gewerkschaftsbewegung*.

Deppe, F., G. Fülberth, and J. Harrer, eds., 1977. *Geschichte der deutschen Gewerkschaftsbewegung*. 3d ed. Cologne: Pahl-Rugenstein Verlag.

Deutschmann, Christoph. 1988. "The Japanese Organisation and Its Influence on Management and Industrial Relations in Western Europe." Paper prepared for the conference "Industrial Relations in Times of Deregulation," Bad Homburg, Werner Reimers-Stiftung, 29 September–1 October 1988.

DGB (Deutscher Gewerkschaftsbund). 1985a. *Grundsätze des DGBs zur Weiterentwicklung des Betriebsverfassungsrechts*. Schriftenreihe Mitbestimmung. Frankfurt: Union Verlag, May.

DGB (Deutscher Gewerkschaftsbund). 1985b. *Konzeption zur Mitbestimmung am Arbeitsplatz*. Schriftenreihe Nr. 7 Mitbestimmung. Frankfurt: DGB, March.

Diamant, Alfred. 1977. "Democratizing the Workplace: The Myth and Reality of Mitbestimmung in the Federal Republic of Germany." In G. David Garson, ed., *Worker Self-Management in Industry*.

Dunlop, John T. 1958. *Industrial Relations Systems*. New York: Henry Holt.

Dunlop, John T., and Walter Galenson, eds., 1978. *Labor in the Twentieth Century*. New York: Academic Press.

Dybowski-Johannson, Gisela. 1980. *Die Interessenvertretung durch den Betriebsrat*. Frankfurt: Campus Verlag.

Edinger, Lewis J. 1986. *West German Politics*. New York: Columbia University Press.

Edlund, Sten, and Birgitta Nyström. 1988. *Developments in Swedish Labour Law*. Stockholm: The Swedish Institute.

Erd, Rainer. 1978. *Verrechtlichung industrieller Konflikte*. Frankfurt: Campus Verlag.

Esser, Josef, and Wolfgang Fach. 1980. "Gewerkschaften als Säule im 'Modell Deutschland'?" In Otto Jacobi, Eberhard Schmidt, and Walther Müller-Jentsch, eds., *Moderne Zeiten—Alte Rezepte: Kritisches Gewerkschaftsjahrbuch 1980/81*. Berlin: Rotbuch Verlag.

Esser, Josef, and Wolfgang Fach. 1989. "Crisis Management 'Made in Germany': The Steel Industry." In Peter J. Katzenstein, ed., *Industry and Politics in West Germany.*

Farthmann, Friedhelm. 1972. "Grundzüge der neuen Betriebsverfassung." *Gewerkschaftliche Monatshefte* 1 (January).

Feldman, Gerald D. 1981. "German Interest Group Alliances in War and Inflation, 1914–1923." In Suzanne Berger, ed., *Organizing Interests in Western Europe: Pluralism, Corporatism, and the Transformation of Politics.* New York: Cambridge University Press.

Flanagan, Robert J., David W. Soskice, and Lloyd Ulman. 1983. *Unionism, Economic Stabilization and Incomes Policies: European Experience.* Washington, D.C.: The Brookings Institution.

Fraenkel, Ernst. 1930. "Zehn Jahre Betriebsrätegesetz." In Rudolf Hilferding, ed., *Die Gesellschaft.* Vol. 1. Frankfurt: Verlag Sauer and Auvermann.

Freeman, Richard B., and James L. Medoff. 1984. *What Do Unions Do?* New York: Basic Books.

Fricke, Werner, Karl Krahn, and Gerd Peter. 1985. *Arbeit und Technik als politische Gestaltungsaufgabe.* Bonn: Verlag Neue Gesellschaft.

Fürstenberg, Friedrich. 1958. "Der Betriebsrat: Strukturanalyse einer Grenzinstitution." *Kölner Zeitschrift für Soziologie und Sozialpsychologie* 10.

Garson, G. David, ed. 1977. *Worker Self-Management in Industry: The West European Experience.* New York: Praeger.

Gartman, David. 1986. *Auto Slavery: The Labor Process in the American Automobile Industry, 1897–1950.* New Brunswick: Rutgers University Press.

George, Alexander. 1979. "Case Studies and Theory Development: The Method of Structured, Focused Comparison." In Paul Gordon Lauren, ed., *Diplomacy: New Approaches in History, Theory and Policy.* New York: The Free Press.

German Press and Information Office. 1979. *Facts about Germany.* Gütersloh: Verlagsgruppe Bertelsmann.

Gesamtmetall. 1989. *Metallindustrie in Zahlen: Beilage zum Gesamtmetall Geschäftsbericht, 1987–1989.* Cologne: Gesamtmetall.

Gester, Heinz. 1972. "Zur Stellung der Gewerkschaften im Betrieb nach dem neuen Betriebsverfassungsgesetz." *Gewerkschaftliche Monatshefte* 1 (January).

Golden, Miriam. 1986. "Interest Representation, Party Systems, and the State: Italy in Comparative Perspective." *Comparative Politics* 18 (April).

Golden, Miriam, and Jonas Pontusson, eds., Forthcoming. *Union Politics in Comparative Perspective: Economic Change and Intra-Class Conflict.* Ithaca: Cornell University Press.

Goldthorpe, John H. 1984a. Introduction to John H. Goldthorpe, ed., *Order and Conflict in Contemporary Capitalism.*

Goldthorpe, John H., ed. 1984b. *Order and Conflict in Contemporary Capitalism.* Oxford: Oxford University Press.

Gourevitch, Peter. 1986. *Politics in Hard Times: Comparative Responses to International Economic Crises.* Ithaca: Cornell University Press.

Gourevitch, Peter, Andrew Martin, George Ross, and Stephen Bornstein. 1984. *Unions and Economic Crisis: Britain, West Germany, and Sweden.* London: George Allen and Unwin.

Grohmann, Peter, and Horst Sachsteller, eds., 1979. *Plakat: 10 Jahre Betriebsarbeit bei Daimler-Benz.* Berlin: Rotbuch Verlag.

Guillebaud, C. W. 1928. *The Works Council: A German Experiment in Industrial Democracy.* Cambridge: Cambridge University Press.

Gustavsen, Bjorn. 1985. "Technology and Collective Agreements: Some Recent Scandinavian Developments." *Industrial Relations Journal* 16.

Hall, Peter A. 1986. *Governing the Economy: The Politics of State Intervention in Britain and France*. New York: Oxford University Press.

Hautsch, Gert, and Bernd Semmler. 1983. *Betriebsbesetzung*. Frankfurt: Institut für Marxistische Studien und Forschungen.

Heclo, Hugh, and Henrik Madsen. 1987. *Policy and Politics in Sweden: Principled Pragmatism*. Philadelphia: Temple University Press.

Helm, Jutta. 1986. "Codetermination in West Germany: What Difference Has It Made?" *West European Politics* 9.

Hemken, R., ed., n.d. *Sammlung der vom Alliierten Kontrollrat und der Amerikanischen Militärregierung Erlassenen Proklamationen, Gesetze, Verordnungen, Befehle, Direktiven*. Stuttgart: Deutsche Verlags-Anstalt.

Herzenberg, Stephen. 1987. "From Sitdowns to Saturn: Implications for the UAW." Paper presented at the conference "Union Politics, Labor Militancy, and Capital Accumulation," Ithaca, New York, Cornell University, 2–5 April.

Herzer, Hans, Bernd Kaßebaum, Gerd Rohde, and Joachim Sauer. 1988. "Gruppenarbeit und sozialintegrative Beteilingungsformen: Merkmale einer veränderten Produktionsstruktur." *Internal discussion paper*, IG Metall Vorstandsverwaltung, Frankfurt, 8 October.

Hibbs, Douglas A., Jr., 1976. "Industrial Conflict in Advanced Industrial Societies." *American Political Science Review* 70.

Hibbs, Douglas A., Jr. 1977. "Political Parties and Macroeconomic Policy." *American Political Science Review* 71.

Hibbs, Douglas A., Jr. 1978. "On the Political Economy of Long-Run Trends in Strike Activity." *British Journal of Political Science* 7.

Hildebrandt, Eckart. 1981. "Der VW-Tarifvertrag zur Lohndifferenzierung." IIVG *Discussion Paper* pre81–216. Berlin: IIVG, February.

Hildebrandt, Eckart. 1982. "Defensive und offensive Ansätze der Besitzstandssicherung in der Tarifpolitik am Beispiel der IG Metall." IIVG *Discussion Paper* pre82–204. Berlin: IIVG, April.

Hirsch, Fred, and John H. Goldthorpe, eds., 1978. *The Political Economy of Inflation*. London: Martin Robertson.

Hoffmann, Reinhard. 1968. "Erweiterung der innerbetrieblichen Mitbestimmung durch Arbeitsgruppen." *Gewerkschaftliche Monatshefte* 12 (December).

Hoffmann, Reinhard. 1978. "Zum Betriebsräteproblem heute." Introduction to R. Crusius, G. Schiefelbein, and M. Wilke, eds., *Die Betriebsräte in der Weimarer Republik*. Vol. 2.

Hohn, Hans-Willy. 1988. *Von der Einheitsgewerkschaft zum Betriebssyndikalismus: Soziale Schließung im dualen System der Interessenvertretung*. Berlin: Sigma Rainer Bohn Verlag.

Höland, Armin. 1985. *Das Verhalten von Betriebsräten bei Kündigungen: Recht und Wirklichkeit im betrieblichen Alltag*. Frankfurt: Campus Verlag.

IG Metall. 1952. "Sondermerkblatt: Aufbau des gewerkschaftlichen Vertrauensmännerkörpers." Letter sent by IG Metall Vorstand to all union locals and district offices, Frankfurt, 1 November (IG Metall archives).

IG Metall. 1965. *Automation: Risiko und Chance*. Vols. 1 and 2. Frankfurt: Europäische Verlagsanstalt.

IG Metall. 1970. "Einige Bemerkungen zur Diskussion über die Arbeitsgruppensprecher." Discussion paper sent to union locals and regional offices by IG Metall Vorstand, Frankfurt, 9 July (IG Metall archives).

IG Metall. 1971. *Computer und Angestellte*. Vols. 1 and 2. Frankfurt: Europäische Verlagsanstalt.

IG Metall. 1972. *Aufgabe Zukunft: Qualität des Lebens*. 10 vols. Proceedings of the fourth international workshop of the IG Metall, 11–14 April, Oberhausen. Frankfurt: Europäischen Verlagsanstalt.

IG Metall. 1977a. *Strukturwandel in der Metallindustrie: Analytische und konzeptionelle Ansätze der IG Metall zur Strukturpolitik 1975 bis 1977.* Frankfurt: IG Metall.

IG Metall. 1977b. *Strukturelle Arbeitslosigkeit durch technologischen Wandel?* Schriftenreihe der IG Metall, Nr. 72. Frankfurt: IG Metall.

IG Metall. 1977c. *Wirtschaftlicher und sozialer Wandel in der Bundesrepublik.* Schriftenreihe der IG Metall, Nr. 73. Frankfurt: IG Metall.

IG Metall. 1978. *Arbeitsmaterialien zum Tarifvertrag zur Sicherung der Eingruppierung und zur Verdienstsicherung bei Abgruppierung.* Stuttgart: Bezirksleitung Stuttgart, July.

IG Metall. 1983. *"Maschinen wollen sie—uns Menschen nicht": Rationalisierung in der Metallwirtschaft.* Frankfurt: IG Metall, October.

IG Metall. 1984a. *"Aktionsprogramm Arbeit und Technik: Der Mensch Muβ Bleiben.* Frankfurt: IG Metall, November.

IG Metall. 1984b. "Entschließung des Beirates der IG Metall gegen die geplanten Verschlechterung des Betriebsverfassungsgesetzes." Frankfurt: IG Metall, 11 December.

IG Metall. 1984c. *Neue Formen der Gruppenarbeit: Qualitätszirkel.* Frankfurt: IG Metall, Abteilung Betriebsräte.

IG Metall. 1985a. "Aktionsmappe zur Verteidigung des Betriebsverfassungsgesetzes." Materials sent to all union locals, district offices, and educational facilities by IG Metall Vorstand. Frankfurt: IG Metall Vorstand, 8 March.

IG Metall. 1985b. *Unterhaltungselektronik: Arbeitsplätze wie Schnee in der Sonne.* Vorschläge der IG Metall zur Beschäftigungssicherung und zur Strukturpolitik in diesem Industriebereich (Suggestions from IG Metall toward job security and structural policy in this industry). Frankfurt: IG Metall.

IG Metall. 1986. "Arbeitszeitflexibilisierung und Arbeitnehmerinteressen—Positionspapier der IG Metall." Frankfurt: IG Metall, June.

IG Metall. 1987a. *Daten, Fakten, Informationen.* Frankfurt: IG Metall.

IG Metall. 1987b. "Auszüge aus den regionalen Verhandlungsergebnissen, Tarifbewegung 1986/87." Frankfurt: IG Metall Vorstand, Abteilung Tarifpolitik, 26 May.

IG Metall. 1988a. "Lohn- und Gehaltsrahmentarifvertrag I: Analytische Arbeitsbewertung." Arbeitspapiere (Teilnehmerunterlage) and Referentenleitfaden (working papers, materials for participants and manual for seminar leaders), IG Metall, Abteilung Bildungswesen/Bildungspolitik, Abteilung Tarifpolitik, and Bezirksleitung Stuttgart, July.

IG Metall. 1988b. "Qualitätszirkel." Unpublished Handbuchbeitrag (Handbook contribution). Frankfurt: IG Metall Vorstandsverwaltung, May.

IG Metall. 1988c. *Tarifpolitik im Strukturwandel.* Materialband Nr. 6 der Diskussionsforen "Die Andere Zukunft: Solidarität und Freiheit." Cologne: Bund Verlag.

IG Metall. 1988d. *Technologieentwicklung und Techniksteurerung.* Materialband Nr. 4 der Diskussionsforen "Die andere Zukunft: Solidarität und Freiheit." Cologne: Bund Verlag.

IG Metall. 1989a. "Die Andere Zukunft: Solidarität und Freiheit: Leitlinien der IG Metall zur gesellschaftlichen und gewerkschaftlichen Reform." Materials sent to all union locals, district offices, and educational facilities by the IG Metall Vorstand, Frankfurt, April.

IG Metall. 1989b. "Entgeltrahmentarifvertrag der Zukunft." Internal draft proposal for discussion. Frankfurt: IG Metall Vorstandsverwaltung, Abteilung Tarifpolitik, 6 April.

IG Metall. 1990a. "Tarifbewegungen der IG Metall, Metallindustrie, 1948/49 bis 1990." Frankfurt: IG Metall Vorstandsverwaltung, Abteilung Tarifpolitik, June.

IG Metall. 1990b. "Tarifbewegung 1990: Metallindustrie." Frankfurt: IG Metall Vorstandsverwaltung, Abteilung Tarifpolitik, July.

IG Metall. 1990c. "Das Ziel ist Erreicht! Umsetzungshilfe für das Tarifergebnis 1990." Frankfurt: IG Metall Vorstandsverwaltung, Abteilung Tarifpolitik, June.

IG Metall. Various years. *Geschäftsberichte, 1952–1985*. Frankfurt: IG Metall Vorstand.

IG Metall. Various years. *Gewerkschaftstage*. Proceedings of IG Metall congresses (*Gewerkschaftstage der IG Metall*). Frankfurt: IG Metall.

IG Metall. Various years. *Vertrauensleute*. Proceedings of IG Metall conferences for shop stewards and works councillors (*Konferenzen der IG Metall für Vertrauensleute und Betriebsratsmitglieder*). Frankfurt: IG Metall.

Ikenberry, G. John. 1988. "Conclusion: An Institutional Approach to American Foreign Economic Policy." In G. John Ikenberry, David A. Lake, and Michael Mastanduno, eds., *The State and American Foreign Economic Policy*. Ithaca: Cornell University Press.

ILO. 1986. *Yearbook of Labour Statistics*. Geneva: International Labour Office.

ILO. 1988. *Yearbook of Labour Statistics*. Geneva: International Labour Office.

Ingham, Geoffrey K. 1974. *Strikes and Industrial Conflict: Britain and Scandinavia*. London: MacMillan.

Jacobi, Otto. 1986a. "Economic Development and Trade Union Collective Bargaining Policy since the Middle of the 1970s." In Otto Jacobi, Bob Jessop, Hans Kastendiek, and Marino Regini, eds., *Economic Crisis, Trade Unions, and the State*. London: Croom Helm.

Jacobi, Otto. 1986b. "Trade Unions, Industrial Relations, and Structural Economic 'Ruptures.'" In Otto Jacobi, Bob Jessop, Hans Kastendiek, and Marino Regini, eds., *Economic Crisis, Trade Unions, and the State*. London: Croom Helm.

Jacoby, Sanford M. 1985. *Employing Bureaucracy: Managers, Unions, and the Transformation of Work in American Industry, 1900–1945*. New York: Columbia University Press.

Janβen, Hans. 1980. "Technischer Wandel und Rationalisierung aus tarifpolitischer Sicht." *Gewerkschaftliche Monatshefte* 4 (April).

Janzen, Karl-Heinz. 1979. "Noch wächst das unbehagen." *Der Gewerkschafter* 3.

Janzen, Karl-Heinz. 1980. "Technologiepolitik und Gewerkschaften." *Gewerkschaftliche Monatshefte* 4 (April).

Jenkins, David. 1973. *Job Power: Blue and White Collar Democracy*. Garden City: Doubleday & Co.

Johnson, Chalmers. 1982. *MITI and the Japanese Miracle*. Stanford: Stanford University Press.

Kahn, Peggy. 1987. "Political Economy, Internal Union Politics, and Union Strategies in the British Coal Industry, 1947–87." Paper presented at the workshop "Union Politics, Labor Militancy, and Capital Accumulation," Ithaca, New York, Cornell University, April.

Kahn-Freund, Otto. 1981. *Labour Law and Politics in the Weimar Republic*. Edited by Roy Lewis and Jon Clark. Oxford: Basil Blackwell.

Kaβebaum, Bernd. 1990. *Betriebliche Technologiepolitik: Arbeitsgestaltung in der Politik der IG Metall*. Frankfurt: Campus Verlag.

Kaβebaum, Bernd, and Kathleen Thelen. 1989. "Arbeitsstrukturuierung und Beteiligung: Betriebliche Fallbeispiele aus den USA, Schweden, und der Bundesrepublik." Interim Report to the Hans-Böckler-Stiftung, September.

Katz, Harry. 1985. *Shifting Gears: Changing Labor Relations in the U.S. Automobile Industry*. Cambridge: MIT Press.

Katz, Harry C., and Charles F. Sabel. 1985. "Industrial Relations and Industrial Adjustment in the Car Industry." *Industrial Relations* 24 (Fall).

Katzenstein, Peter J. 1984. *Corporatism and Change*. Ithaca: Cornell University Press.

Katzenstein, Peter J. 1985. *Small States in World Markets: Industrial Policy in Europe*. Ithaca: Cornell University Press.

Katzenstein, Peter J. 1987. *Policy and Politics in West Germany: The Growth of a Semisovereign State*. Philadelphia: Temple University Press.

Katzenstein, Peter J. 1989a. "Stability and Change in the Emerging Third Republic." In Peter J. Katzenstein, ed., *Industry and Politics in West Germany.*

Katzenstein, Peter J., ed., 1989b. *Industry and Politics in West Germany: Toward the Third Republic.* Ithaca: Cornell University Press.

Kern, Horst, and Michael Schumann. 1984. *Das Ende der Arbeitsteilung?* Munich: C. H. Beck.

Kerr, Clark, John T. Dunlop, Frederick H. Harbison, and Charles A. Myers. 1960. *Industrialism and Industrial Man.* Cambridge: Harvard University Press.

Kissler, Leo. 1989. "Co-determination Research in the Federal Republic of Germany: A Review." In Cornelis J. Lammers and György Széil, eds., *International Handbook of Participation in Organizations for the Study of Organizational Democracy, Co-operation, and Self-Management.* Vol. 1. New York: Oxford University Press.

Kittner, Michael, ed. 1984. *Arbeits- und Sozialordnung.* 9th ed. Cologne: Bund Verlag.

Kittner, Michael. 1985. *Beschäftigungsförderungsgesetz.* Cologne: Bund Verlag.

Kochan, Thomas A., and Joel Cutcher-Gershenfeld. 1988. "Institutionalizing and Diffusing Innovations in Industrial Relations." Washington, D.C.: U.S. Department of Labor, Bureau of Labor-Management Relations and Cooperative Programs monograph BLMR 128.

Kochan, Thomas A., and Harry C. Katz. 1988. *Collective Bargaining and Industrial Relations.* 2d ed. Homewood, Ill.: Irwin.

Kochan, Thomas A., Harry C. Katz, and Robert McKersie. 1986. *The Transformation of U.S. Industrial Relations.* New York: Basic Books.

Kochan, Thomas A., Harry C. Katz, and Nancy R. Mauer. 1984. *Worker Participation and American Unions: Threat or Opportunity?* Kalamazoo, Mich.: W. E. Upjohn Institute for Employment Research.

Kohl, Wilfrid, and Giorgio Basevi, eds., 1980. *West Germany: A European and Global Power.* Lexington, Mass.: Lexington Books.

König, Otto, Adi Ostertag, and Hartmut Schulz, eds. 1985. *"Unser Beispiel könnte ja Schule machen!"* Cologne: Bund Verlag.

Koopmann, Klaus. 1979. *Gewerkschaftliche Vertrauensleute.* Vols. 1 and 2. Munich: Minerva Publikation.

Koopmann, Klaus. 1981. *Vertrauensleute: Arbeitervertretung im Betrieb.* Frankfurt: Büchergilde Gutenberg.

Korpi, Walter, and Michael Shalev. 1979. "Strikes, Industrial Relations, and Class Conflict in Capitalist Societies." *British Journal of Sociology* 30 (June).

Kotthoff, Hermann. 1979. "Zum Verhältnis von Betriebsrat und Gewerkschaft, Ergebnisse einer empirischen Untersuchung." In Joachim Bergmann, ed., *Beiträge zur Soziologie der Gewerkschaften.* Frankfurt: Suhrkamp.

Kotthoff, Hermann. 1981. *Betriebsräte und betriebliche Herrschaft.* Frankfurt: Campus Verlag.

Krasner, Stephen D. 1984. "Approaches to the State: Alternative Conceptions and Historical Dynamics." *Comparative Politics* 16 (January).

Kreile, Michael. 1978. "West Germany: The Dynamics of Expansion." In Peter J. Katzenstein, ed., *Between Power and Plenty: Foreign Economic Policies of Advanced Industrial States.* Madison: University of Wisconsin Press.

Kreye, Otto. 1986. "Arbeitslosigkeit in Westeuropa: Arbeitsmarktpolitik versus Beschäftigungspolitik." *Gewerkschaftliche Monatshefte* 7 (July).

Kritisches Jahrbuch. Various years. Frankfurt: Fischer Taschenbuch Verlag.

Krusche, Reinhard. 1982. "Analyse der Entwicklungslinien qualitativer Tarifpolitik der NGG." IIVG *Discussion Paper* dp82–209. Berlin: IIVG, July.

Krusche, Reinhard, and Dagmar Pfeiffer. 1975. *Betriebliche Gewerkschaftsorgane und Interessenvertretung: Zur Betriebsräte- und Vertrauensleutepolitik der IG Metall.* Berlin: Verlag Die Arbeitswelt.

Kurz-Scherf, Ingrid. 1985. "Tarifpolitik und Arbeitskämpfe." In Michael Kittner, ed., *Gewerkschaftsjahrbuch 1985*. Cologne: Bund Verlag.

Kurz-Scherf, Ingrid. 1988a. "Tarifpolitik und Arbeitskämpfe." In Michael Kittner, ed., *Gewerkschaftsjahrbuch 1988*. Cologne: Bund Verlag.

Kurz-Scherf, Ingrid. 1988b. "Tarifbewegungen im 1. Halbjahr 1988." *WSI Mitteilungen* 41 (September).

Kurz-Scherf, Ingrid. 1989. "Tarifpolitik und Arbeitskämpfe." In Michael Kittner, ed., *Gewerkschaftsjahrbuch 1989*. Cologne: Bund Verlag.

Landau, Martin, and Eva Eagle. 1981. "On the Concept of Decentralization." Unpublished manuscript, University of California, Berkeley.

Lang, Klaus. 1988. "Strukturwandel: Chancen und Gefahren für solidarische Tarifpolitik." Speech delivered at an IG Metall conference, "Die andere Zukunft", 20–22 June (Arbeitseinheit II).

Lange, Peter. 1984. "Unions, Workers, and Wage Regulation: The Rational Bases of Consent." In John H. Goldthorpe, ed., *Order and Conflict in Contemporary Capitalism*. London: Oxford University Press.

Lange, Peter, and Geoffrey Garrett. 1985. "The Politics of Growth: Strategic Interaction and Economic Performance in the Advanced Industrial Democracies, 1974–1980." *Journal of Politics* 47:3 (August).

Lange, Peter, George Ross, and Maurizio Vannicelli. 1982. *Unions, Change, and Crisis: French and Italian Union Strategy and the Political Economy, 1945–1980*. London: George Allen and Unwin.

Laube, Ulrich. 1981. *Gewerkschaftliche Tarifpolitik und industrielle Arbeitsbedingungen in der BRD*. Cologne: Pahl-Rugenstein Verlag.

Lecher, Wolfgang. 1991. "Den Tiger reiten: Soziale Produkivität und direkte Mitbestimmung." *Gewerkschaftliche Monatshefte* 2 (February).

Lehmbruch, Gerhard. 1977. "Liberal Corporatism and Party Government." *Comparative Political Studies* 10 (April).

Lehmbruch, Gerhard, and Phillipe Schmitter, eds. 1982. *Patterns of Corporatist Policy-Making*. Beverly Hills, Calif.: Sage.

Leminsky, Gerhard. 1980. "Humanisierung der Arbeit aus eigener Kraft." *Gewerkschaftliche Monatshefte* 4 (April).

Lichtenstein, Nelson. 1982a. "Industrial Democracy, Contract Unionism, and the National War Labor Board." *Labor Law Journal* 33 (August).

Lichtenstein, Nelson. 1982b. *Labor's War at Home: The CIO in World War II*. New York: Cambridge University Press.

Lichtenstein, Nelson. 1988. "The Union's Early Days: Shop Stewards and Seniority." In Mike Parker and Jane Slaughter, eds., *Choosing Sides*.

Lindberg, Leon N., and Charles S. Maier, eds. 1985. *The Politics of Inflation and Economic Stagnation*. Washington, D.C.: The Brookings Institution.

Lobodda, Gerd. 1988. "Beschäftigungspläne: Eine erste Bewertung über Stellenwert, Perspektiven, Grenzen, und Möglichkeiten." Speech delivered to an IG Metall workshop on employment plans, IG Metall Verwaltungsstelle Nürnberg, 16 April.

Locke, Richard M. 1987. "Strategic Choice and Its Constraints: Italian Labor Politics in Transition—the Case of FIAT." Paper presented at the conference "Union Politics, Labor Militancy, and Capital Accumulation," Ithaca, New York, Cornell University, 2–5 April.

Löhrlein, Klaus. 1989. "Mitgliederzahlen: Entwicklung und Verteilung der Gewerkschaftsmitglieder in den DGB–Landesbezirken." In Michael Kittner, ed., *Gewerkschaftsjahrbuch 1989: Daten, Fakten, Analysen*. Cologne: Bund Verlag.

Ludwig, Franz. 1979. "Mitbestimmung aus der Sicht eines Arbeitsdirektors." In Rudolf Judith, ed., *Montanmitbestimmung: Geschichte, Idee, Wirklichkeit*. Cologne: Bund Verlag.

Luebbert, Gregory M. 1987. "Social Foundations of Political Order in Interwar Europe." *World Politics* 39 (July).

Macbeath, Innis. 1973. *The European Approach to Worker-Management Relationships.* London and Washington: British–North American Committee.

McPherson, William. 1940. *Labor Relations in the Automobile Industry.* Washington, D.C.: The Brookings Institution.

McPherson, William. 1955. "Codetermination in Practice." *Industrial and Labor Relations Review* 8.

Maier, Charles S. 1975. *Recasting Bourgeois Europe: Stabilization in France, Germany, and Italy in the Decade after World War I.* Princeton: Princeton University Press.

March, James G., and Johan P. Olsen. 1984. "The New Institutionalism: Organizational Factors in Political Life." *American Political Science Review* 78 (September).

Markovits, Andrei. 1986. *The Politics of the West German Trade Unions.* Cambridge: Cambridge University Press.

Markovits, Andrei S., and Christopher S. Allen. 1979. "The 1978–79 Steel Strike: German Unions at a Crossroad." Unpublished manuscript.

Markovits, Andrei S., and Christopher S. Allen. 1980. "Power and Dissent: The Trade Unions in the Federal Republic of Germany Re-Examined." *West European Politics* 3 (January).

Markovits, Andrei S., and Christopher S. Allen. 1981. "Trade Union Responses to the Contemporary Economic Problems in Western Europe: The Context of Current Debates and Policies in the Federal Republic of Germany." *Economic and Industrial Democracy* 2.

Markovits, Andrei S., and Christopher S. Allen. 1984. "Trade Unions and the Economic Crisis: The West German Case." In Peter Gourevitch, Andrew Martin, George Ross, and Stephen Bornstein, eds., *Unions and Economic Crisis.*

Martin, Andrew. 1977. "Sweden: Industrial Democracy and Social Democratic Strategy." In G. David Garson, ed., *Worker Self-Management in Industry.*

Martin, Andrew. 1984. "Trade Unions in Sweden: Strategic Responses to Change and Crisis." In Peter Gourevitch, Andrew Martin, George Ross, and Stephen Bornstein, eds., *Unions and Economic Crisis.*

Matthöfer, Hans. 1968a. "Die Bedeutung der Mitbestimmung am Arbeitsplatz und im Betrieb für die politische Bildungsarbeit der Gewerkschaften." *Die Neue Gesellschaft* 15.

Matthöfer, Hans. 1968b. "Betriebsnahe Tarifpolitik." *Express International* 60 (20 August).

Matthöfer, Hans. 1968c. "Das Dokument: Vorschlag von Hans Matthöfer zur Novellierung des Beriebsverfassungsgesetzes." *Gewerkschaftliche Monatshefte* (December).

Matthöfer, Hans. 1968d. "Mitbestimmung am Arbeitsplatz." *Express International* 60 (20 August).

Matthöfer, Hans. 1968e. "Raus aus der Konzertierte Aktion?" *Express International* 63 (16 November).

Matthöfer, Hans. 1976. *Für eine menschliche Zukunft.* Düsseldorf: Econ Verlag.

Matthöfer, Hans. 1980. *Humanisierung der Arbeit und Produktivität in der Industriegesellschaft.* Cologne: Bund Verlag.

Mausolff, Anneliese. 1952. *Gewerkschaft und Betriebsrat im Urteil der Arbeitnehmer.* Darmstadt: Eduard Roether Verlag.

Miller, Doug. 1982. "Social Partnership and the Determinants of Workplace Independence in West Germany." *British Journal of Industrial Relations* 20 (March).

Milner, Henry. 1989. *Sweden: Social Democracy in Practice.* London: Oxford University Press.

Moses, John A. 1982. *Trade Unionism in Germany from Bismarck to Hitler 1869–1933.* Vol. 2, 1919–1933. Totowa, N.J.: Barnes and Noble.

Muhr, Gerd. 1972. "Zur Neuregelung des Betriebsverfassungsgesetzes." *Gewerkschaftliche Monatshefte* 1 (January).

Müller, Alfred. 1968. "Technischer Fortschritt und gewerkschaftliche Tarifpolitik." *WWI Wirtschaftswissenschaftliche Mitteilungen* 4/5 (April/May).

Müller-Jentsch, Walther. 1984. "The Changing Balance between Workplace Representation and Industrywide Representation in West Germany." In Tokunaga Shigeyoshi and Joachim Bergmann, eds., *Industrial Relations in Transition.*

Müller-Jentsch, Walther, and Hans-Joachim Sperling. 1978. "Economic Development, Labour Conflicts, and the Industrial Relations System in West Germany." In Colin Crouch and Alessandro Pizzorno, eds., *The Resurgence of Class Conflict in Western Europe Since 1968. Vol. 1.*

Muster, Manfred. 1988a. "Eckpunkte zur Gruppenarbeit." Internal position paper, Vorstandsverwaltung der IG Metall, Abteilung Automation/Technologie/HdA, 20 June.

Muster, Manfred. 1988b. "Zum Stand der Gruppenarbeit in der Automobilindustrie der Bundesrepublik Deutschland." Internal position paper, Vorstandsverwaltung der IG Metall, Abteilung Automation/Technologie/HdA, 28 January.

Muster, Manfred, and Manfred Wannöffel. 1989. *Gruppenarbeit in der Automobilindustrie.* Bochum: IG Metall Verwaltungsstelle Bochum in Zusammenarbeit mit der Gemeinsamen Arbeitsstelle Ruhr Universität Bochum/IG Metall.

Naschold, Frieder. 1980. "Humanisierung der Arbeit zwischen Staat und Gewerkschaften." *Gewerkschaftliche Monatshefte* 4.

Nedelmann, Birgitta, and Kurt G. Meier. 1977. "Theories of Contemporary Corporatism: Static or Dynamic?" *Comparative Political Studies* 10 (April).

Neumann, Franz. 1944. *Behemoth: The Structure and Practice of National Socialism 1933–1944.* New York: Harper Torchbooks.

OECD. 1983. *Positive Adjustment Policies: Managing Structural Change.* Paris: OECD.

OECD. 1986a. *Economic Outlook: Historical Statistics.* Paris: OECD.

OECD. 1986b. *OECD Economic Outlook.* Paris: OECD, December.

OECD. 1988. *Economic Outlook: Historical Statistics: 1960–86.* Paris: OECD.

OECD. 1989. *Economic Outlook: Historical Statistics: 1960–87.* Paris: OECD.

OECD. Various years. *Main Economic Indicators.* Paris: OECD.

Oertzen, Peter von. 1963. *Betriebsräte in der Novemberrevolution.* Düsseldorf: Droste Verlag.

Oertzen, Peter von. 1968. "SPD und Mitbestimmung." *Express International* 54/55 (2 March).

Olson, Mancur. 1982. *The Rise and Decline of Nations.* New Haven: Yale University Press.

Panitch, Leo. 1976. *Social Democracy and Industrial Militancy: The Labour Party, the Trade Unions, and Incomes Policy, 1945–1974.* Cambridge: Cambridge University Press.

Panitch, Leo. 1977. "The Development of Corporatism in Liberal Democracies." *Comparative Political Studies* 10 (April).

Parker, Mike. 1985. *Inside the Circle: A Union Guide to QWL.* Boston: South End Books.

Parker, Mike, and Jane Slaughter. 1988. *Choosing Sides: Unions and the Team Concept.* Boston: South End Books.

Pejovich, Svetozar. 1983. "Codetermination in the West: The Case of Germany." In Svetozar Pejovich, ed., *Philosophical and Economic Foundations of Capitalism.* Lexington, Mass.: Lexington Books.

Peter, Gerd. 1979. "Zur ideologiekritischen Auseinandersetzung mit dem Humanisierungsprogramms." In Willi Pöhler, ed., *. . . damit die Arbeit menschlicher wird: Fünf Jahre Aktionsprogramm Humanisierung des Arbeitslebens.* Bonn: Verlag Neue Gesellschaft.

Peter, Gerd. 1982. "Konflikte um das Humanisierungsprogramm." In Gotthard Bechmann, et al., eds., *Technik und Gesellschaft.* Frankfurt: Campus Verlag.

Pfeiffer, Dagmar, and Reinhard Krusche. 1975. *Betriebliche Gewerkschaftsorgane und Interessenvertretung: Zur Betriebsräte- und Vertrauensleutepolitik der IG Metall.* Berlin: Verlag Die Arbeitswelt.

Pinther, Helmut. 1970. "Mitbestimmung am Arbeitsplatz." *Gewerkschaftliche Monatshefte* 5 (May).

Piore, Michael J. 1982. "American Labor and the Industrial Crisis." *Challenge* 25:1 (March/April).

Piore, Michael J., and Charles F. Sabel. 1984. *The Second Industrial Divide: Possibilities for Prosperity.* New York: Basic Books.

Pirker, Theo. 1979. *Die Blinde Macht: Die Gewerkschaftsbewegung in der Bundesrepublik.* Vol. 1 and 2. Berlin: Verlag Olle & Wolter.

Pizzorno, Alessandro. 1978. "Political Exchange and Collective Identity in Industrial Conflict." In Colin Crouch and Alessandro Pizzorno, eds., *The Resurgence of Class Conflict in Western Europe Since 1968.* Vol. 2.

Pöhler, Willi. 1979. "Fünf Jahre Humanisierungsprogramm im Bereich des Bundesminsters für Forschung und Technologie." In Willi Pöhler, ed., ...*damit die Arbeit menschlicher wird: Fünf Jahre Aktionsprogramm Humanisierung des Arbeitslebens.* Bonn: Verlag Neue Gesellschaft.

Pöhler, Willi. 1980. "Staatliche Förderung für die Verbesserung der Arbeits- und Lebensqualität." *Gewerkschaftliche Monatshefte* 4 (April).

Pontusson, Jonas. 1988. "Unions, Management, and Industrial Innovation: Volvo and British Leyland Compared." Paper presented at the annual meeting of the American Political Science Association, Washington, D.C., September.

Pontusson, Jonas. 1989. "The Micro and Macro Politics of Industrial Innovation: A Comparison of Volvo and British Leyland." Unpublished manuscript, Cornell University.

Pontusson, Jonas. 1990. "The Politics of New Technology and Job Redesign: A Comparison of Volvo and British Leyland." *Economic and Industrial Democracy* 11.

Radke, Olaf. 1968. "Mitbestimmung am Arbeitsplatz?" *Express International* 63 (16 November).

Radke, Olaf. 1969. *Betriebsnahe Tarifpolitik.* Arbeitsheft 400, Abteilung Bildungswesen. Frankfurt: IG Metall, June.

Reich, Nathan. 1938. *Labour Relations in Republican Germany: An Experiment in Industrial Democracy, 1918–1933.* New York: Oxford University Press.

Riemer, Jeremiah. 1982. "Alterations in the Design of Model Germany: Critical Innovations in the Policy Machinery for Economic Steering." In Andrei Markovits, ed., *The Political Economy of West Germany: Modell Deutschland.* New York: Praeger.

Riemer, Jeremiah. 1983. "Crisis and Intervention in the West German Economy: A Political Analysis of Changes in the Policy Machinery during the 1960s and 1970s." Ph.D. diss., Cornell University.

Rogers, Joel E. 1984. "Divide and Conquer: The Legal Foundations of Postwar U.S. Labor Policy." Ph.D. diss., Princeton University.

Röpke, Wilhelm. 1982. "The Guiding Principles of the Liberal Programme." In Horst Friedrich Wünche, ed., *Standard Texts on the Social Market Economy.* Stuttgart and New York: Gustav Fischer Verlag.

Rose, Gunter. 1973. "Mitbestimmung auf Betriebsebene: Ansätze und Schwerpunkte nach dem Betriebsverfassungsgesetz 1972." *Gewerkschaftliche Monatshefte* 10 (October).

Ross, Arthur M., and Paul T. Hartmann. 1960. *Changing Patterns of Industrial Conflict.* New York: Wiley.

Roth, Siegfried, and Heribert Kohl, eds. 1988. *Perspektive: Gruppenarbeit.* Cologne: Bund Verlag.

Sabel, Charles F. 1981. "The Internal Politics of Trade Unions." In Suzanne Berger, ed., *Organizing Interests in Western Europe: Pluralism, Corporatism, and the Transformation of Politics.* Cambridge: Cambridge University Press.

Sabel, Charles F. 1982. *Work and Politics*. Cambridge: Cambridge University Press.

Sabel, Charles F. 1986. "Struktureller Wandel der Produktion und neue gewerkschaftliche Strategien." *Prokla* 62 (March).

Säcker, Franz Jürgen, and Ernst Zander, eds. 1981. *Mitbestimmung und Effizienz*. Stuttgart: Fachverlag für Wirtschafts- und Steuerrecht.

Sandberg, Åke. 1984. "Über die Möglichkeiten der Gewerkschaften, Entwicklung und Anwendung von Produktionstechniken zu beeinflussen." In Werner Fricke and Wilgart Schuchardt, eds., *Beteiligung als Element gewerkschaftlicher Arbeitspolitik*. Bonn: Verlag Neue Gesellschaft

Sandberg, Åke. 1986. "Trade Union Strategies in Production Issues: Some Swedish Experiences." Paper presented at the Eleventh World Congress of Sociology, New Dehli, August. Swedish Center for Working Life Discussion Paper. Stockholm: Arbetslivscentrum.

Scharpf, Fritz W. 1980. "Beschäftigungsorientierte Strukturpolitik." IIM-LMP *Discussion Paper* 80–42. International Institute of Management, Wissenschaftszentrum Berlin.

Scharpf, Fritz W. 1984. "Economic and Institutional Constraints of Full-Employment Strategies: Sweden, Austria, and West Germany, 1973–1982." In John H. Goldthorpe, ed., *Order and Conflict in Contemporary Capitalism*.

Scharpf, Fritz, Bernd Reissert, and Fritz Schnabel. 1976. *Politikverflechtung: Theorie und Empirie des kooperativen Föderalismus in der Bundesrepublik*. Kronberg: Scriptor.

Schmidt, Eberhard. 1970. *Die Verhinderte Neuordnung, 1945–1952*. Frankfurt: Europäische Verlagsanstalt.

Schmidt, Eberhard. 1973. "Die Rolle der Betriebsräte in der Gewerkschaftsbewegung." In Otto Jacobi, Walther Müller-Jentsch, and Eberhard Schmidt, eds., *Gewerkschaften und Klassenkampf: Kritisches Jahrbuch 1973*. Frankfurt: Fischer Taschenbuch Verlag.

Schmidt, Eberhard. 1974. "Die Auseinandersetzungen um die Rolle der Vertrauensleute in der IG Metall." In Otto Jacobi, Walther Müller-Jentsch, and Eberhard Schmidt. *Gewerkschaften und Klassenkampf: Kritisches Jahrbuch 1974*. Frankfurt: Fischer Taschenbuch Verlag.

Schmidt, Eberhard. 1975. *Ordnungsfaktor oder Gegenmacht: Die Politische Rolle der Gewerkschaften*. 3d ed. Frankfurt: Suhrkamp Verlag.

Schmidt, Edgar. 1968. "Gegenmacht im Betrieb." *Express International* 64 (14 December).

Schmitter, Philippe C. 1974. "Still the Century of Corporatism?" *The Review of Politics* 36. Reprinted in Philippe Schmitter and Gerhard Lehmbruch, eds., *Trends Toward Corporatist Intermediation*. Beverly Hills, Calif.: Sage, 1979.

Schmitter, Philippe C. 1977. "Modes of Interest Intermediation and Models of Societal Change in Western Europe." *Comparative Political Studies* 10 (April).

Schmitter, Philippe C. 1981: "Interest Intermediation and Regime Governability in Contemporary Western Europe and North America." In Suzanne Berger, ed., *Organizing Interests in Western Europe*. Cambridge: Cambridge University Press.

Schmitter, Philippe, and Gerhard Lehmbruch, eds. 1979. *Trends toward Corporatist Intermediation*. Beverly Hills, Calif.: Sage.

Schneiders, Volker. 1987. "Krise der Massenproduktion, technologischer Wandel und Gewerkschaftspolitik in der Bundesrepublik: Eine Skizze." Unpublished manuscript, University of Osnabrück, January.

Schuchman, Abraham. 1957. *Codetermination: Labor's Middle Way in Germany*. Washington, D.C.: Public Affairs Press.

Schultz-Wild, Rainer. 1978. *Betriebliche Beschäftigungspolitik in der Krise*. Frankfurt: Campus Verlag.

Schumann, Michael. 1969. "Möglichkeiten der Mitbestimmung am Arbeitsplatz." *Gewerkschaftliche Monatshefte* 4 (April).

Schwerin, Don S. 1984. "Historic Compromise and Pluralist Decline? Profits and

Capital in the Nordic Countries." In John H. Goldthorpe, ed., *Order and Conflict in Contemporary Capitalism.*

Sengenberger, Werner. 1984. "West German Employment Policy: Restoring Worker Competition." *Industrial Relations* 23 (Fall).

Shirai, Taishiro, ed. 1983. *Contemporary Industrial Relations in Japan.* Madison: University of Wisconsin Press.

Shirer, William L. 1960. *The Rise and Fall of the Third Reich.* New York: Simon and Schuster.

Shonfield, Andrew. 1969. *Modern Capitalism: The Changing Balance of Public and Private Power.* London: Oxford University Press.

Silvia, Stephen. 1988. "The West German Labor Law Controversy: A Struggle for the Factory of the Future." *Comparative Politics* 20 (January).

Skocpol, Theda. 1979. *States and Social Revolutions: A Comparative Analysis of France, Russia, and China.* Cambridge and New York: Cambridge University Press.

Skocpol, Theda. 1985. "Bringing the State Back In: Strategies of Analysis in Current Research." In Peter Evans, Dietrich Rueschemeyer, and Theda Skocpol, eds., *Bringing the State Back In.* New York: Cambridge University Press.

Skowronek, Stephen. 1982. *Building a New American State: The Expansion of National Administrative Capacities.* New York: Cambridge University Press.

Slichter, Sumner. 1941. *Union Policies and Industrial Managment.* Washington, D.C.: The Brookings Institution.

Slichter, Sumner, James J. Healy, and E. Robert Livernash. 1960. *The Impact of Collective Bargaining on Management.* Washington, D.C.: The Brookings Institution.

Spiro, Herbert. 1958. *The Politics of German Codetermination.* Cambridge: Harvard University Press.

Statistisches Jahrbuch für die Bundesrepublik Deutschland. Various Years. Wiesbaden: W. Kohlhammer.

Steinkühler, Franz. 1984 "Einbahnstraße Technik? Das Verhältnis der Gewerkschaften zur den 'neuen Technologien.'" *Blätter für deutsche und internationale Politik* 2.

Steinmo, Sven. 1989. "Political Institutions and Tax Policy in the United States, Sweden, and Britain." *World Politics* 41 (July).

Steinmo, Sven, and Kathleen Thelen. Forthcoming. Introduction to Sven Steinmo, Kathleen Thelen, and Frank Longstreth, eds., *Institutional Perspectives: State, Society, and Economy.* New York: Cambridge University Press.

Stephens, Evelyne Huber, and John D. Stephens. 1982. "The Labor Movement, Political Power, and Workers' Participation in Western Europe." In Maurice Zeitlin, ed., *Political Power and Social Theory.* Vol. 3. Greenwich, Conn.: JAI Press.

Stern, Boris. 1925. *Works Council Movement in Germany.* Bulletin of the U.S. Bureau of Labor Statistics (Misc. series) No. 383. Washington, D.C.: Government Printing Office.

Streeck, Wolfgang. 1979. "Gewerkschaftsorganisation und industrielle Beziehungen: Einige Stabilitätsprobleme industriegewerkschaftlicher Interessenvertretung und ihre Lösung im System der industriellen Beziehungen der Bundesrepublik Deutschland." IIM *Discussion Paper* 79–30. Wissenschaftszentrum Berlin.

Streeck, Wolfgang. 1981. "Qualitative Demands and the Neo-Corporatist Manageability of Industrial Relations." *British Journal of Industrial Relations* 19 (July).

Streeck, Wolfgang. 1983. "Co-determination: The Fourth Decade." IIM-LMP *Discussion Paper* 83-1. Wissenschaftszentrum Berlin. Published in *International Yearbook of Organizational Democracy.* Vol. 2. Chichester: John Wiley and Sons, 1984.

Streeck, Wolfgang. 1984a. "Guaranteed Employment, Flexible Manpower Use, and Cooperative Manpower Management: A Trend Towards Convergence?" In Tokunaga Shigeyoshi and Joachim Bergmann, eds., *Industrial Relations in Transition.*

Streeck, Wolfgang. 1984b. *Industrial Relations in West Germany: A Case Study of the Car Industry.* London: Heinemann.

Streeck, Wolfgang. 1984c. "Neo-Corporatist Industrial Relations and the Economic Crisis in West Germany." In John H. Goldthorpe, ed., *Order and Conflict in Contemporary Capitalism.*

Streeck, Wolfgang. 1987. "Industrial Relations in West Germany: Agenda for Change." IIM-LMP *Discussion Paper* 87-5. Wissenschaftszentrum Berlin, April.

Streeck, Wolfgang. 1989. "Successful Adjustment to Turbulent Markets: The Automobile Industry." In Peter J. Katzenstein, ed., *Industry and Politics in West Germany.*

Swedish Employers' Confederation. 1982. "Agreement on Efficiency and Participation, SAF-LO-PTK." Stockholm: SAF.

Swedish Metal Workers' Union. 1985a. "Erneuerungfonds." Internal memorandum (German translation), Svenska Metall, Förbundsmeddelande 85/28, Arbetsmarknadsärenden, 4 February.

Swedish Metal Workers' Union. 1985b. *Rewarding Work.* Union pamphlet, first published in the Swedish Metal Workers' Union's report "Det goda arbetet," to the 1985 congress. Stockholm: Svenska Metallindustriarbetareförbundet.

Swenson, Peter. 1989. *Fair Shares: Unions, Pay, and Politics in Sweden and West Germany.* Ithaca: Cornell University Press.

Tegtmeier, Werner. 1973. *Wirkung der Mitbestimmung der Arbeitnehmer.* Göttingen: Vandenhoeck & Ruprecht.

Teschner, Eckart. 1977. *Lohnpolitik im Betrieb.* Frankfurt: Campus Verlag.

Teuteberg, Hans Jürgen. 1961. *Geschichte der Industriellen Mitbestimmung in Deutschland.* Tübingen: J.C.B. Mohr (Paul Siebeck).

Thelen, Kathleen. 1987a. "Codetermination and Industrial Adjustment in the German Steel Industry: A Comparative Interpretation." *California Management Review* 29 (Spring).

Thelen, Kathleen. 1987b. "Union Structure and Strategic Choice: The Politics of Flexibility in the German Metalworking Industries." Paper presented at the workshop "Union Politics, Labor Militancy, and Capital Accumulation," Ithaca, N.Y., Cornell University, April. Forthcoming in Miriam Golden and Jonas Pontusson, eds., *Union Politics in Comparative Perspective: Economic Change and Intra-Class Conflict.* Ithaca: Cornell University Press.

Thelen, Kathleen. 1989a. "Neoliberalism and the Battle over Working-Time Reduction in West Germany." In Richard E. Foglesong and Joel D. Wolfe, eds., *The Politics of Economic Adjustment: Pluralism, Corporatism, and Privatization.* Westport, Conn.: Greenwood Press.

Thelen, Kathleen. 1989b. "Worker Participation and Work Reorganization in U.S. Industry." In Bernd Kaßebaum and Kathleen Thelen, "Arbeitsstrukturierung und Beteiligung: Betriebliche Fallbeispiele aus den USA, Schweden, und der Bundesrepublik." Interim report to the Hans-Böckler-Stiftung, September.

Thelen, Kathleen. 1991. Arbeitsumstrukturierung und Gewerkschaftspolitik in den USA. Final report to the Hans-Böckler-Stiftung.

Thimm, Alfred L. 1980. *The False Promise of Codetermination: The Changing Nature of European Workers' Participation.* Lexington, Mass.: Lexington Books.

Thimm, Alfred L. 1981. "How Far Should German Codetermination Go?" *Challenge* 11 (July/August).

Tilch, Wolfgang, Oswald Todtenberg, and Fritz Vilmar. n.d. "Kritik und Revidiertes Konzept der 'Mitbestimmung am Arbeitsplatz.'" Internal document, Vorstandsverwaltung der IG Metall.

Tokunaga Shigeyoshi, and Joachim Bergmann, eds. 1984. *Industrial Relations in Transition: The Cases of Japan and the Federal Republic of Germany.* Tokyo: University of Tokyo Press.

Trautwein-Kalms, Gudrun, and Gerhard Gerlach. 1980. *Gewerkschaften und Humanisierung der Arbeit.* Vol. 5 of *Schriftenreihe HdA.* Frankfurt: Campus Verlag.

Turner, Lowell. 1988. "Are Labor-Management Partnerships for Competitiveness

Possible in America?" BRIE *Working Paper* 36. Berkeley: University of California, Berkeley Roundtable on the International Economy.

Turner, Lowell. 1991. *Democracy at Work: Changing World Markets and the Future of Labor Unions.* Ithaca, New York: Cornell University Press.

Ullmer, Richard. 1980. "Die Krise der AEG." In Otto Jacobi, Eberhard Schmidt, and Walther Müller-Jentsch, eds., *Moderne Zeiten—Alte Rezepte: Kritisches Gewerkschaftsjahrbuch 1980/81.* Berlin: Rotbuch Verlag.

Vilmar, Fritz. 1968. "Die Mitbestimmung muß am Arbeitsplatz beginnen." *Gewerkschaftliche Monatshefte* 8.

Vilmar, Fritz. 1970. "Arbeitsgruppenbesprechungen im Betriebsverfassungsgesetz verankern!" *Gewerkschaftliche Monatshefte* 3 (March).

Vilmar, Fritz. 1971. *Mitbestimmung am Arbeitsplatz: Basis demokratischer Betriebspolitik.* Berlin: Hermann Luchterhand Verlag.

Webber, Douglas. 1983a. "Combatting and Acquiesing in Unemployment? Economic Crisis Management in Sweden and West Germany." *West European Politics* 6 (January).

Webber, Douglas. 1983b. "A Relationship of 'Critical Partnership'? Capital and the Social-Liberal Coalition in West Germany." *West European Politics* 6 (April).

Weber, Hajo. 1986. "Desynchronisation, Dezentralisierung—und Dekomposition?" Arbeitsberichte und Forschungsmaterialien, Nr. 19, Universität Bielefeld, Department of Sociology, May.

Wedderburn, K. W., Roy Lewis, and Jon Clark. 1983. *Labour Law and Industrial Relations: Building on Kahn-Freund.* Oxford: Clarendon Press.

Weiss, Manfred. 1978. *Gewerkschaftliche Vertrauensleute.* Cologne: Europäische Verlagsanstalt.

Weiß-Hartmann, Anne, and Wolfgang Hecker. 1977. "Die Entwicklung der Gewerkschaftsbewegung 1945–1949." In F. Deppe, G. Fülberth, and J. Harrer, eds., *Geschichte der deutschen Gewerkschaftsbewegung.*

Wilensky, Harold L. 1976. *The "New Corporatism," Centralization, and the Welfare State.* Contemporary Political Sociology Series 06-020. Beverly Hills, Calif.: Sage.

Wilensky, Harold L. 1981. "Leftism, Catholicism, and Democratic Corporatism: The Role of Political Parties in Recent Welfare State Development." In Peter Flora and A. J. Heidenheimer, eds., *The Development of Welfare States in Europe and America.* Brunswick, N.J.: Transaction Books.

Wilensky, Harold L. 1983. "Political Legitimacy and Consensus: Missing Variables in the Assessment of Social Policy." In S. E. Spiro and E. Yuchtman-Yaar, eds., *Evaluating the Welfare State: Social and Political Perspectives.* New York: Academic Press. Also Institute of Industrial Relations Reprint Number 453. Berkeley: University of California.

Wilensky, Harold L., and Lowell Turner. 1987. *Democratic Corporatism and Policy Linkages: The Interdependence of Industrial, Labor Market, Incomes, and Social Policies in Eight Countries.* Research Monograph Series Number 69, Berkeley: University of California, Institute of International Studies.

Windolf, Paul. 1984. "Industrial Robots in the Automobile Industry." Paper prepared for the International Automobile Conference, Wissenschaftszentrum Berlin, August.

Windolf, Paul, and Hans-Willy Hohn. 1984. *Arbeitsmarktschancen in der Krise: Betriebliche Rekrutierung und soziale Schließung.* Frankfurt: Campus Verlag.

Winschuh, Josef. 1922. *Betriebsrat oder Gewerkschaft? Beiträge zur Soziologie des Betriebsrätewesens.* Essen: G. D. Baedeker.

Winschuh, Josef. 1923. "Auszüge aus *Praktische Werkspolitik.*" Dokument 30 in R. Crusius, G. Schiefelbein, and M. Wilke, eds., *Die Betriebsräte in der Weimarer Republik: Von der Selbstverwaltung zur Mitbestimmung.* Vol. 1. Berlin: Verlag Olle & Wolter.

Wirtschaftvereinigung Eisen- und Stahlindustrie. 1984. *Statistisches Jahrbuch der Eisen- und Stahlindustrie.* Düsseldorf: Verlag Stahleisen M.B.H.

WSI (Wirtschafts- und Sozialwissenschaftliches Institute des DGB). 1986. "Informationsblätter Arbeit, Gesundheit, Humanisierung." Düsseldorf: WSI, November.

Ziegenfuβ, Hans, Heiner Heseler, and Hans Jürgen Kröger, eds., 1984. *"Wer kämpft, kann verlieren, wer nicht kämpft, hat schon verloren."* Hamburg: VSA Verlag.

Zoll, Rainer. 1981. *Partizipation oder Delegation: Gewerkschaftliche Betriebspolitik in Italien und in der Bundesrepublik Deutschland.* Frankfurt: Europäische Verlagsanstalt.

Zysman, John. 1983. *Governments, Markets, and Growth: Financial Systems and the Politics of Industrial Change.* Ithaca: Cornell University Press.

Index

INDEX

Library of Congress Cataloging-in-Publication Data

Thelen, Kathleen Ann.
    Union of parts : labor politics in postwar Germany / Kathleen A.
Thelen.
        p.   cm. — (Cornell studies in political economy)
    Includes bibliographical references and index.
    ISBN 0-8014-2586-7 (alk. paper)
        1. Labor policy—Germany.   2. Trade-unions—Germany.
3. Industrial relations—Germany.   4. Works councils—Germany.
5. Collective bargaining—Germany.   6. Industriegewerkschaft Metall
für die Bundesrepublik Deutschland.   I. Title.   II. Series.
HD8451.T44   1991
322'.2'0943—dc20   91-55050

Cornell Studies in Political Economy

EDITED BY PETER J. KATZENSTEIN